Study Guide

to Accompany

Psychological Testing

ANNE ANASTASI
Fordham University

Sixth Edition

Susana P. Urbina
University of North Florida

MACMILLAN PUBLISHING COMPANY
New York

COLLIER MACMILLAN PUBLISHERS
London

Macmillan Publishing Company
866 Third Avenue, New York, New York 10022

Collier Macmillan Canada, Inc.

Printing: 4 5 6 7   Year: 2 3 4 5

ISBN 0-02-303040-2

FOREWORD

This *Study Guide* is basically new and *not* a revision of an earlier guide. It is fully as updated as the text itself and focuses attention on significant current and ongoing developments in psychological testing.

The introductory summaries of each chapter should prove particularly helpful to students because they identify key points in the text with unusual succinctness and clarity. The informal, lively style of the *Guide,* along with the game-like nature of many of its exercises, should make learning fun.

A diversity of ingenious item types and exercises are specially designed to reflect the varied content of separate chapters. The material provided was chosen to appeal to users with different levels of prior knowledge and sophistication.

The *Guide* encourages students to think through and understand in depth the topics covered in the text, rather than memorize facts. It also stimulates students to delve into the theoretical implications and practical applications of what they read in the text, as well as to go beyond the text and become familiar with important sources in the field.

All in all, Dr. Urbina has set a high standard in study guides and has demonstrated that such guides can be both effective and enjoyable to the user.

My personal good wishes to all who use this *Study Guide.* May you find it a profitable and happy experience.

Anne Anastasi

CONTENTS

PART FIVE
PERSONALITY TESTS

PREFACE

Unlike textbooks, which are usually required reading, study guides are typically optional items for students to purchase and use as they see fit. It, therefore, stands to reason that the paramount consideration in writing a study guide must be to make it as useful as possible for the student who chooses to acquire it. This *Study Guide* has been prepared, with that goal in mind, for use with the sixth edition of Anne Anastasi's *Psychological Testing* (1988). Its primary purposes are to be a reliable, comprehensive, and versatile companion to that text and a learning tool that will prove useful for students at various levels. It contains material that can be used in different ways, and to different extents, by beginning as well as advanced students.

The *Guide* begins with a section, addressed to the student, on how to make the most effective use of this tool. The chapters that follow contain some common features that are appropriate for every chapter of the textbook, namely, a Chapter Outline, a Chapter Summary, a set of Study Questions that cover the major topics of each chapter, a Multiple Choice self-test, and a section on Miniprojects and Suggested Outreach Activities. In addition, each chapter contains a number of structured activities presented in formats tailored to the content of the respective textbook chapters. These structured activities include statistical exercises, fill-in-the-blanks, matching, and true/false items, with answers provided for all of them. The Appendix contains the Table of Areas under the Normal Curve, which is needed for many statistical exercises, and directions on how to use that table.

I wish to express my appreciation to Anne Anastasi for the contribution she has made to the preparation of this *Guide.* Her comments and suggestions, at every step of the process, have been invariably cogent and helpful.

The *Study Guide* for the fifth edition of the textbook (1982) was prepared by Henry J. Oles and Jack B. McMahon. Small portions of the material from that *Guide,* that were still appropriate for the sixth edition, have been included in this one, with the permission of the copyright owner.

ABOUT THE AUTHOR

Susana P. Urbina is an Associate Professor of Psychology at the University of North Florida, in Jacksonville, Florida. She received her Ph.D., in Psychometrics, at Fordham University in 1972 and was licensed in Florida in 1976. Her principal areas of teaching and research are psychological testing and assessment.

TO THE STUDENT

The textbook for which this *Study Guide* was written, *Psychological Testing* by Anne Anastasi, has been described by various reviewers as impeccable, essential, lucid, authoritative, scrupulously fair, and, simply, as the standard in its field. It has never, to my knowledge, been described as easy. Your instructor's choice of that textbook should indicate to you that you are about to embark on a fairly rigorous course in what is generally considered to be a fairly rigorous field. Your instructor could probably have chosen an easier text, but she or he could not have chosen a better one. This *Study Guide* has been prepared to ease your way through a textbook which, though written with unusual clarity, is massive in scope. Read this section of the Guide thoroughly, to familiarize yourself with its contents and to devise a plan on how it can best serve your purposes.

Each chapter of the *Study Guide* follows the respective textbook chapter quite closely and contains five major sections: a Chapter Outline, a Chapter Summary, a Comprehensive Review, a series of Multiple Choice/Test Yourself items, and a section on Miniprojects/Suggested Outreach Activities. What follows is a rationale for each major section of the *Guide* and suggestions on how to use them most effectively.

Chapter Outline

The *Study Guide*'s outlines contain the headings for *all* of the sections of each chapter, including all subheadings. These outlines should be reviewed before you read the textbook chapters so that you will, at one glance, get a sense of their scope.

Chapter Summary

This section of the *Guide* condenses the most important ideas presented in each chapter into a segment of text that can be read in a few minutes. You can use the summaries in two ways. First, you can read each summary *before* you read the textbook chapter, note ideas and terms that seem entirely new to you and/or complex, and make it a point to study those most carefully in the textbook. An initial reading of the *Guide*'s summaries will also introduce you to the main ideas contained in the chapters in a more detailed way than the outlines so that, when you read the textbook, they will seem more familiar to you than they otherwise would. A second reading of the *Guide*'s chapter summaries can serve an obvious and important function in your review and preparation for tests, by quickly reminding you of what you have learned. However, it should be noted that although the summaries touch upon all the *major* ideas discussed in the text, they can only convey a small portion of the information in it and can never substitute for a thorough reading of the book.

Comprehensive Review

This section contains a variety of items that you will want to use, for the most part, *after* you have read the textbook chapters. The activities in this section of the Guide are tailored to the contents of the chapters and include the following:

1. *Study Questions.* This is the only segment of the comprehensive review section that is common to every chapter of the Guide. The study questions break down the content of the chapters into topical areas. They can serve both as a list of learning objectives, before you approach the textbook chapter, and as a means of checking what you have learned, after you study the chapter. To use them in the most conscientious manner, you would actually write down answers to each of the study questions as though they were essay questions in a test. If time will not allow for this, you could select at least a few study questions and

prepare answers to those. If your instructor informs you that course examinations will include essay items, you will want to make the study questions a central part of your reviews.

2. *Exercises.* In all of the chapters that contain a significant amount of statistical material, some computational exercises are included. Chapter 4, which is the beginning of Part Two of the textbook (Technical and Methodological Principles), is the first one in which statistical exercises appear and, therefore, includes a brief review of basic statistics to which you may want to turn later on in the text as well. In addition, the Appendix of the *Guide* contains the Table of Areas under the Normal Curve, along with directions on how to use it. A thorough understanding of that table is simply indispensable in psychological testing, and many of the exercises will require you to use it. Although the exercises may seem daunting to some students, the statistical concepts they encompass are fairly basic and simply unavoidable in this field, as they are in much of psychology. You may want to survey all the exercises in a given chapter first and start by attempting those that seem most manageable. As the level of difficulty increases, you may need to look at the answers and explanations that are provided and then rework the solutions by yourself to make sure that you have understood the process by which they were reached. In some cases, you may need to consult a good textbook in basic statistics, and review material connected with the exercises.

3. *Fill-in-the-Blanks and Matching Items.* Most of the chapters in the *Guide* contain many fill-in-the-blanks items aimed at helping you to study and review the key terms, concepts, and names contained in the textbook chapters. These and the matching items, which typically cover test titles, are meant to be relatively easy to answer; the fill-in items, for example, provide you with a cue to the correct answers by showing the same number of blank spaces as the number of letters in the terms, concepts, and names to be filled in. Matching and fill-in items can help you to learn key material in three ways. First, you can try to answer them after your initial reading of the textbook chapter and, if you cannot, you should reread the respective portions of the text. Second, you can use the items as a way to help you commit some of the information about key material to memory. Third, you can gauge your knowledge of the important terms, concepts, names, and tests covered in the chapters by looking over the lists of answers to the fill-in items, and the lettered portions of the matching items, and making sure you can define and/or identify them in your own words.

4. *True/False and Why?* Several items of this type are included in chapters that highlight important issues and/or research findings related to testing. You can use them first in an easy, straightforward fashion, after your initial reading of the textbook chapter, by simply deciding whether the statements are true or false. The second approach to these items, which could come after you have studied the text in greater depth and are preparing for a test, would be to actually answer the question "Why?" and write down the reason(s) for your true/false responses. Having to write down the reasons for your answers should help to clarify your understanding of the issues or findings involved in the items.

Multiple Choice: Test Yourself

These items can, of course, be used as a self-test at any point. However, it would probably be best to reserve them for your last review before a test, to gauge your knowledge of the chapter and make sure you are well prepared. This suggestion is made for several reasons. First, multiple choice items are used by most instructors, so it is likely that answering the items in the self-test will be a good "dress rehearsal" for the real test. Second, unlike the items in the comprehensive review section of the *Guide,* the multiple choice items sample the content of each chapter rather sparsely, as a real examination is likely to do, and thus they are more appropriately used as a minitest than for reviewing the material in any kind of systematic fashion. Finally, if you leave the self-tests for the last part of your review, you can get a fairly good idea of how well prepared you are for the upcoming tests. If your score on the minitest for a certain chapter is below 75 percent, you should take that as an indication that you need to do more studying prior to the real test.

Miniprojects/Suggested Outreach Activities

The goals of this section of the *Guide* go beyond helping you to master the material in the textbook and helping you prepare for examinations. The miniprojects and activities that are suggested in the last section of each chapter of the *Guide* are addressed, by and large, to students who want not only to do well in the psychological testing course, but also in the psychological testing field. Many activities involve readings of outside sources that are very important in the field, or representative of its major aspects, or both. There are also a number of miniprojects that encourage you to go beyond the literature of psychological testing and actively involve yourself in an experience that will deepen your knowledge of how testing is applied. The intention that guided the choice of miniprojects was to make them varied and enjoyable enough so that you would want to follow through with one or two from every chapter. In spite of the fact that the miniprojects are meant to expand your knowledge beyond the text, to the extent that you pursue them, your knowledge of what is *in* the text is very likely to deepen and increase.

Chapter 1

FUNCTIONS AND ORIGINS OF PSYCHOLOGICAL TESTING

CHAPTER OUTLINE

I Q

g. born

CHAPTER SUMMARY

Psychological testing developed in response to the practical need to select and classify people in settings such as schools and the military. This fact is largely responsible for the popularity and growth of psychological testing as well as for many of the weaknesses that became inherent in their use.

The major historical influences that led to and shaped the development of modern psychological testing in the late nineteenth century were the awakening of interest in the humane treatment and training of the mentally retarded and the emergence of psychology as an experimental discipline. Francis Galton, in England, and James McKeen Cattell, in the United States, pioneered in the attempt to measure intellectual functions through tests of sensory discrimination and reaction time. However, it was Alfred Binet, in France, who devised the first successful tests of intelligence which centered on tasks that directly assessed functions such as judgment, reasoning, and comprehension.

Further developments in psychological testing came around the time of World War I, when the need to classify a large number of recruits into the armed forces in the United States gave rise to group testing which, among other things, introduced "objective" types of items. The need to differentiate among an individual's performance on various types of abilities, along with the development of factor analysis, led to aptitude testing. In the meantime, standardized achieve-

Binet Tests.
who successful
in school?
who successful
in life?

2

ment tests were also being developed for the purpose of assessing the outcomes of school instruction. Techniques for the assessment of personality or nonintellectual aspects of behavior, including self-report inventories and projective devices, were also developed around the time of World War I but, on the whole, they have lagged behind tests of abilities in terms of their accomplishments.

The rapidity of changes in the area of psychological testing requires familiarity with the major sources of information in the field. Organizations such as the Buros Institute, which publishes the *Mental Measurements Yearbook* (MMY) and *Tests in Print* (TIP), as well as the Educational Testing Service (ETS), monitor the publication of new tests and changes in existing tests to keep test users abreast of developments. In addition, test publishers provide information directly to test users through their catalogs and test manuals. An indispensable guide for anyone wishing to evaluate psychological tests is the *Standards for Educational and Psychological Testing*.

COMPREHENSIVE REVIEW

STUDY QUESTIONS:

1. Identify the traditional function of psychological tests and describe how that function has affected their development and their role in contemporary psychology.

2. Describe the historical precursors of psychological testing that existed prior to the nineteenth century.

3. Identify three historical events that propelled the development of modern psychological testing in the nineteenth and early twentieth centuries.

4. Discuss the contributions of Sir Francis Galton to the development of psychology and testing.

5. Describe the Binet-Simon scales in terms of their content and the procedures used in their development.

6. Identify the major differences between individual and group testing.

7. Discuss how aptitude testing developed and identify the two major types of tests that fall in that category.

8. Discuss the ways in which achievement tests resemble and differ from intelligence and aptitude tests.

9. Describe three major approaches to the assessment of personality.

10. List the major sources of information on testing that are currently available.

FILL IN THE BLANKS: Key Terms and Concepts

1. A major legacy of the early psychological labs to the field of psychological testing was an emphasis on rigorous control of experimental conditions; in testing, this feature became known as __Standardization__ of procedures.

2. The term _ _ _ _ _ _ _ _ _ _ _ _ was used for the first time by Cattell to describe measures of sensory and motor processes.

3. The term _ _ _ _ _ _ _ _ _ _ _ _ _ _ was used by Binet to express a child's score on his entire test.

4. Tests that are administered to only one person at a time are called *individual scales*.

5. The testing movement underwent tremendous growth after the development of _ _ _ _ _ _ _ _ _ _ _ made large scale testing programs possible.

6. _ _ _ _ _ _ _ _ _ _ _ _ _ _ _ _ _ _ _ tests were developed especially for use in vocational counseling and in the selection and classification of personnel in order to supplement global intelligence tests.

7. _ _ _ _ _ _ _ _ _ _ _ _ _ _ _ _ _ _ _ batteries are especially suitable for intraindividual comparisons because they provide separate scores on several traits.

8. *Factor Analysis* is a statistical method for studying the interrelatedness among scores obtained by many persons on a variety of different tests.

9. _ _ _ _ _ _ _ _ _ _ _ _ _ _ tests are educational tools that were originally devised to assess the outcomes of school instruction.

10. The term *personality* tests refers to measures concerned with nonintellectual aspects of behavior, such as emotional states, motivation, and interests.

11. The term used to describe the use of the questionnaire technique in personality testing is _ _ _ _ _ _-_ _ _ _ _ _ _ inventory.

12. In the context of personality measurement, a task that simulates everyday-life settings is called a _ _ _ _ _ _ _ _ _ _ _ _ _ test.

13. The approach to the study of personality that consists of presenting a person with a relatively unstructured task meant to assess characteristic modes of response is known as

_ _.

FILL IN THE BLANKS: Key People

1. _ _ _ _ _ _ _ _ _ _ was a French physician who established the use of language as the main criterion of intellectual level.

2. _ _ _ _ _ _ _ _ was a French physician who pioneered sense- and muscle-training techniques for the mentally retarded.

3. *Binet* was the originator of the first successful scale of intelligence.

from retarded kids to decide what kids would be successful

4. The founder of the first major psychology laboratory established in Leipzig, Germany in 1879 was __ __ __ __ __.

5. __ __ __ __ __ __ was an English biologist who contributed to the testing movement through his interest in the study of heredity.

6. __ __ __ __ __ __ __ was an American psychologist whose work merged experimental psychology with the testing movement.

7. __ __ __ __ __ __ __ __ __ was a German psychologist whose pioneering work in testing grew out of his interest in the clinical examination of psychiatric patients.

8. __ __ __ __ __ __ __ __ __ __ was a German psychologist who advanced testing through his use of sentence completion, memory span, and arithmetical tasks in the lab.

9. The American psychologist who prepared the most famous revision of the Binet-Simon scales was __ __ __ __ __ __.

10. __ __ __ __ __ __ was the director of a committee formed by psychologists to assist the United States government in the World War I effort.

11. The psychologist who introduced multiple-choice items to testing was __ __ __ __.

12. __ __ __ __ __ __ __ __ was an Englishman who pioneered studies of trait organization through the use of correlational analysis.

13. __ __ __ __ __ __ __ __ __ was the American psychologist whose work spearheaded the development of standardized achievement tests.

14. __ __ __ __ __ was the originator of some of the most important publications for information about tests.

ANSWERS TO FILL-IN-THE-BLANKS:

Key Terms and Concepts

1. standardization
2. mental test
3. mental level
4. individual scales
5. group tests
6. special aptitude (tests)
7. multiple aptitude (batteries)
8. factor analysis

9. achievement (tests)

10. personality (tests)

11. self-report (inventory)

12. situational (test)

13. projective techniques

Key People

1. Esquirol

2. Seguin

3. Binet

4. Wundt

5. Galton

6. Cattell

7. Kraepelin

8. Ebbinghaus

9. Terman

10. Yerkes

11. Otis

12. Spearman

13. Thorndike

14. Buros

MATCHING: Early Tests (One letter per number)

___ 1. Early procedure for the assessment of intelligence through nonverbal channels;

___ 2. Prototype of the personality questionnaire;

E 3. Group test for general routine testing developed during World War I;   Army Alpha

A 4. The first test to use the intelligence quotient (IQ) as a score;   Stanford Binet

___ 5. First nonlanguage group scale of intelligence;

C 6. First successful individual intelligence test;   Benet-Simon Scale

      A. Stanford-Binet

      B. Seguin Form Board

      C. Binet-Simon Scale

      D. Army Alpha

      E. Army Beta

      F. Woodworth Personal Data Sheet

ANSWERS:

1 - B;   2 - F;   3 - D;   4 - A;   5 - E;   6 - C.

MATCHING: Sources of Information about Tests

___ 1. Comprehensive guide for evaluating practices in psychological testing;

D (2.) Source which should provide essential information for administering, scoring, and evaluating a test; *test manual*

___ 3. Buros Institute publication that serves as an index for the MMY;

A (4.) One of the earliest and most important sources of information on published tests; *Mental Measurements Yearbook*

___ 5. Best source of information for purchasing a published test;

___ 6. Source of current information on unpublished tests;

        A. *Mental Measurements Yearbook* (MMY)

        B. *Tests in Print* (TIP)

        C. *Tests in Microfiche* (ETS)

        D. Test manual

        E. Test publishers' catalog

        F. *Standards for Educational and Psychological Testing*

ANSWERS:

1 - F;   2 - D;   3 - B;   4 - A;   5 - E;   6 - C.

MATCHING: Organizations concerned with Testing

___ 1. Organization which offers access to the Buros Institute database;

___ 2. Major professional association for psychologists which is responsible for publishing the *Testing Standards.*

___ 3. Current publisher of the MMY series;

___ 4. Organization established at the turn of the century to reduce duplication in testing entering college freshmen;

___ 5. Organization responsible for major testing programs on behalf of universities, professional schools, and government agencies;

        A. Buros Institute of Mental Measurements

        B. Bibliographic Retrieval Services

        C. Educational Testing Service

        D. American Psychological Association

        E. College Entrance Examination Board

*State mad testing
4th 8th + 11th grade* 7

ANSWERS:

1 - B;   2 - D;   3 - A;   4 - E;   5 - C.

MULTIPLE CHOICE: TEST YOURSELF

1. More tests are used for _____
   than for any other application.

   a. counseling and guidance
   b. educational purposes
   c. research in differential psychology
   d. selection of employees and promotions

2. The principal reason for the development of psychological tests has been _____

   _____ .

   a. research into the psychological components of man
   b. the need for information to aid the counseling process
   c. the desire to collect more information about people
   d. the need to select and classify people more accurately

3. Intelligence testing began in the early twentieth century from Seguin's and Binet's work

   with _____ .

   a. retarded children
   b. gifted children
   c. the mentally ill
   d. normal children

4. Sir Francis Galton believed intelligence could be assessed by _____

   _____ .

   a. evaluating a child's verbal development
   b. using the method of free association
   c. measuring sensory discrimination and reaction time
   d. testing for memory span

5. According to the Binet test, if a child had a mental level of six, his performance *6 y.o.*

   _____ .

   a. was definitely retarded
   b. matched that of the average six-year-old
   c. indicated a readiness for school
   d. showed he was incapable of making judgments based on reason

6. The Binet scale placed most of its emphasis on _____ .

   a. reasoning
   b. comprehension
   c. judgments
   d. all of the above

7. The first group tests of intelligence were prepared for _____

    Army _____.

    a. identifying the retarded for special educational programs
    b. research conducted at the Columbian Exposition of 1893
    c. quickly assessing the intelligence of army draftees
    d. the evaluation of normal school children

8. Compared with the Army Alpha, the Army Beta placed more emphasis on _____.

    a. nonlanguage items
    b. verbal items
    c. discrimination items
    d. reading

9. Multiple aptitude test batteries _____

    _____.

    a. were among the first group tests developed
    b. are based mostly on numerical reasoning items
    c. were a practical outcome of factor analysis
    d. are not suitable for differential diagnosis

10. The major difference between aptitude and achievement tests is that aptitude tests _____

    _____.

    a. place more emphasis on performance-type skills
    b. go through more rigorous technical development
    c. depend less on specific content learning
    d. none of the above

11. Which of the following is the best example of an achievement test? _____

    _____.

    a. The Stanford-Binet
    b. A final exam in Physics
    c. The Army Alpha
    d. A sentence completion test

12. Some persons are placed in a setting in which it would be very easy for them to cheat. They

    do not know that their behavior is being closely observed. This type of test is best classified

    as a _____.

    a. situational test
    b. self-report
    c. projective test
    d. free association evaluation

13. The Woodworth Personal Data Sheet was developed to _____
    _____.

    a. identify mental retardation in school children
    b. summarize an individual's life history
    c. predict student success in college
    d. screen military recruits for severe emotional disturbance

14. The best known source of critical information about published tests is _____
    _____.

    a. a textbook on educational and psychological tests
    b. *Tests in Print*
    c. the *Mental Measurements Yearbook*
    d. *The Journal of Educational Measurement*

15. The most complete source of information about any particular test should be found in ____
    _____.

    a. the test's manual
    b. the *Mental Measurements Yearbook*
    c. *Tests in Print*
    d. the *Standards for Educational and Psychological Testing*

MINIPROJECTS/SUGGESTED OUTREACH ACTIVITIES:

1. Although most of the terms and concepts essential to psychological testing have already been listed in the comprehensive review, there are other important terms in this chapter that you may not know. Many of these words are part of the basic vocabulary of psychology and related disciplines. As a vocabulary-building exercise, you should underline any unfamiliar words and look them up in a good, preferably unabridged, dictionary. Here is a sample of terms with which you may not, but ought to, be familiar:

   anthropometric

   intraindividual

   stimulus (singular) and stimuli (plural)

   phenomenon (singular) and phenomena (plural)

   kinesthetic

   reaction time

   aesthetic

   psychopathology

   homogeneous and heterogeneous

   psychometrics

2. Two of the most useful sources of information on psychological tests, available in many libraries, are the *Mental Measurements Yearbook* (MMY) series and *Tests in Print* (TIP). Locate the latest editions of these works and familiarize yourself with them by reading their respective Introduction sections. These sections are only a few pages long and should not take much time to read. However, they are as good an investment of time as possible for

students starting to get acquainted with the field of testing. If time allows, look up the entries of one or two tests in each series to become even more familiar with these works.

3. Chapter 1 contains many names of people important in the history of testing; the more you know about them, the easier it will be to remember them. A quick way to learn more about the people mentioned in this chapter is to look up their names in the *Encyclopedia of Psychology* edited by R. J. Corsini (New York: Wiley, 1984). A more time-consuming, but probably more enjoyable, way to learn more about the pioneers of psychological testing is to read Raymond Fancher's book *The Intelligence Men: Makers of the IQ Controversy* (New York: Norton, 1985), which is now available in paperback.

4. Some worthwhile follow-up reading is to be found in the review entitled "Mental Measurement: Some Emerging Trends," which is contained in the Ninth MMY, immediately following the Introduction. This article, written by Anne Anastasi, takes both a prospective and a retrospective view at the field of psychological testing and should help deepen your understanding of the material contained in the first three chapters of the textbook.

ANSWERS TO MULTIPLE CHOICE/TEST YOURSELF ITEMS:

1. b	4. c	7. c	10. c	13. d
2. d	5. b	8. a	11. b	14. c
3. a	6. d	9. c	12. a	15. a

Chapter 2
NATURE AND USE OF PSYCHOLOGICAL TESTS

CHAPTER OUTLINE

What is a Psychological Test?
    Behavior Sample
    Standardization
    Objective Measurement of Difficulty
    Reliability
    Validity

Why Control the Use of Psychological Tests?
    Qualified Examiner
    Security of Test Content

Test Administration
    Advance Preparation of Examiners
    Testing Conditions
    Introducing the Test: Rapport and Test-Taker Orientation

Examiner and Situational Variables

Test Anxiety

Effects of Training on Test Performance
    Coaching
    Test Sophistication
    Instruction in Broad Cognitive Skills
    Overview

CHAPTER SUMMARY

A psychological test is defined as an objective and standardized measure of a sample of behavior. The adequacy of coverage of a test depends on the number and nature of its items, whereas its predictive or diagnostic value depends on the empirical relationship between its items and the behavior in question. Standardization of a test consists of developing uniform procedures for its administration and scoring, as well as generating normative data on which to base the interpretation of scores. Tests are primarily evaluated in terms of their reliability, or consistency of their scores, and in terms of their validity, which is the extent to which we know what they measure.

The use of psychological tests needs to be controlled in order to ensure that they are used only by those people who are qualified to select and apply them properly. In addition, access to the content of most tests needs to be controlled in order to preserve their integrity and usefulness.

?# 3
answer

One of the most important objectives in psychological testing is to reduce or eliminate the influence of any variables extraneous to what the test is measuring. To this end, good testing practice requires the examiner to be prepared to deal with all eventualities related to the administration of the test and to establish rapport with the individuals to be tested. In addition, attention should be given to ensuring that the testing environment and other testing conditions do not interfere with the performance of examinees. Skilled examiners try to detect, and whenever possible eliminate, the operation of extraneous influences in a testing situation, whether such influences arise from their own expectations, from the context of the testing or from special characteristics of examinees. One such characteristic is the amount of anxiety experienced by some test takers. This variable has been studied extensively and, although its operation appears to be quite complex, it has generally been found to correlate negatively with scores on tests of achievement and intelligence. Treatment programs that address both test anxiety and study skills appear to be the most promising in this regard.

Another variable which can affect performance on psychological tests, and thus potentially alter their validity, is the extent of training individuals receive prior to the testing. Training can encompass activities that range from coaching, which is test specific and may reduce validity, to instruction in broader skills, which falls in the realm of education and does not affect validity. Many procedures designed to orient examinees and to equalize their test-taking experience are also available now. Such procedures may actually enhance validity by reducing the influence of test sophistication as an extraneous variable.

COMPREHENSIVE REVIEW

STUDY QUESTIONS:

1. Define what a psychological test is and explain the meaning of each term in that definition.

2. Identify and describe the two principal ways in which psychological tests are currently evaluated.

3. Discuss the major reasons why the use of tests needs to be controlled.

4. List and discuss the reasons why testing information needs to be communicated effectively to test takers, concerned professionals, and the general public.

5. Discuss the function that advance preparation of examiners and knowledge and control of conditions serve in testing.

6. Describe the ways in which the process of establishing rapport may vary with different types of tests and test takers.

7. Identify the major variables pertaining to the examiner which might affect test results.

8. Discuss the effects of test anxiety on test results, in light of the research findings cited in the text.

9. Compare and contrast coaching with education in terms of how each might affect testing.

10. Describe the types of test familiarization materials that are currently available.

FILL IN THE BLANKS: Key Terms and Concepts

1. A(n) _ _ _ _ _ _ _ _ _ _ _ _ _ _ _ _ _ _ _ _ is an objective and standardized measure of a sample of behavior.

2. A(n) Sample is a small portion or subset selected from a population or universe.

3. A test is _ _ _ _ _ _ _ _ _ _ _ _ _ _ _ _ when control of testing conditions is established through uniformity of procedures in administration and scoring.

4. The average performance of a representative sample of the types of persons for whom a test is designed is called the Norm.

5. Although _ _ _ _ _ _ _ _ _ _ _ refers to a determination of a present condition based on test results, the term also implies a prediction regarding behaviors in situations other than the present test.

6. A test's norms are based on a group that is called the Standardization Sample.

7. A(n) Raw Score, is an objective measure of test performance that is, by itself, meaningless.

8. Reliability → dependable _ refers to the consistency of test scores across time, forms, or scorers.

9. Validity refers to the degree to which a test fulfills its purported function. measures what it says it measures

10. A(n) _ _ _ _ _ _ _ _ _ _ _ is an independent measure of performance on the function assessed by a test that can be used to validate the test.

11. A(n) Validity co-efficient is a measure of correlation between test scores and a criterion.

12. The _ _ _ _ _ _ _ _ _ _ _ group is a representative sample of persons on whom a test's validity is investigated.

13. The difficulty value is an empirically established measure of the difficulty of a test item that is used to determine whether an item is selected and where it is placed.

14. _ _ _ _ _ _ _ _ _ is a term that refers to the examiner's efforts to arouse interest in, and elicit cooperation from, test takers.

15. The Self-fulfilling prophecy is an effect on the test taker's responses that can occur as a function of the examiner's expectations.

16. __ __ __ __ __ __ __ __ is a term that refers to intensive drills on items similar to those on a test to be taken.

17. The difference between coaching and __ __ __ __ __ __ __ __ __ is that the results of the latter extend to the broader behavior that the test is designed to assess whereas the effects of the former are limited to the test.

18. __ __ __ __   __ __ __ __ __ __ __ __ __ __ __ __ __ is an examinee variable that consists of test-taking practice and generally results in score gains.

19. __ __ __ __ _–_ __ __ __ __ __ __ __ __ procedures are techniques designed to rule out or equalize differences in the prior test-taking experience of examinees.

20. __ __ __ __   __ __ __ __ __ __ is an examinee variable that consists of cognitive and emotional components and generally results in score decrements.

ANSWERS TO FILL-IN-THE-BLANKS: (Key Terms and Concepts)

1. psychological test
2. sample
3. standardized
4. norm
5. diagnosis
6. standardization sample
7. raw score
8. reliability
9. validity
10. criterion
11. validity coefficient
12. validation (group)
13. difficulty value
14. rapport
15. self-fulfilling (prophecy)
16. coaching
17. education
18. test sophistication
19. test orientation (procedures)
20. test anxiety

TRUE/FALSE and WHY?

1. The goal of psychological testing is to obtain a direct measurement of the behavior sample covered by the test. (T/F) Why? _F_____

2. In personality testing, responses are usually evaluated in terms of norms that represent the most desirable pattern of performance. (T/F) Why? _F_____

    _____

3. In individual assessment an experienced examiner may occasionally depart from standardized test procedures provided that the information thus elicited is not used in arriving at scores. (T/F) Why? _T_____

4. In general, children are more susceptible to examiner and situational variables than are adults. (T/F) Why? _____

5. Studies of the relation between anxiety and test performance indicate that even a slight amount of anxiety is detrimental to performance. (T/F) Why? _F_____ _is common_

    _____

6. Promoting some sense of mystery about tests is an effective device that examiners may use to build rapport. (T/F) Why? _____

7. Proper interpretation of test scores cannot proceed without some background data on the test taker. (T/F) Why? _T_____

8. The state laws regarding disclosure of testing information enacted in New York in the late 1970's have been quite effective in accomplishing the goals that prompted their enactment. (T/F) Why? _____

9. Empirical verification of equivalence is necessary when any test materials, such as answer sheets, differ from those used with the standardization sample. (T/F) Why? _T_____

    _____

10. The single most important requirement for proper test administration is the advance preparation of the examiner. (T/F) Why? _____

    _____

11. General motivational feedback has been found more effective than corrective feedback in improving the performance of low scorers on subsequent tests. (T/F) Why? _____

    _____

12. In order to be qualified to administer most group tests some supervised training in the administration of the particular test is usually essential. (T/F) Why? _____

_____

ANSWERS TO TRUE/FALSE:

1. False	4. True	7. True	10. True
2. False	5. False	8. False	11. False
3. True	6. False	9. True	12. False

MULTIPLE CHOICE: TEST YOURSELF

1. All psychological tests fundamentally depend upon the measurement of _____

_____.

   a. basic mental processes
   b. aptitudes
   c. behavior samples
   d. traits

2. In the final analysis, the worth of a test item or an entire test depends upon _____

_____.

   a. how closely the material covered by the test resembles the behavior that is to be predicted
   b. the norms that are published in the test manual
   c. the standardization procedures
   d. its empirical correspondence with the criterion

3. The major distinction between "diagnosis" and "prediction" centers upon _____

_____.

   a. time factors
   b. whether behavior external to the test is involved
   c. whether a physician is involved
   d. accuracy

4. Standardization in testing basically refers to _____

_____.

   a. a printed test form
   b. the use of trained examiners to evaluate performance
   c. measurement against a proven standard
   d. complete uniformity of procedure

5. A ten-year-old boy takes an intelligence test and gets only 8 out of 40 questions correct. Based on this we can say _____.

    a. that the test was too difficult for him
    b. that he is definitely below average in IQ
    c. that he should be retested
    d. nothing, since we do not know the norms

6. A person scores exactly at the norm on an aptitude test. This means that the person _____

_____.

    a. achieved an "average" score
    b. had the highest score possible
    c. answered 50% of the questions correctly
    d. showed "ideal" performance

7. The standardization sample is used in test development to _____

_____.

    a. test the test
    b. generate test items
    c. establish the norms
    d. determine test validity

8. Reliability in testing is best defined as _____.

    a. objectivity
    b. exactness
    c. consistency
    d. accuracy

9. The most important consideration regarding any test is its _____

_____.

    a. norms
    b. accuracy
    c. reliability
    d. validity

10. It has been said that persons who score well on a medical aptitude test also do very well in medical school. This would mean that the medical aptitude test is _____.

    a. reliable
    b. valid
    c. qualified
    d. standardized

11. A test is designed to predict success in graduate school. Success in graduate school is therefore the _____.

    a. criterion
    b. validation factor
    c. empirical validity
    d. objective

12. Some controls must be placed on the availability of psychological tests in order to _____
    _____.

    a. protect the content from disclosure
    b. ensure that the test is administered by qualified people
    c. prevent test misuse
    d. all of the above

13. Rapport is best defined in the testing situation as _____
    _____.

    a. ensuring total objectivity
    b. arousing the examinee's interest and cooperation
    c. making special efforts to motivate those students who do not show normal interest
    d. being especially friendly with the examinees

14. Test anxiety _____.

    a. is always detrimental to test performance
    b. generally causes an examinee to work harder
    c. is more of a problem for some examinees than others
    d. should be eliminated on good objective tests

MINIPROJECTS/SUGGESTED OUTREACH ACTIVITIES:

1. The most direct way to learn how the use of tests is controlled in practice is to obtain one or more of the catalogs of test publishers and look up the sections that deal with restrictions on sales of their tests, qualifications purchasers must meet, and issues of test security. Some catalogs are more explicit than others in outlining their policies and some, e.g., Consulting Psychologists Press, Inc.'s catalog, even contain sections outlining the elements of good testing practice discussed in Chapter 2. Catalogs can be obtained by writing to some of the publishers listed in Appendix C of the textbook or, more easily, through your professor or a local testing center.

2. One fringe benefit from the study of psychological testing is, or at least ought to be, an increase in one's test sophistication. Chapter 2 contains a good deal of information which, if followed up, could prove useful in that regard. The activities listed below may be more or less appropriate, depending on your individual circumstances, but either one of them would serve to deepen your understanding of the material in the chapter and might also increase your success as a test-taker.

   A. If you are prone to experience test anxiety to an extent that is bothersome, find out the resources available in your area, perhaps in the Counseling Center in your school, to help you deal with that problem. First, you may want to assess objectively the extent to which test anxiety is a problem by taking the Test Anxiety Inventory or a similar instrument. Afterwards, if the results warrant it or simply for the sake of the experience, you could go through a test anxiety reduction treatment program, preferably one that addresses the cognitive and emotional aspects of test anxiety.

   B. If you are planning to enter a graduate or professional school, a very worthwhile investment of your time would be to investigate what materials are available in your area to prepare for the appropriate entrance examinations. Test-preparation software packages, such as the one available for the GRE General Test that is mentioned in the text, would be among the most useful. In addition, there is an ample supply of books, such as the Barron's and Monarch's series, available in most college bookstores. These guides contain helpful information and practice items for every major entrance examination used by universities and professional schools. As you go through the practice items, keep track of the time they take, as well as your scores, and try to gauge "practice effects" by noting any improvements in your speed and accuracy.

ANSWERS TO MULTIPLE CHOICE/TEST YOURSELF ITEMS:

1. c	4. d	7. c	10. b	13. b
2. d	5. d	8. c	11. a	14. c
3. a	6. a	9. d	12. d	

Chapter 3
SOCIAL AND ETHICAL CONSIDERATIONS IN TESTING

CHAPTER OUTLINE

Ethical Issues in Psychological Testing

User Qualifications

Responsibilities of Test Publishers

Protection of Privacy

Confidentiality

Communicating Test Results

Testing Cultural Minorities
    The Setting
    Legal Regulations
    Test-related Factors
    Interpretation and Use of Test Scores
    Objectivity of Tests

CHAPTER SUMMARY

Psychologists' longstanding concern with professional ethics was first codified formally with the publication of the *Ethical Principles of Psychologists* in 1953. Since then, that publication has undergone periodic revisions and several others have appeared, focusing on various aspects of the profession, but especially those that pertain to the delivery of psychological services.

The latest edition of the *Ethical Principles,* published in 1981, contains three principles that specifically address issues in psychological testing and they, along with the current *Standards for Educational and Psychological Testing* and the *Guidelines for Computer-based Tests and Interpretations,* published in 1986, help to define the responsible use of tests.

The major responsibility for the proper use of tests rests with the individual user. Qualifications for using tests vary depending on the type of test involved as well as with different aspects of testing. In general, administrative and scoring tasks may be delegated to properly trained technicians but appropriate interpretation and adequate communication of test results require the perspective of a psychologist who is qualified by virtue of education and experience in the area of testing. Test publishers share in the responsibility to prevent the misuse of tests through their control of the distribution and marketing of test materials.

Two very important aspects of psychological testing practice concern the need to protect the privacy of test takers and to maintain the confidentiality of test data. Although these issues are related, protection of privacy centers primarily on the requirements that the test taker be made aware of the purposes of testing, or informed consent, and that the information gathered from the test taker be relevant to those purposes. Confidentiality, on the other hand, centers on issues of access to test results by test takers and other persons as well as retention of records by institutions. Proper testing practice also extends to the communication of test results in a manner that is understandable to the recipients and that takes into account their characteristics and the context of the communication.

Over the past three decades, societal concerns about the civil rights of cultural minorities and women have helped to focus much attention on psychological tests. This attention derives primarily from the role tests play in employment and educational decision-making and centers around the notion that the test scores of minority group members are unfairly lowered by cultural conditions that are beyond their control. In the realm of employment, the *Uniform Guidelines on Employee Selection Procedures* adopted by the Equal Employment Opportunity Commission (EEOC) in 1978 have played a crucial role in delineating what constitutes discriminatory practices. However, many ambiguities remain in this and other areas of test use that require continuous interpretations by the courts which, in turn, have not always been consistent. The essential problem with regard to the testing of minorities lies in differentiating between cultural influences that are limited to the test, and should be eliminated or ruled out, and those that affect both test and criterion behaviors, which may need to be addressed by appropriate remediation but cannot be ignored.

COMPREHENSIVE REVIEW

STUDY QUESTIONS:

1. Discuss the major reasons why the use of psychological tests needs to be restricted to those who are competent in their use.

2. Describe how you would gauge whether someone is a "qualified" psychologist.

3. List three examples of practices concerning the distribution and marketing of psychological tests that are deemed as unacceptable and explain why they might be harmful.

4. Discuss how the purpose for which testing is conducted affects the issue of protecting the privacy of test takers.

5. Explain what is meant by "informed consent" as fully as possible.

6. Discuss the issue of access to test results from the standpoint of test takers, parents, third persons, and institutions.

7. Identify and discuss the major precautions that should apply to the communication of test results to the individual test taker.

8. Describe the major provisions of the *Uniform Guidelines on Employee Selection Procedures*.

9. Discuss the issue of relevant versus irrelevant cultural factors as it applies to the content of psychological tests.

10. Describe the rationale used by those who view standardized testing as having a positive function with regard to protecting the civil rights of minorities and women.

FILL IN THE BLANKS: Key Terms, Concepts, and Organizations

1. The group that investigates and adjudicates complaints lodged against members of the American Psychological Association (APA) is the APA's _ _ _ _ _ _

   _ _ _ _ _ _ _ _ _.

2. The group that publishes illustrative ethics cases in the various specialty areas of psychology on an annual basis is the APA's Committee on _ _ _ _ _ _ _ _ _ _ _ _ _ _

   _ _ _ _ _ _ _ _ _.

3. The _ _ _ _ _ _ _ _ _   _ _ _ _ _ _ of _ _ _ _ _ _ _ _ _ _ _ _ _

   _ _ _ _ _ _ _ _ _ _ (ABPP) is the organization that certifies diplomates in areas such as clinical, counseling, and school psychology.

4. The _ _ _ _ _   _ _ _ _ _ _ _ _ _ _ _ _   _ _ _ _ _ _ _ _ _ _ _ _

   _ _ _ _ _ _ _ _ _ _ (EEOC) is the organization charged with implementing and enforcing Title VII of the Civil Rights Act of 1964.

5. The legal statutes that control the practice of psychology are usually called

   _ _ _ _ _ _ _ _ _ _   _ _ _ _.

6. ~~Certification~~ usually refers to the legal procedure whereby the use of the title "psychologist" is protected.

7. ~~Relevance~~ is the ethical concept that requires that instruments used in assessment be valid and appropriate to their purposes.

8. ~~informed consent~~ is the ethical concept that requires that test takers be made aware of the reasons for and intended use of tests.

9. ~~Confidentiality~~ is the ethical principle that limits the disclosure of information obtained by psychologists in the course of their work.

10. _ _ _ _ _ _ _ _ _ _ _ _ is the ethical principle that aims to forestall misuse of tests by unqualified users.

11. _ _ _ _ _ _ _ _ _   _ _ _ _ _ _ _ refers to the situation that occurs when the use of a selection procedure results in a substantially higher rate of rejection for minority than for nonminority candidates.

12. _ _ _ _ _ _ _ _ _ _ _ _ _   _ _ _ _ _ _ _ is the term applied to efforts aimed at compensating for the residual effects of past social inequities.

ANSWERS TO FILL-IN-THE-BLANKS: (Key Terms, Concepts, and Organizations)

1. Ethics Committee
2. (Committee on) Professional Standards
3. American Board of Professional Psychology (ABPP)
4. Equal Employment Opportunity Commission (EEOC)
5. licensing laws
6. certification
7. relevance
8. informed consent
9. confidentiality
10. competence
11. adverse impact
12. affirmative action

TRUE/FALSE and WHY?

1. The independent practitioner of psychology needs to meet higher standards of professional qualifications than the institutional psychologist. (T/F) Why? _____
   _____

2. Publication of psychological tests in newspapers or magazines is a good way to promote their use. (T/F) Why? _____
   _____

3. The question of invasion of privacy is more likely to arise in personality than in intelligence testing. (T/F) Why? _____
   _____

4. For purposes of testing effectiveness it is sometimes necessary to subject a person to a testing program under false pretenses. (T/F) Why? _____
   _____

5. In clinical situations clients basically surrender their rights to the protection of their privacy in order to obtain help. (T/F) Why? _F_____
   _____

6. Evidence from national and statewide surveys suggests that the goal of designing testing procedures that protect individuals' rights *and* yield meaningful data cannot be achieved. (T/F) Why? _____

_____

7. The underlying principle regarding confidentiality of test records is that such records should not be released without the consent of the test taker. (T/F) Why? T_____

_____

8. When test records are retained for legitimate use in longitudinal research, access to them needs to be controlled even more stringently than usual. (T/F) Why? _____

_____

9. Computerized data banks are sure to eventually destroy the possibility of protecting the security of individual records. (T/F) Why? _____

_____

10. Once a selection procedure has been satisfactorily validated, even if disproportionate rejection rates occur for minorities, the EEOC *Uniform Guidelines'* requirements can be presumed to have been met. (T/F) Why? _____

_____

ANSWERS TO TRUE/FALSE:

1. True	4. False	7. True	10. False
2. False	5. False	8. True	
3. True	6. False	9. False	

MULTIPLE CHOICE: TEST YOURSELF

1. The use of tests by professional psychologists is controlled by a set of rules known as _____

_____.

   a. APA Testing Regulations
   b. Standards for Educational and Psychological Testing
   c. EEOC Rules and Regulations
   d. Federal law 21.176

2. Sales of psychological tests should be restricted to those with _____

_____.

   a. at least a Master's degree in psychology
   b. a Ph.D. or doctoral degree
   c. a state license and/or certification
   d. appropriate training and experience for the test

3. Aptitude and personality testing by mail is _____
_____.

    a. perfectly acceptable
    b. acceptable under some conditions
    c. unacceptable under nearly any condition
    d. illegal

4. The privacy of test scores, such as those obtained by adults on personality tests, is best

    protected by _____
_____.

    a. establishing strict laws with severe punishment for those who do not abide by them
    b. never releasing the scores to anyone for any reason
    c. sharing test results only with qualified personnel
    d. informing the examinee about the tests and their intended use

5. Examinees will be less sensitive about the privacy of their test scores if they _____
_____.

    a. obtain socially acceptable scores
    b. understand their intended use
    c. realize that the score represents only a sampling of behavior
    d. all of the above are true

6. Who should make the final decision about the release of psychological test scores? _____
_____

    a. The examinee, or if the examinee is not of age, the parent.
    b. The researcher who collected the data.
    c. The chief executive officer of the institution involved.
    d. The law.

7. If a testing session has been handled in a very professional and ethical manner, how many
individuals will refuse to allow their test scores to be used for research? _____
_____

    a. More than 50% will refuse.
    b. Between 30 and 50% will refuse.
    c. Between 10 and 30% will refuse.
    d. Only a negligible number will refuse to cooperate.

8. Psychological test information obtained on children _____
_____.

    a. should never be divulged to parents
    b. may, in some cases, be communicated to the parent
    c. must legally be shared with the parent
    d. should be made available to the child's whole family

9. The major problem in educational and psychological testing is _____
   _____.

   a. improper test standardization
   b. poor norms that do not apply to a given situation
   c. poor communication of test results to the examinee
   d. tests that have low reliability and validity

10. In communicating test results to an examinee _____.

   a. all technical information should be released
   b. the characteristics of the examinee must be considered
   c. no one else should be in the room
   d. normative information should not be divulged

11. Minorities may, on the average, score lower on psychological tests because _____
   _____.

   a. they may have less test-taking experience
   b. of poor rapport with the examiner
   c. they may not have the same level of motivation as others
   d. all of the above are factors

12. The most frequent misgivings in terms of the use of tests with minority group members

   stem from _____.

   a. the subjectivity of tests
   b. biases in test content
   c. misinterpretation of scores
   d. their lack of rapport with nonminority examiners

13. Tests on which minority group members score significantly lower than nonminorities _____
   _____.

   a. should be thrown out
   b. should be modified until average minority scores equal average nonminority scores
   c. may not be biased but instead demonstrate a deficiency
   d. none of the above

14. The EEOC *Uniform Guidelines* _____
   _____.

   a. recommend the abolishment of testing
   b. apply to tests but not to interview procedures
   c. are based on the current *Testing Standards*
   d. apply to both private and governmental employers

MINIPROJECTS/SUGGESTED OUTREACH ACTIVITIES:

1. Generate a list of all the publications cited in Chapter 3 that contain the words "principles,"
   "standards" or "guidelines" in their titles. You should come up with a list of seven works
   that, together, define the proper practice of psychology and psychological testing, from the
   standpoint of the profession. Note the dates of publication and the publishers of each of

these works and then locate and review the two that interest you the most (one of the seven is contained in Appendix A of the textbook).

2. The *American Psychologist,* which is the official journal of the American Psychological Association, has been publishing cases which highlight the application of the *Ethical Principles of Psychologists* annually since 1981. From 1981 to 1986 these cases appeared in the June issue; since then, they have appeared in the issue for July. A review of some of these illustrative cases should prove interesting and should greatly enhance your understanding of the ethical issues discussed in Chapter 3.

3. As mentioned in the textbook, almost every state has some laws that govern the practice of psychology and/or the use of the title "psychologist." Find out what the licensing/certification laws are in your state and in another state that interests you and compare them. Applicable state statutes can be located through library research or by contacting the Department of Professional Regulation of the state in question.

ANSWERS TO MULTIPLE CHOICE/TEST YOURSELF ITEMS:

1. b	4. d	7. d	10. b	13. c
2. d	5. d	8. c	11. d	14. d
3. c	6. a	9. c	12. c	

Chapter 4

NORMS AND THE INTERPRETATION OF TEST SCORES

CHAPTER OUTLINE

Statistical Concepts

Developmental Norms
   Mental Age
   Grade Equivalents
   Ordinal Scales

Within-Group Norms
   Percentiles
   Standard Scores
   The Deviation IQ
   Interrelationships of Within-Group Scores

Relativity of Norms
   Intertest Comparisons
   The Normative Sample
   National Anchor Norms
   Specific Norms
   Fixed Reference Group
   Item Response Theory

Computer Use in the Interpretation of Test Scores
   Technical Developments
   Hazards and Guidelines

Criterion-Referenced Testing
   Nature and Uses
   Content Meaning
   Mastery Testing
   Relation to Norm-Referenced Testing

Expectancy Tables

CHAPTER SUMMARY

Raw scores on psychological tests are meaningless and can only be interpreted in terms of a clearly defined and uniform frame of reference. The most commonly used frame of reference for score interpretation consists of normative information derived from the performance of representative samples of individuals against which a test taker's own performance can be compared. In order to allow for meaningful use of the information extracted from tests, raw scores typically are converted into derived scores which express test results in ways that permit comparisons of an individual's performance to the standardization sample and also of an individual's performance across various tests.

Statistical methods used to organize and summarize quantitative score data for normative purposes begin by grouping the data into frequency distributions and plotting them graphically in distribution curves that frequently approximate the mathematical model of the normal curve. In addition, score distributions are described in terms of measures of central tendency, such as the mean, and measures of variability, such as the standard deviation.

Developmental regularities, such as chronological age, progression through school grades, and invariant sequences in the unfolding of certain behaviors, allow for the use of developmental level attained as a frame of reference for the interpretation of test scores. Developmental norms, which include mental ages, grade equivalents, and ordinal scales based on developmental stages, are derived by gathering data on the typical performance of individuals who are at various points within a given sequence. Although these norms have popular appeal, they tend to be either qualitative or psychometrically crude and thus do not lend themselves to precise statistical treatment.

Within-group norms which evaluate an individual's performance in terms of the most nearly comparable standardization group, on the other hand, have a uniform and clearly defined quantitative meaning, and can be used in most statistical analyses. The main types of within-group norms are percentiles and standard scores. Percentile scores express an individual's relative position within the standardization group in terms of the percentage of persons whose scores fall below that of the individual. Standard scores express the distance between an individual's score and the group mean in terms of the standard deviation of the distribution of scores. The most basic type of standard scores, which are called "z scores," can either be derived linearly or can be "normalized," i.e., obtained by referring to tables of percentages of cases at various points within the normal curve; both types of standard scores can be transformed further into scales that are more convenient, such as T scores or deviation IQs.

The comparability of test scores depends not just on the use of comparable scale units, but also on test content and on the composition of the groups from which norms are derived. Norms can be derived from large samples that are representative of broadly defined populations, e.g., national norms for elementary school children, from more narrowly defined subgroups, or even locally within a particular setting, depending on the purpose of the test. Comparability of scores can also be achieved without the use of a normative sample, as such, either by scaling a test in terms of a fixed reference group or by deriving a common scale unit from item data representing a wide range of ability and item difficulty, with the use of item response theory (IRT) mathematical models.

The use of computers has had an impact on every aspect of psychological testing, including test construction, administration, scoring, and interpretation. The speed and flexibility that computers bring to data-processing is also allowing the exploration of new approaches to testing, such as IRT models of sample-free scaling and interactive computer systems. However, computerized testing procedures have also given rise to new concerns regarding the proper evaluation and use of the computer-generated test data.

Criterion-referenced testing is an approach that uses a specified content domain, rather than a specified population of persons, as its interpretive frame of reference. This approach, which has been applied primarily in educational settings, requires the delineation of a clearly defined domain of knowledge or skills to be assessed by the test as well as a determination of what constitutes mastery of that domain. Both of these requirements limit the applicability of criterion-referenced testing.

Test scores can also be interpreted in terms of existing data about the relationship between them and criterion performance. Expectancy tables and expectancy charts are two of the methods used to represent the relationship between scores on a test or predictor and the outcome on a criterion.

COMPREHENSIVE REVIEW

STUDY QUESTIONS:

1. Define three measures of central tendency and three measures of variability that are used to describe a group of scores.

2. Describe mental age units and grade equivalents and discuss their similarities and their shortcomings.

3. Describe the approach to developmental norms exemplified by ordinal scales and cite two areas of development in which this approach can be applied.

4. Define and compare percentile scores and standard scores in terms of how they are derived and how they are interpreted.

5. Describe the traditional ratio IQ score and contrast it with the deviation IQ.

6. List and discuss the major factors that need to be taken into consideration if test scores are to be compared.

7. Discuss the issues that are pertinent to the selection of a normative sample and describe two ways in which score comparability can be achieved through nonnormative scales.

8. Describe two of the examples of testing innovations that have come about through the use of computers.

9. Contrast and compare criterion-referenced testing with norm-referenced testing.

10. Describe how test scores can be interpreted in terms of expected criterion performance.

EXERCISES: Review of Basic Statistics and Standard Scores

NOTE: All of the following exercises, as well as those in subsequent chapters, are based on the formulas given in the textbook and use the same notations that the textbook uses.

TABLE 1   RESULTS OF A TEST TAKEN BY 50 STUDENTS

N = 50

70	74	80	86	89	90	60	41	62	51
67	63	65	66	59	66	69	55	72	73
75	80	82	83	94	97	47	54	63	71
66	70	76	80	75	77	78	78	81	57
68	69	71	72	74	74	84	85	89	93

1. In order to make the data in Table 1 more manageable, set up a grouped frequency distribution through the following steps:

   A. List all of the scores in descending order;

   B. Determine the range of the distribution by subtracting the lowest score obtained from the highest one and adding 1;

   C. Divide the range by 12, which is an arbitrary but appropriate (i.e., between 10 and 20) number of groups to cover the score distribution in Table 1. Round the result to the next whole number which will then be the interval size or i.

   D. Build the grouped frequency distribution from the bottom, making sure that the lowest class interval starts with a multiple of the interval size, i, and includes the lowest score obtained. Continue building additional class intervals, all with the same i, until you reach a group that includes the highest obtained score.

   E. Tally the number of raw scores that occur within each class interval in the distribution and place the sum of the tallies for each interval in a column labelled "f", for "frequencies", next to the respective intervals. The sum of the f column should equal N, the number of cases.

2. Draw a frequency polygon to represent the data in the grouped frequency distribution based on Table 1 by following these steps:

   A. On normal graph paper, draw a perpendicular axis, or ordinate (usually labelled the "Y" axis) to present all the frequencies in column f from zero to the highest one.

   B. Draw a horizontal axis, or abscissa (usually labelled the "X" axis) to present the midpoint or middle score of each interval from the lowest to one above the highest one in the grouped distribution. Note that the length of the Y axis should be approximately 60% of the length of the X axis.

   C. Place a point on the graph at the appropriate frequency for each point on the X axis and connect these points with straight lines. The lowest and highest points should be connected with the baseline at the next lowest and highest X values.

3. Draw a histogram to represent the same data by duplicating the X and Y axes used for the frequency polygon and drawing a bar with the midpoint as its center for each score interval. The height of each bar will be the frequency, on the Y axis, that corresponds to each interval.

4. Set up a cumulative frequency distribution from the grouped version of the data in Table 1 that you prepared in Exercise 1. In order to do this you will need to:

   A. Start a column for cumulative frequencies, labelled "cf". The cf column will consist of the total number of scores up to and including each class interval, starting from the lowest one to the highest one. The cf for the highest interval should equal N.

   B. Add a cumulative proportion column, labelled "cp", by dividing each cumulative frequency value by N. Then create a cumulative percentage column, labelled "C%", by multiplying each cp value by 100.

   C. Prepare a cumulative percentage distribution graph by creating an X axis listing the upper real limit for each interval, which is the top score in each interval plus .5. The Y axis should list the cumulative percentages, C%, from zero to 100% at intervals of 10.

Plot the C% values corresponding to each of the values on the X axis and connect all the points with straight lines.

5. For the following set of raw score data:

| 52 | 54 | 56 | 58 | 60 | 61 | 61 | 63 | 67 | 68 |

   A. Describe the central tendency of the data by finding the mean, median and mode;

   B. Describe the variability of the data by finding the range, standard deviation (SD), and variance;

   C. Express each score in terms of its distance from the mean in standard deviation units by calculating the z score for each raw score.

6. Assume that a large tenth grade class took achievement tests known to be highly reliable and valid in the areas of Geography, Spelling, and Mathematics. The scores on all three of these tests were normally distributed, but the tests differed in the following respects:

	Number of Items	Mean	Standard Deviation
Geography Test	75	60	10
Spelling Test	150	100	20
Math Test	40	25	5

Assume that you are particularly interested in comparing three of the students who took these tests (Alan, Betty, and Carlos) in terms of how they did in relation to each other, in relation to their classmates, and also in terms of designating the one who performed best in all areas. The students' scores are as follows:

	Alan	Betty	Carlos
Geography Test	46	72	60
Spelling Test	110	100	140
Math Test	30	33	37

   A. Prepare a table showing the percentage scores for each student on each test. Note, however, that since the percentage scores on each test come from different distributions, they cannot be justifiably averaged across tests or otherwise compared with the percentage scores from the other tests.

   B. Prepare a table showing linearly derived z scores for Alan, Betty, and Carlos. Note that although z scores can be averaged, the presence of decimals and negative values will make it more difficult to do so than it would be otherwise.

   C. Using the Table of Areas under the Normal Curve in the Appendix of this guide, look up the percentile equivalents for each z score.

   D. Convert each of the z scores into T scores (Mean = 50, SD = 10) and make up a table showing them and showing the average T score for each student. The initial goal of obtaining scores that are intra-and interindividually comparable will have been achieved most suitably with this final step.

7. Using the table of z scores prepared for Exercise 6 B, convert each z score into the following types of scores through linear transformations (New score = (z score x SD) + Mean):

   A. Deviation IQs (Mean = 100 and SD = 15);

B. College Entrance Examination Board (CEEB) scores (Mean = 500 and SD = 100).

8. Convert each of the percentile scores you obtained in Exercise 6 C into stanine scores by using Table 4-4 of the textbook. You will need to obtain cumulative percentages for each stanine by adding the normal curve percentages shown in Table 4-4 from left to right. Note that these are the first nonlinearly derived standard scores you have obtained thus far in these exercises.

9. Assume that the scores and cumulative percentages given below were taken from a distribution whose shape deviated somewhat from the normal curve. Obtain normalized z scores for each raw score point given by referring to the Table of Areas under the Normal Curve in the Appendix of this guide.

Raw Scores:	60	50	40	30	20	10
Cumulative %:	95%	75%	65%	45%	15%	5%

10. Assume that 100 students took a test and that the test scores were normally distributed and had a mean of 20 and a standard deviation of 2.

A. What are the z scores for the following raw scores?

   16   18   19   20   21   22   24

B. Using the Table of Areas under the Normal Curve in the Appendix of this guide, with the z scores you have just obtained, determine the percentage of the scores that fall between the following raw score ranges:

   18 and 22   19 and 21   16 and 24

ANSWERS TO EXERCISES: (Review of Basic Statistics and Standard Scores)

1. A.   **TABLE 2**   **TEST RESULTS ARRANGED IN DESCENDING ORDER**

N = 50

97				72	72	
94				71	71	
93				70	70	
90				69	69	
89	89			68		
86				67		
85				66	66	66
84				65		
83				63	63	
82				62		
81				60		
80	80	80		59		
78	78			57		
77				55		
76				54		
75	75			51		
74	74	74		47		
73				41		

B. Range = 97 − 41 + 1 = 57

C. Interval size = 57/12 = 4.75 or 5

D. and E. **TABLE 3**   **GROUPED FREQUENCY DISTRIBUTION**

$$N = 50 \qquad i = 5$$

X Scores	Tallies	f Frequencies
95-99	I	1
90-94	III	3
85-89	IIII	4
80-84	ⅢⅡ II	7
75-79	ⅢⅡ I	6
70-74	ⅢⅡ ⅢⅡ	10
65-69	ⅢⅡ III	8
60-64	IIII	4
55-59	III	3
50-54	II	2
45-49	I	1
40-44	I	1

2. See Figure 1

Figure 1 – Frequency polygon for test data

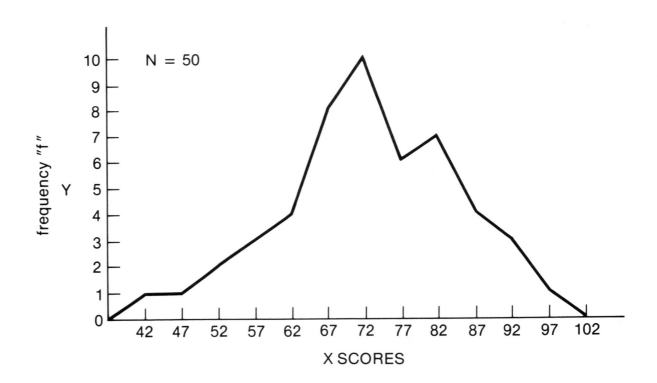

3. See Figure 2

Figure 2 – Histogram for test data

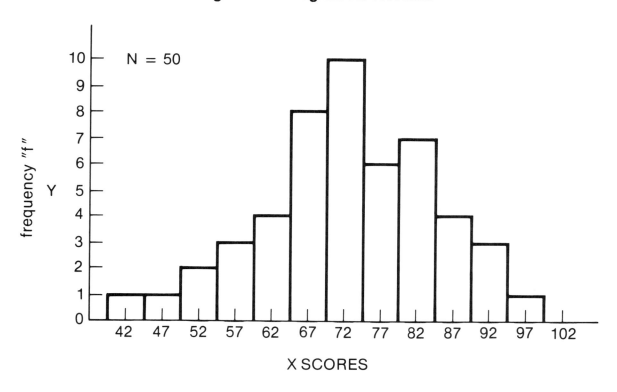

4. A. and B.

TABLE 4   **CUMULATIVE FREQUENCIES, PROPORTIONS, AND PERCENTAGES**

X	f	cf	cp	C%
95-99	1	50	1.00	100
90-94	3	49	.98	98
85-89	4	46	.92	92
80-84	7	42	.84	84
75-79	6	35	.70	70
70-74	10	29	.58	58
65-69	8	19	.38	38
60-64	4	11	.22	22
55-59	3	7	.14	14
50-54	2	4	.08	8
45-49	1	2	.04	4
40-44	1	1	.02	2

C. See Figure 3

Figure 3 – Cumulative percentage distribution

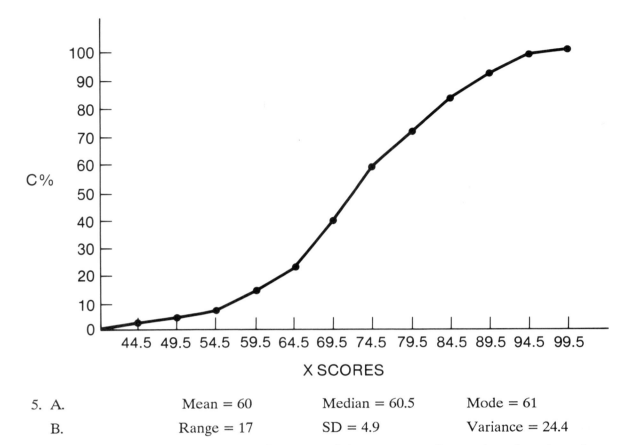

X SCORES

5. A.   Mean = 60   Median = 60.5   Mode = 61

   B.   Range = 17   SD = 4.9   Variance = 24.4

NOTE: All of the variability measures (but none of the measures of central tendency) you have obtained from this exercise coincide exactly with those in the illustration contained in Table 4-2 of the textbook. The reason is, of course, apparent if you examine the data for this exercise and for the one in Table 4-2 of the text and realize that the scores for this exercise were altered only by adding a constant of 20 to each of the scores in Table 4-2. This illustrates an important difference between measures of variability and measures of central tendency.

C.

Raw Scores	z scores
52	−1.63
54	−1.22
56	−0.82
58	−0.41
60	0.00
61	+0.20
61	+0.20
63	+0.61
67	+1.43
68	+1.63

6. A.

PERCENTAGE SCORES FOR ALAN, BETTY, AND CARLOS

	Alan	Betty	Carlos
Geography Test	61	96	80
Spelling Test	73	67	93
Math Test	75	83	93

B.

LINEARLY DERIVED z SCORES FOR ALAN, BETTY, AND CARLOS

	Alan	Betty	Carlos
Geography Test	−1.4	+1.2	0.0
Spelling Test	+0.5	0.0	+2.0
Math Test	+1.0	+1.6	+2.4

C.

PERCENTILE SCORES FOR ALAN, BETTY, AND CARLOS

	Alan	Betty	Carlos
Geography Test	8th	88th	50th
Spelling Test	69th	50th	98th
Math Test	84th	95th	99th

D.

T SCORES FOR ALAN, BETTY, AND CARLOS

	Alan	Betty	Carlos
Geography Test	36	62	50
Spelling Test	55	50	70
Math Test	60	66	74
Average T scores	50	59	65

7. A.

DEVIATION IQ SCORES FOR ALAN, BETTY, AND CARLOS

	Alan	Betty	Carlos
Geography Test	79	118	100
Spelling Test	108	100	130
Math Test	115	124	136

B.

CEEB SCORES FOR ALAN, BETTY, AND CARLOS

	Alan	Betty	Carlos
Geography Test	360	620	500
Spelling Test	550	500	700
Math Test	600	660	740

NOTE: Although school achievement test scores typically are not reported in terms of deviation IQs or CEEB-type scores, there is no reason, other than custom or convenience, for using certain combinations of means and SDs for standard score transformations. Since these standard scores were all derived linearly, they stand in the same relative positions to one another regardless of the differences in units, a fact that is quite noticeable upon inspection of these results.

8.

STANINES FOR ALAN, BETTY, AND CARLOS

	Alan	Betty	Carlos
Geography Test	2	7	5
Spelling Test	6	5	9
Math Test	7	8	9

9.

Raw Scores	C%	Normalized z Scores
60	95	+1.64
50	75	+0.67
40	65	+0.39
30	45	−0.13
20	15	−1.04
10	5	−1.64

NOTE: These z scores, which were obtained through a nonlinear transformation, could be further transformed into other types of derived scores, as was done in Exercises 7 A and 7 B.

10. A.

Raw Scores	z Scores
16	−2.0
18	−1.0
19	−0.5
20	0.0
21	+0.5
22	+1.0
24	+2.0

B. 68 percent would fall between 18 and 22;
38 percent would fall between 19 and 21; and
95 percent would fall between 16 and 24.

FILL IN THE BLANKS: Key Terms and Concepts

1. When test scores are interpreted in terms of how far along the normal developmental path an individual has progressed, the frame of reference is that of *developmental norms*.

2. The major types of developmental norms described in the textbook are *mental* ages, *grade* equivalents, and *ordinal* scales.

3. A mental age score from a test whose items are grouped into year levels consists of the sum of the *basal age*, which is the highest age at and below which all tests were passed, and the additional credits earned at higher age levels.

4. *Grade equivalents* are a type of developmental norm that is obtained by computing the average raw scores obtained by children in various grade levels.

5. The _____ _____ Schedules are one example of an ordinal scale which shows the developmental level a child has attained in motor, adaptive, language, and personal-social behavior.

6. _____-_____ norms are a frame of reference for score interpretation based on an evaluation of the individual's performance in terms of the most nearly comparable group.

7. Whereas the 50th percentile corresponds to the *median*, the 25th and 75th percentiles are known as the first and third *quartile* points, respectively.

8. A(n) _____ _____ chart is a graphic representation of scores that is plotted on paper especially designed to show percentile points spaced in the same way they are in a normal distribution.

9. Comparability of norms can be achieved by using an anchor test to develop equivalency tables for scores on different tests. One way to do this is by the _____ method, in which scores on two tests are considered equivalent when they have equal percentiles in a given group.

10. The Scholastic Aptitude Test uses the 11,000 candidates who took the test in 1941 as a _____ _____ group to provide comparability and continuity of scores without evaluating performance normatively each year.

11. The approach to test equating known as _____ _____ theory uses a uniform and "sample-free" scale of measurement based on data derived from anchor items or anchor tests representing a wide range of ability and item difficulty.

12. _____ computer interpretations of test results are produced by means of a computer program that associates prepared verbal statements with particular patterns of test responses.

13. _____ computer systems allow an individual to, in effect, engage in a dialogue with a computer and have been used primarily for educational and career planning.

14. The kind of testing that uses a specified content domain as its interpretive frame of reference is called *criterion-referenced* testing. The major feature of this type of assessment is the procedure of testing for _____.

15. __ __ __ __ __ __ __ __ __ __ __ __ __ __ __ __ and __ __ __ __ __ __ __ __ __ __ __ __

__ __ __ __ __ __ __ are two of the methods that can be used to express test scores in terms of the probability of different criterion outcomes.

ANSWERS TO FILL-IN-THE-BLANKS: (Key Terms and Concepts)

1. developmental norms
2. mental (ages)/grade (equivalents)/ordinal (scales)
3. basal age
4. grade equivalents
5. Gesell Developmental (Schedules)
6. within-group (norms)
7. median/quartile
8. normal percentile (chart)
9. equipercentile (method)
10. fixed reference (group)
11. item response (theory) (IRT)
12. narrative (computer interpretations)
13. interactive (computer systems)
14. criterion-referenced/mastery
15. expectancy tables/expectancy charts

MULTIPLE CHOICE: TEST YOURSELF

1. Norms for an educational or psychological test are established by _____

_____.

   a. the opinion of experts in the field covered by the test
   b. testing a representative sample of people
   c. examining the performance of the top and bottom 10% of a population
   d. using item analysis procedures for each item and combining the results for those taking the test

2. The major advantage of converting raw test scores to derived scores is that _____

_____.

   a. derived scores show a test taker's relative standing compared with others taking the test
   b. some derived scores permit the direct comparison of scores made on different tests
   c. derived scores show the test taker's score in relation to perfect performance
   d. a and b

3. The normal curve is _____.

    a. bilaterally symmetrical
    b. more likely to be approximated when small groups are used
    c. one that has a mean value that is less than 10% higher than the median
    d. one that shows only positive standard scores

4. Which of the following is a measure of central tendency? _____.

    a. Standard deviation
    b. Average deviation
    c. Mean
    d. Variance

5. What is the mean for the following set of scores? _____.

    10, 8, 7, 2, 1

    a. 7
    b. 28
    c. 5.6
    d. none of the above

6. The most simple measure of variability is the _____.

    a. average deviation
    b. mean
    c. variance
    d. range

7. What is the median for the following set of scores? _____.

    64, 53, 50, 57, 61, 56, 58, 59

    a. 57
    b. 58
    c. 57.5
    d. 57.25

8. The mental age units used in revisions of the Stanford-Binet prior to 1986 _____

_____.

    a. remain constant with advancing age
    b. shrink with advancing age
    c. become larger with advancing age
    d. bear no real relationship to age

9. The major problem associated with the use of percentiles is that _____

_____.

    a. they are difficult to interpret
    b. they are more difficult to calculate than most other derived scores
    c. in a normal distribution percentile units are not equal throughout the scale
    d. they show little relationship to other derived scores

10. Linearly derived standard scores or z scores are based on _____
    _____.
    a. a raw score's distance from the mean in SD units
    b. derived percentile ranks
    c. the relation of a raw score to a normalized distribution
    d. expectancy scores

11. A stanine is an example of a (an) _____.
    a. ordinal scale value
    b. standard score
    c. z score
    d. norm-equivalent score

12. A person obtains a percentile score of 76. This means that the person _____
    _____.
    a. answered 76% of the items correctly
    b. did not score as well as 76% of those taking the test
    c. has a z score of –0.76
    d. outperformed 76% of those who also took the test

13. Systematic variations among the scores obtained by a single individual on different tests
    might be due to _____.
    a. differences in test content
    b. differences in scale units among the tests
    c. the composition of the standardization samples of the different tests
    d. any or all of the above

14. The main focus of criterion-referenced testing is on _____
    _____.
    a. score comparisons with a known group
    b. what individuals know within a specified domain
    c. how students compare with their classmates
    d. expectancies of how a person will do in the future

15. An expectancy table _____
    _____.
    a. gives the probabilities of different criterion outcomes for persons who obtain each test score
    b. shows the relationship between raw scores and expected standard scores
    c. is presented in terms of z scores
    d. is an important feature in mastery testing

MINIPROJECTS/SUGGESTED OUTREACH ACTIVITIES:

A thorough understanding of the concepts presented in Chapter 4 is crucial to an effective grasp of most of the material in the rest of the textbook. Therefore, instead of going beyond the subject matter covered in this chapter, your follow-up should consist of deepening your knowledge of what *is* covered. To this end it may be helpful for you to pinpoint the topics or concepts you may need to study further. Chances are that a review of your performance in the statistical exercises will reveal those areas to you as many students find that their working knowledge of statistics is somewhat limited.

1. Find a good basic textbook in statistics, preferably one geared to the behavioral and social sciences, such as *Applied Statistics for the Behavioral Sciences,* 2nd edition, by D. E. Hinkle, W. Wiersma, and S. G. Jurs (Boston: Houghton Mifflin, 1988.) A review of such a text is likely to strengthen both your grasp of and your self-confidence in this area.

2. Take the time to study the nature and characteristics of the normal distribution in as much detail as possible. Review carefully the Table of Areas under the Normal Curve presented in the Appendix of this guide as well as the relationships among various types of scores presented in Figure 4-6 of the textbook. An expanded version of that figure can be found in *Test Service Notebook 148,* which is a four-page pamphlet published by The Psychological Corporation (TPC) and available from them (see Appendix C of the textbook for TPC's address).

3. Investigate how distributions can differ from the normal curve in terms of their shape. Review concepts such as the "skewness" and "kurtosis" of distributions and what they mean as far as the data they represent are concerned.

4. Replicate, or expand on, some of the exercises in this chapter of the guide, especially any that were troublesome for you, with a different set of data. You could, for example, ask an instructor to provide you with the raw scores for an examination from a class with a large enrollment. With this "data bank" you could proceed to calculate measures of central tendency and variability, compute percentiles, z scores, T scores or stanines for each student and draw a frequency polygon or a histogram to represent the performance of the class.

5. Study Table 4-5 of your textbook and, using the Table of Areas under the Normal Curve, see if you can arrive at the percentage data for the standard deviation values given in Table 4-5, or for different SD values (e.g., 10 or 20), within the IQ intervals listed. This will allow you to practice standard score transformations and will increase your understanding of the impact that the value chosen for the SD has on the meaning of deviation IQs.

ANSWERS TO MULTIPLE CHOICE/TEST YOURSELF ITEMS:

1. b	4. c	7. c	10. a	13. d
2. d	5. c	8. b	11. b	14. b
3. a	6. d	9. c	12. d	15. a

Chapter 5
RELIABILITY

CHAPTER OUTLINE

CHAPTER SUMMARY

Measures of the reliability or consistency of test scores allow us to estimate the proportions of total variance attributable to error variance and to true variance. Reliability is gauged by the degree of relationship between two independently derived sets of scores from the same test. The degree of relationship between two sets of scores can be graphically represented by a scatter diagram and/or expressed numerically by a correlation coefficient which can range from +1.00 to −1.00. The most common type of correlation coefficient is the Pearson Product-Moment Correlation Coefficient or Pearson r, which is actually the mean of the cross-products of two sets of standard scores. Although the degree of correlation desirable for reliability coefficients is in the .80s or higher, a correlation coefficient can be statistically significant at a much lower value.

The types of reliability that are applicable for a given test depend on the nature of the sources of error or irrelevant fluctuations that are likely to enter into test scores. Methods of gauging reliability include some that assess a single source of error variance, such as split-half reliability which estimates variance due to content sampling, and some that assess two sources of error variance, such as delayed alternate-form reliability which estimates variance due to time *and* content sampling. Methods of gauging reliability also vary with regard to whether they utilize a single administration of a single test form, such as Kuder-Richardson reliability and coefficient alpha which are measures of interitem consistency influenced by content sampling and content heterogeneity, or whether they use two administrations of a single test form separated by an interval, such as test-retest reliability which assesses time sampling error. Yet another method, i.e., immediate alternate-form reliability, utilizes contiguous administrations of two test forms and results in an estimate of content sampling error only. In addition, for tests in which scorer differences may be a potential source of error, scorer reliability coefficients can be used to gauge the extent of those differences.

Another issue that needs to be considered in the process of investigating the reliability of tests is the extent to which speed plays a role in determining test scores. If a significant proportion of the total variance of test scores is attributable to speed, single-trial reliability coefficients are not applicable unless procedures used in obtaining them are modified to take time into account.

Correlation coefficients are affected by the variability of the samples in which they are found as well as by the composition of those samples. Therefore, every reliability coefficient should be accompanied by a description of the type of group on which it was obtained to allow for a determination of whether such a coefficient applies to the groups with which a test will be used. In addition, in situations wherein the variability of scores is likely to be reduced, such as in criterion-referenced or mastery testing, the procedures used to evaluate reliability need to be suitably modified.

The standard error of measurement is an alternative way of expressing test reliability and is suitable to the interpretation of individual scores in terms of the reasonable limits within which they are likely to fluctuate as a function of measurement error. When a comparison of the significance of the differences between scores on different tests is needed, the standard error of the difference is a very useful statistic that takes into account the combined errors of measurement of the two tests.

COMPREHENSIVE REVIEW

STUDY QUESTIONS:

1. Define reliability and relate it to the concept of error of measurement.

2. Describe the meaning of correlation and of correlation coefficients.

3. Discuss the notion of statistical significance as it applies to the evaluation of correlation coefficients used as measures of reliability.

4. Describe the procedures involved in gathering test-retest, alternate-form, split-half, and Kuder-Richardson estimates of reliability.

5. Describe the procedure involved in estimating scorer reliability and explain how this type of reliability differs from the other types.

6. Discuss the considerations that are pertinent to the selection of each method of estimating reliability.

7. Describe the difference between a pure speed test and a pure power test and the impact of the role of speed on the procedures used to gauge the reliability of a test.

8. List and discuss two important sample characteristics that can affect the size of a reliability coefficient.

9. Compare and contrast the standard error of measurement with the reliability coefficient in terms of their derivation and applicability.

10. Explain why the standard error of the difference between two scores is always larger than the standard error of measurement of either of the two scores.

EXERCISES: Statistical Aspects of Reliability

1. Prepare a scatter diagram for the following set of bivariate data:

Person	Variable X	Variable Y
A	10	3
B	2	7
C	9	1
D	7	5
E	3	8
F	5	5
G	1	7
H	3	7

2. For the above data, calculate the Pearson product-moment correlation coefficient, using the formula given in the textbook.

3. A test of 100 items has a reliability of .88. What would be the estimated reliability if the length of the test were:

   A. doubled;

   B. cut to only 25 items?

4. The following set of data represents the raw scores of students A through F on the odd and even halves of a 40-item multiple choice test from a course in Psychological Testing. Calculate the split-half (odd-even) reliability and use the Spearman-Brown formula to estimate the reliability of the entire test.

RAW SCORES

Student	Odd Half	Even Half	Total Score
A	20	18	38
B	19	17	36
C	19	17	36
D	15	17	32
E	15	16	31
F	13	13	26

5. As a follow-up to the previous exercise, calculate the Kuder-Richardson Formula 20 (K-R 20) reliability coefficient for the same 40-item multiple choice test. Use the data that follow along with the K-R 20 formula. You will also need to refer back to the total test scores for the students (given in the last column in the previous item) in order to compute the variance (SD_t^2) term for the K-R 20. After you have calculated the K-R 20 reliability

coefficient, compare it to the odd-even coefficient you obtained in the previous item and explain the difference between the two coefficients.

$$\text{K-R 20 Formula:} \quad r_{tt} = \left(\frac{n}{n-1}\right) \frac{SD_t^2 - \Sigma\, pq}{SD_t^2}$$

where

n   = the number of items in the test

SD_t = the standard deviation of total test scores

p   = the proportion of students who passed each item

q   = the proportion of students who failed each item

TABLE 5. ITEM STATISTICS

Item #	p	q	Item #	p	q
1	1.00	0.00	21	0.83	0.17
2	0.50	0.50	22	0.83	0.17
3	1.00	0.00	23	0.50	0.50
4	0.83	0.17	24	1.00	0.00
5	0.83	0.17	25	1.00	0.00
6	1.00	0.00	26	0.67	0.33
7	0.83	0.17	27	0.83	0.17
8	0.83	0.17	28	0.67	0.33
9	0.83	0.17	29	0.83	0.17
10	1.00	0.00	30	0.67	0.33
11	1.00	0.00	31	1.00	0.00
12	1.00	0.00	32	1.00	0.00
13	1.00	0.00	33	0.50	0.50
14	0.83	0.17	34	0.50	0.50
15	0.67	0.33	35	0.83	0.17
16	1.00	0.00	36	1.00	0.00
17	0.67	0.33	37	0.67	0.33
18	0.33	0.67	38	0.67	0.33
19	1.00	0.00	39	1.00	0.00
20	1.00	0.00	40	1.00	0.00

Note: Consult p. 123 of the textbook for a more complete explanation of the Kuder-Richardson Formula 20.

6. A test has a standard deviation of 9 and a reliability of .88. What is the standard error (SE) of measurement for the test?

7. Calculate the standard errors of measurement for each of the following reliability coefficients:

    .90   .75   .50   .25

with each of the following standard deviation values:

    10   15   20   25

(For a total of 4 x 4 = 16 standard errors of measurement)

8. A student obtains a Verbal IQ (VIQ) of 90 and a Performance IQ (PIQ) of 101 on an intelligence test. The standard errors of measurement are 3 for the VIQ and 4 for the PIQ. Using the Table of Areas under the Normal Curve in the appendix of this guide, determine the level of significance for the difference between the two IQ scores and explain the meaning of the level of significance you find.

9. Using the Table of Areas Under the Normal Curve (again), determine how far apart a Verbal IQ (VIQ) and a Performance IQ (PIQ) must be in order for the difference between them to be significant at the .01 level, given that the standard errors of measurement are 4 for the VIQs and 6 for the PIQs.

ANSWERS TO EXERCISES: (Statistical Aspects of Reliability)

1. See Figure 4

Figure 4 – Scatter diagram of bivariate data

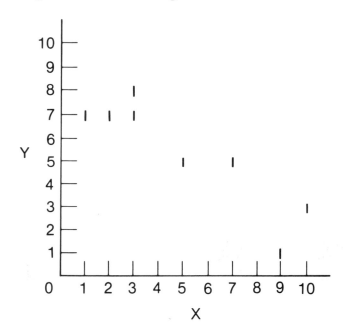

2. Pearson r = – 0.898 or – 0.90

3. A.   r = 0.936 or 0.94   B.   r = 0.647 or 0.65

4. Odd-even reliability = 0.81

   Spearman-Brown estimate for the whole test = 0.895

5. The K-R 20 reliability coefficient is 0.75, which is somewhat lower than the odd-even reliability coefficient obtained in the previous exercise. The difference is due to the fact that the K-R 20 takes into account content heterogeneity as well as content sampling error whereas the odd-even reliability only takes into account content sampling error.

6. Standard error (SE) of measurement = 3.12

7.

TABLE 6. STANDARD ERRORS OF MEASUREMENT

Reliability	SD = 10	SD = 15	SD = 20	SD = 25
.90	3.16	4.74	6.32	7.91
.75	5.00	7.50	10.00	12.50
.50	7.07	10.61	14.14	17.68
.25	8.66	12.99	17.32	21.65

Notice that the standard errors of measurement for a given reliability coefficient are a constant proportion of the standard deviation values. Study this table and extend it to other reliability coefficients and SD values, if possible. Consider, for example, what the SE of measurement would be if reliability were perfect (+ 1.00) or zero.

8. Standard error (SE) of the difference between scores = 5

Absolute difference between the scores = 11

$$z = \frac{\text{Difference between scores}}{\text{SE of the difference}} = \frac{11}{5} = 2.2$$

The Table of Areas under the Normal Curve indicates that the probability of obtaining a difference of 11 points between the scores (in either direction) if there were no difference at all between the two "true" scores is less than 3 out of 100 (p is exactly 0.0139 (2) or 0.0278).

9. The Table of Areas under the Normal Curve indicates that the z value necessary for a significance level of .01 is 2.58. Since the SE of the difference between VIQs and PIQs is 7.21, the difference between IQs would have to be at least 19 points for it to be significant at that level (7.21 (2.58) = 18.60 or 19).

FILL IN THE BLANKS: Key Terms and Concepts

1. The concept of *Reliability* or consistency of scores underlies the computation of the *error* of *measurement* which, in turn, allows us to predict the range of fluctuation likely to occur in a score as a result of irrelevant or chance factors.

2. The total variance of test scores is made up of differences in the characteristic being measured by a test or "_ _ _ _" variance and chance factors or _ _ _ _ _ variance.

3. A _ _ _ _ _ _ _ _ _ _ _ _ _ _ _ _ _ _ _ _ _ _ _ or _ _ _ _ _ _ _ _ _ _ _ _ _ _ _ _ _ is a graphic representation of the relationship between two variables wherein each person's scores on both variables are simultaneously represented by a single tally mark.

4. The probable fluctuation to be expected from sample to sample in the size of correlations, means, and any other group measures can be estimated by determining a _ _ _ _ _ of _ _ . _ _ _ _ _ _ _ _ _ _ for the value of those statistics.

5. Test-Retest reliability is found by administering the identical test on two occasions and correlating the scores obtained on each occasion. This method estimates the amount of error variance attributable to time sampling.

6. The _ _ _ _ _ _ formula is an alternate method for finding split-half reliability that is based on the variance of differences between scores on the two half-tests as a proportion of total variance.

7. A major difference between the usual split-half methods of investigating reliability and measures of interitem consistency, such as Kuder-Richardson reliability, is that the former assess error variance due to content sampling whereas the latter assess error variance due to content sampling and content heterogeneity.

8. The manual for a test of creativity in which the judgment of the scorer enters into the scoring process should include one or more estimates of _ _ _ _ _ _ _ _ _ _ _ _ _ _ _ _ _ _.

9. A major problem inherent in two-trial methods of establishing reliability, such as test-retest and alternate forms, is that the correlation between the two trials may be spuriously high due to Recall.

10. In a pure power test the proportion of total test variance attributable to individual differences in speed would be zero, whereas in a pure speed test that proportion would be 1.00.

11. The reliability coefficient and the standard error of measurement are alternative ways of expressing test reliability. The former is useful in comparing different tests whereas the latter is more appropriately used to interpret individual scores.

12. Measures of correlation, such as reliability coefficients, are affected by the range of individual differences or _ _ _ _ _ _ _ _ _ _ _ _ _ _ in the groups used to calculate them. The main effect of a restriction in the range of one or both of the correlated variables is that the _ _ _ _ _ _ _ _ _ _ _ _ between them will be lowered.

ANSWERS TO FILL-IN-THE-BLANKS: (Key Terms and Concepts)

1. reliability/error (of) measurement
2. "true" (variance)/error (variance)
3. bivariate distribution (or) scatter diagram

4. level (of) significance

5. test-retest (reliability)/time (sampling)

6. Rulon (formula)

7. Kuder-Richardson (reliability)/content (sampling)/content heterogeneity

8. scorer reliability

9. recall

10. zero/1.00

11. different tests/individual scores

12. variability/correlation

TRUE/FALSE and WHY?

1. A correlation coefficient of + 0.30 indicates a stronger relationship between the correlated variables than a correlation coefficient of – 0.67. (T/F) Why? _F_ _____

   _____

2. The .01 and the .05 levels of significance are applied in most psychological research because they indicate 99% and 95% levels of confidence, respectively, that the data support the hypothesis being tested. (T/F) Why? _T_ _____

   _____

3. When retest reliability and/or delayed alternate-form reliability are reported it is desirable to give some indication of relevant intervening experiences that might have occurred between the two administrations of the test. (T/F) Why? _____

   _____

4. The technique of retesting with the identical test is appropriate for finding the reliability coefficient of most psychological tests. (T/F) Why? _____

   _____

5. All other things being equal, the longer a test is, the more reliable it will be in terms of content sampling. (T/F) Why? _____

6. If the criterion one is trying to predict with a test is highly heterogeneous, the content heterogeneity of test items is not necessarily a source of error variance. (T/F) Why? _____

   _____

7. Most aptitude and intelligence tests, whether speeded or not, are designed to prevent the achievement of perfect scores. (T/F) Why? _T_ _____

   _____

8. If the reliability coefficient reported in a test manual was calculated for a group ranging across all high school years, it can be safely assumed that the reliability would be at least as high if recomputed within a single year level. (T/F) Why? _____

_____

ANSWERS TO TRUE/FALSE:

1. False	3. True	5. True	7. True
2. True	4. False	6. True	8. False

MULTIPLE CHOICE: TEST YOURSELF

1. The best definition of reliability is _____ .
   a. consistency
   b. exactness of measurement
   c. correlational coefficient
   d. validity of measurement

2. A correlation of – 1.24 means _____ .
   a. an inverse relationship between two variables
   b. a direct negative correlation
   c. there is a moderate negative correlation
   d. an error has been made

3. A correlation of + 0.32 is found to be significant at the .01 level. This means that _____
   _____ .
   a. the correlation is definitely real
   b. the correlation is significant at the 99% level
   c. there is a 1% chance or less that the true r is zero
   d. the minimum real value for r is greater than zero

4. The most basic method of determining reliability involving the administration of a test on more than one occasion is known as _____ .
   a. coefficient alpha
   b. test-retest reliability
   c. Kuder-Richardson 21
   d. the Rulon method

5. If a test shows high split-half reliability, it probably means that _____
   _____ .
   a. the test is valid
   b. the correlation is negative
   c. variation due to content sampling is not a large problem
   d. the proportion of error variance to true variance is high

6. The time interval between the first and second administrations for test-retest reliability should be _____.

    a. one hour or less
    b. between one hour and two days
    c. reported along with the obtained coefficient
    d. determined by the validity coefficient

7. When reliability is determined by the delayed alternate-form method, error variance is contributed by each of the following except _____.

    a. differences between the test takers
    b. content sampling
    c. time between form 1 and form 2
    d. differences in the test takers' emotional state

8. The Spearman-Brown formula is used to estimate changes in the reliability of a test when _____.

    a. more persons are added to or taken from the sample
    b. alternate forms are used to determine reliability
    c. the test has undergone revision
    d. the length of the test is varied

9. A test with 30 items and a reliability of .60 is lengthened to 60 items. What is its expected reliability? _____.

    a. .75
    b. −.75
    c. .69
    d. .84

10. The coefficient alpha is used to determine the interitem consistency of tests with items _____.

    a. which are extremely heterogeneous
    b. of varying levels of difficulty
    c. which are multiple-scored
    d. which are scored as right or wrong

11. A test has a reliability coefficient of .91. This means that _____.

    a. 9% of the variance is real
    b. 82.8% of the variance is real
    c. 91% of the variance is true
    d. 91% of the questions were answered correctly

12. The reliability for a speeded test _____

_____ .

    a. can be calculated as for an unspeeded test
    b. will be lower than for an unspeeded test
    c. is found by the split-half method
    d. will be spuriously high if found by the usual single-trial methods

13. A test writer wishes to ensure that his test will show the highest reliability possible. He

    should _____

_____ .

    a. increase the number of items on the test
    b. try to maintain item homogeneity
    c. administer the test to a very heterogeneous standardization sample
    d. all of the above will increase reliability

14. A test has a standard deviation of 5 and a reliability of .91. What is the standard error of

    measurement? _____ .

    a. 15
    b. 1.5
    c. 2.5
    d. 6

15. The standard error of measurement for test 1 is 2.5. The standard error of measurement for

    test 2 is 3.1. The standard error of the difference between the two tests will be _____

_____ .

    a. less than 3.1
    b. between 2.5 and 3.1
    c. less than 2.5
    d. greater than 3.1

MINIPROJECTS/SUGGESTED OUTREACH ACTIVITIES:

1. As was the case in Chapter 4, the present chapter presupposes some familiarity with the basic statistical techniques that underlie the topic of reliability. Therefore, once again, a review of the pertinent areas of a good basic statistics textbook is highly recommended. Use your performance in the statistical exercises for this chapter as a guide to the areas in which you need to strengthen or expand your knowledge. In particular, the notion of *correlation* and the specific techniques used to measure it, such as the Pearson r, should be thoroughly understood in order to achieve a good grasp of the material on reliability, as well as validity, and related topics. In addition, the concept of *statistical significance,* which is part of the much larger topics of *probability* and *statistical estimation* using the normal curve as the underlying distribution, should be well understood for a meaningful grasp of the material on "standard errors" in this and later chapters.

2. Locate a table of the critical values of the Pearson r (which is discussed on page 115 of the textbook) in a statistics textbook. Study the table and notice the impact that sample size and the different levels of significance have on the critical values listed in the table. Try to

explain the meaning of the table to someone else in your own words or write a short essay describing the table.

ANSWERS TO MULTIPLE CHOICE/TEST YOURSELF ITEMS:

1. a	4. b	7. a	10. c	13. d
2. d	5. c	8. d	11. c	14. b
3. c	6. c	9. a	12. d	15. d

Chapter 6
VALIDITY: BASIC CONCEPTS

CHAPTER OUTLINE

Content-Related Validation
    Nature
    Specific Procedures
    Applications
    Face Validity

Criterion-Related Validation
    Concurrent and Predictive Validation
    Criterion Contamination
    Some Common Criteria
    Validity Generalization

Construct-Related Validation
    Developmental Changes
    Correlations with Other Tests
    Factor Analysis
    Internal Consistency
    Convergent and Discriminant Validation
    Experimental Interventions
    Contributions from Cognitive Psychology
    Construct-Related Validation: Advances and Pitfalls

Overview of Validation Concepts
    Comparison of Validation Procedures
    Inclusiveness of Construct-Related Validation
    Validation in the Test Construction Process

CHAPTER SUMMARY

The process of validating a test consists of ascertaining what the test actually measures, and how well it does so, through both logical and empirical methods that illuminate the relationship between performance on the test and independently observable facts about the behavior in question. The validity of a test is not established in the abstract; rather, it must be established with reference to the particular use for which the test is being considered. The specific techniques that are used in validating a test can be grouped into three major categories, namely, content-related, criterion-related, and construct-related validation.

Content-related validation, which is most commonly applied in educational and occupational testing, involves a determination of the adequacy of coverage of the relevant behavior domain through a systematic examination of test content. Content validity is built into a test through the choice of items that sample the specified domain of skills and knowledge to be tested in an appropriate and representative fashion. Content validity differs from "face validity" in that the former is established through objective and empirical procedures whereas the latter refers to what the test superficially appears to measure.

Criterion-related validation procedures are relevant whenever a test is used to predict an individual's performance in specified activities. A major distinction made among criterion-related validation procedures concerns the temporal aspects of the relationship between the test and the criterion. Concurrent criterion-related validation takes place when criterion information is available at the time of testing or when the purpose of testing is the diagnosis of existing status. Predictive criterion-related validation procedures, on the other hand, involve a time interval between the gathering of test and criterion data or pertain to the prediction of a future outcome from test data. The criteria used in test validation can encompass various indices of performance in educational, vocational, or employment settings, membership in contrasted groups, including psychiatric diagnostic categories, ratings developed for the purpose of defining a criterion, and correlations with available tests. Regardless of their source, criterion measures must be gathered independently and guarded against contamination which could take place if test scores were to influence standing on the criterion.

Construct-related validation is a complex and comprehensive concept that involves the accumulation of diverse data that shed light on the extent to which a test measures a theoretical construct or trait. In this sense, construct-related validity encompasses the previous categories of test validation procedures as well as all of the uses and interpretations of tests that expand, enhance or corroborate the meaning of test scores. The data that contribute to construct-related validation range from the internal consistency of the test itself, to the relationship between test performance and a wide network of variables external to the test, including age differentiation, experimental effects, empirically derived factors, and other tests with which the one in question should correlate either positively or negatively or not correlate. In addition, cognitive psychologists have recently expanded the range of construct validation techniques to include those that attempt to study cognitive constructs themselves through a detailed breakdown, analysis, and manipulation of the information-processing components and knowledge stores necessary to perform the tasks set by test items.

As our understanding of the scope of construct validity has expanded, it has been argued that the term validity should be reserved for construct validity alone. If this were done, the concepts presently subsumed under content validity might be labeled "content relevance" and "content coverage" instead and predictive and concurrent criterion-related validity could be labeled, respectively, as the predictive and diagnostic utility of a test.

COMPREHENSIVE REVIEW

STUDY QUESTIONS:

1. Define content validation and explain the specific procedures that are used to determine the content validity of a test.

2. Describe when content validation is an appropriate technique for evaluating tests and explain why this is so.

3. Define face validity and contrast it with other types of validity.

4. Define and compare concurrent and predictive validation.

5. Define criterion contamination and explain its effects on criterion-related **validation** studies.

6. List and describe several types of criteria commonly used in concurrent and predictive validation.

7. Discuss the notions of validity generalization and situational specificity as they are currently understood.

8. Define construct-related validation and describe three methods whereby it can be studied.

9. Describe the multitrait-multimethod matrix design and how the concepts of convergent and discriminant validation fit into that method.

10. Discuss the contributions of cognitive psychology to the area of construct-related validation.

11. Describe the advantages and disadvantages that have resulted from the adoption of the concept of construct validity.

FILL IN THE BLANKS: Key Terms and Concepts

1. In psychological testing, the concept of _Validity_ refers to a determination of what the test measures and how well it does so.

2. The type of validation that is concerned with whether a test covers a representative sample of the knowledge domain to be measured is __ __ __ __ __ __ __ __ __-__ __ __ __ __ __ __ __ __ validation.

3. __ __ __ __ __ __ __ __ validity is built into a test from the outset through the choice of appropriate items. For educational tests, the items are designed to meet the __ drawn-up by subject matter experts.

4. _Face_ validity pertains to whether a test "looks valid" to the people who take it and is not a type of validity in the technical sense.

5. A(n) _Criterion_ is a direct and independent measure of what a test is designed to determine or predict.

6. Concurrent and predictive validation are two aspects of __ __ __ __ __ __ __ __ __ __-__ __ __ __ __ __ __ __ validation that differ in terms of the time relation between criterion and test. In addition, there is a logical distinction between these two aspects of validation in that __ __ __ __ __ __ __ __ __ __ __ validation is relevant to tests used to diagnose existing status whereas in __ __ __ __ __ __ __ __ __ __ __ validation interest is centered on a future outcome.

7. When a person who is involved in the assignment of criterion ratings has knowledge of examinees' test scores, the criterion is said to have undergone

__ __ __ __ __ __ __ __ __ __ __ __ __ __.

8. Whereas the most common criteria used in validating intelligence tests are indices of
   _ _ _ _ _ _ _ _   _ _ _ _ _ _ _ _ _ _ _ _, special aptitude tests are most
   frequently validated with criteria based on performance in
   _ _ _ _ _ _ _ _ _ _   _ _ _ _ _ _ _ _ or actual _ _ _ performance.

9. There are many practical reasons why predictive validation techniques utilize
   _ _ _ _ _ _ _ _ _ _ _ rather than ultimate criteria, chief among which are the
   possible unavailability and multidetermined nature of the latter.

10. Validation by the method of _ _ _ _ _ _ _ _ _ _ _   _ _ _ _ _ _ _ involves a
    composite criterion that reflects the cumulative and uncontrolled selective factors
    operating in daily life that result in survival in, versus elimination from, a certain group.

11. One criterion that may be used in validating certain personality tests, provided it is based on
    prolonged observation and detailed case history data rather than on a cursory interview or
    examination, is _ _ _ _ _ _ _ _ _ _ _   _ _ _ _ _ _ _ _ _.

12. While _ _ _ _ _ _ _ _ can be used as a subsidiary technique in deriving criterion data
    on, for example, academic achievement and job success, they can also be used as the core of
    the criterion measure themselves.

13. The work done by Schmidt, Hunter and their co-workers in the realm of industrial
    validation studies, suggests that as far as some aptitude tests are concerned,
    _ _ _ _ _ _ _ _ _   _ _ _ _ _ _ _ _ _ _ _ _ _ _ can occur far more
    widely across occupations than previously recognized.

14. The CONSTRUCT-Related validity of a test is the extent to which
    the test can be shown to measure a certain trait.

15. The _ _ _ _ _ _ _ _ _ _ validity of a test is essentially the correlation of the test with
    whatever is common to a group of tests or other indices of behavior that have been
    subjected to _ _ _ _ _ _ analysis.

16. When a test is validated by the method of _ _ _ _ _ _ _ _
    _ _ _ _ _ _ _ _ _ _ _, the criterion is the total score on the test itself.

17. The process whereby construct validity is demonstrated by a test's high correlation with
    variables with which it should correlate is called _ _ _ _ _ _ _ _ _ _ _ validation,
    whereas a demonstration that a test does not correlate significantly with variables from
    which it should differ is called _ _ _ _ _ _ _ _ _ _ _ _ _ validation.

18. The work of the cognitive psychologist Susan Embretson expands the concept of construct validation so that it includes two aspects. The first aspect, or __ __ __ __ __ __ __ __ __ __ __ __ __ __ is the same as traditional construct-related validation in that it is concerned with the relations between test performance and a network of other variables. The second aspect, or __ __ __ __ __ __ __ __ __ __ __ __ __ __ __ __ __ __ __ __, on the other hand, is concerned with identifying the specific information-processing components and knowledge required to perform test items.

ANSWERS TO FILL-IN-THE-BLANKS: (Key Terms and Concepts)

1. validity
2. content-related (validation)
3. content (validity)/test specifications
4. face (validity)
5. criterion
6. criterion-related (validation)/concurrent (validation)/ predictive (validation)
7. (criterion) contamination
8. academic achievement/specialized training/job (performance)
9. intermediate (criteria)
10. contrasted groups
11. psychiatric diagnosis
12. ratings
13. validity generalization
14. construct-related (validity)
15. factorial (validity)/factor (analysis)
16. internal consistency
17. convergent (validation)/discriminant (validation)
18. nomothetic span/construct representation

TRUE/FALSE and WHY?

1. In general, the names of tests are quite helpful in providing meaningful clues to the areas of behavior that tests cover. (T/F) Why? _____

_____

2. The task of validating a test is complete once the test has been shown to have high validity. (T/F) Why? _____

_____

3. Content validation is an appropriate technique for educational and occupational achievement tests but not for aptitude or personality tests. (T/F) Why? _____

_____

4. The correlation between a new test and a previously available one is appropriately used as evidence of criterion-related validity only when the former is a shorter or simpler form of the latter. (T/F) Why? _____

_____

5. Since the mid-1970s, the situational specificity of job requirements has been regarded as a more serious limitation in the use of selection tests than was previously thought. (T/F) Why? _____

_____

6. The major advantage of using age differentiation as a criterion of validity is the fact that developmental changes can be assumed to be universal. (T/F) Why? _____

_____

7. In construct-related validation studies, when correlations between a new test and similar earlier tests are obtained, it is desirable that those correlations be as high as possible. (T/F) Why? _____

_____

8. The concept of construct validation has often been misunderstood to imply that validation can be achieved in the absence of data. (T/F) Why? _____

_____

9. The process of validating a test should normally be linked to the last stages of test development. (T/F) Why? _____

_____

10. Experimental interventions wherein test scores are used as the dependent variable are a good source of data for construct validation. (T/F) Why? _____

_____

ANSWERS TO TRUE/FALSE:

1. False	4. True	7. False	10. True
2. False	5. False	8. True	
3. True	6. False	9. False	

MULTIPLE CHOICE: TEST YOURSELF

1. By definition, validity is a measure of _____.
   a. what a test measures
   b. criterion-related reliability
   c. the utility of a test
   d. the accuracy of test scores

2. Which of the following activities would be especially suitable for investigating the content validity of an achievment test? _____

   _____.

   a. Reading the manual
   b. Looking up the test in the *Mental Measurements Yearbook*
   c. Studying the test items
   d. Looking at the norms

3. A table of specifications made up for the purpose of preparing an achievement test should

   _____.

   a. list all the content areas to be included
   b. reflect the importance of each topic
   c. indicate the important instructional objectives
   d. all of the above

4. Content validation is most appropriate for _____.
   a. aptitude tests
   b. achievement tests
   c. personality tests
   d. all of the above

5. Face validity is especially important when testing _____.
   a. children
   b. adults
   c. for aptitude
   d. to assess content validity

6. Criterion-related validity includes _____

   _____.

   a. content validation
   b. concurrent, predictive, and construct validation
   c. construct validation
   d. predictive and concurrent validation

7. Test A has been in use for many years. It is highly respected as a test of intelligence. Test B is a new intelligence test which is much shorter and easier to administer than Test A. The validation of Test B with Test A would be _____.

    a. content validation
    b. concurrent validation
    c. predictive validation
    d. discriminant validation

8. Criterion contamination occurs when _____
_____.

    a. a test is lacking in construct validity
    b. the criterion measure is found to be invalid
    c. knowledge of test scores influences decision-making
    d. errors are made in predicting criterion performance

9. Academic achievement is most often used to validate _____
_____.

    a. intelligence tests
    b. personality tests
    c. interest tests
    d. comprehensive testing programs

10. The ultimate criterion for most tests would be _____
_____.

    a. academic achievement
    b. personality as assessed by other tests
    c. actual performance in real life or on the job
    d. convergent validation with moderator tests

11. A musical aptitude test is given, at the same time, to a number of music majors and to a group of college students in other majors. This method of validating the musical aptitude test is known as _____.

    a. concurrent validation
    b. contrasted groups method
    c. both a and b
    d. neither a nor b

12. Analyses of developmental changes, age differentiation, factor analysis, and internal consistency data are all especially important to _____.

    a. predictive validity
    b. construct validity
    c. synthetic validity
    d. content validity

13. It is found that a new reading test correlates very highly with an intelligence test, but near zero with a personality test. This information is important for _____
_____.

   a. convergent and discriminant validation
   b. predictive validity
   c. establishing normative standards
   d. internal consistency analysis

14. Correlating each item on a test with overall test performance is an example of _____
_____.

   a. factorial validity
   b. content validation
   c. internal consistency validation
   d. factor analysis

15. If two or more traits are measured by two or more different techniques, all of which claim to measure the traits, validity is established through _____
_____.

   a. the predictive approach
   b. the factorial approach
   c. the multitrait-multimethod approach
   d. none of the above

16. A multitrait-multimethod matrix design would contain all of the following except _____
_____.

   a. reliability coefficients
   b. factorial validities
   c. convergent validities
   d. discriminant validities

MINIPROJECTS/SUGGESTED OUTREACH ACTIVITIES:

1. One of the most appropriate activities you could undertake in order to gain a better understanding of content-related validation is to prepare a short achievement test covering a specific segment of this course, such as the section on Statistical Concepts in Chapter 4, for example. To guide you in this activity, you could use a short book by Norman Gronlund entitled *Constructing Achievement Tests,* 3rd edition (Englewood Cliffs, N.J.: Prentice-Hall, 1982) or any other similar publication (several are cited in Chapter 14 of the textbook). Prepare a two-way table of specifications such as the one shown in Table 14-2 of the text and construct items of several types, e.g., multiple choice, matching, true/false. After you have completed your test, give it to one or more of your classmates and then score it and discuss it with them.

2. Criterion-related validation is particularly relevant to tests, such as the SAT and GRE, used for admission into colleges and graduate schools. To investigate this concept further, read the section on Tests for the College Level and Beyond, on pp. 328-335 of the textbook, for information and references on the validity data available for whichever one of those tests is of greatest interest to you.

3. The Strong-Campbell Interest Inventory of the Strong Vocational Interest Blank (SVIB-SCII) is an example of a test in the area of personality which, because of its longevity and widespread use, has been thoroughly investigated in terms of concurrent and predictive, as well as contruct, validity. A review of either the *Manual for the SVIB-SCII* or the *User's Guide for the SVIB-SCII* (both distributed by Consulting Psychologists Press of Palo Alto, California) should provide you with a clearer understanding of several validation techniques, including the method of contrasted groups, internal consistency, and convergent and discriminant validation, among others. If you are able to take this test, perhaps at the Counseling Center in your school, you should do so before reading the manual or the guide and get a copy of the results. The process of reviewing the SVIB-SCII materials will become more meaningful and relevant if you can apply what you learn to your own scores.

ANSWERS TO MULTIPLE CHOICE/TEST YOURSELF ITEMS:

1. a	5. b	9. a	13. a
2. c	6. d	10. c	14. c
3. d	7. b	11. c	15. c
4. b	8. c	12. b	16. b

Chapter 7

VALIDITY: MEASUREMENT AND INTERPRETATION

CHAPTER OUTLINE

CHAPTER SUMMARY

The use of psychological tests requires a consideration of validity in two different stages. The first consists of ascertaining, from test manuals and published data, whether the construct or trait that a test seems to be measuring is compatible with the purposes for which the test will be used. The second stage consists of determining the validity of the test against specific local criteria. The quantitative techniques for expressing and interpreting validity discussed in this chapter pertain to both stages but are especially relevant for the latter.

The relationship between test scores and criteria can be expressed in terms of validity coefficients, bivariate distributions, expectancy tables, or expectancy charts. The kind of correlation coefficient used to express the relationship between test scores and criterion measures depends on how these data are expressed. The Pearson r, which is one of the most frequently used coefficients of correlation, for example, requires that both test and criterion variables be continuous. In addition, the Pearson r assumes that the relationship between the correlated variables is linear and uniform throughout the range.

Validity coefficients can vary in magnitude depending on the nature and heterogeneity of the group on which they are found, but they should be high enough to be statistically significant at least at the .05 or .01 levels. The accuracy of prediction of a test with a given validity can also be interpreted through the standard error of estimate, which shows the margin of error to be expected in a predicted criterion score as a result of the imperfect validity of the test.

Decision theory is an approach that can be useful in evaluating the contribution of a test of known validity to the decision-making process. Essentially, decision theory utilizes quantitative information about the conditions wherein decisions are made, such as base rates and selection ratios, along with validity measures, to project the gains in accuracy and productivity that can be realized through the use of a test. In addition, to the extent that the value of expected outcomes can be quantified, e.g., in terms of dollars, decision theory can be used to calculate the expected utilities of various outcomes. If more parameters are taken into account, more complex decision strategies, such as sequential decision-making and the use of treatments adapted to individual characteristics, can be instituted in order to increase the effectiveness of a test further.

Information from several tests can be combined in a test battery to predict a single criterion. The two main strategies used for combining test data are multiple regression equations and multiple cutoff scores. The former are derived from the correlation of each test in the battery with the criterion and with each of the other tests; they aim to predict criterion standing by weighting the score of each test in direct proportion to its validity and to the uniqueness of its contribution to the battery. The multiple cutoff scores strategy, on the other hand, simply determines the minimum score on each test that is needed for acceptable performance on the criterion and selects only those people who score above the cutoff on all tests. Which of the two strategies should be used, or whether to combine the strategies, depends on the type of relations found between tests and criteria and on the question of critical skills and compensatory qualifications.

Not all of the decisions made on the basis of tests are as simple as whether to accept or reject an individual. In placement decisions, for example, individuals are not rejected but assigned to appropriate "treatments" on the basis of scores on one or more predictors. Classification decisions, which are even more complex, but also hold greater potential benefits, involve the assignment of individuals to "treatments" based on the use of multiple predictors whose validities are determined separately against more than one criterion. The aim of occupational or educational classification decisions is to maximize the utilization of talent by an *a priori*, battery-based determination of the best match between individuals' abilities or predispositions and the requirements of the fields to which they are assigned.

In the past two to three decades there has been a great deal of concern about the possibility that test scores may have a different predictive meaning for people of various subgroups, especially ethnic minorities in the United States. This concern has prompted a good deal of research on whether tests show a bias, or systematic error, in prediction when applied to black Americans in particular. The main questions in this research have been whether tests have differential validities (slope bias) for different groups and whether test scores overpredict or underpredict criterion performance for various groups (intercept bias). Comprehensive surveys done to date have not supported the hypothesis that ability tests are less valid for blacks than for whites and have shown no significant tendencies for tests to underpredict the criterion scores of blacks either. One conclusion that can be drawn tentatively from this research is that classification strategies based on multiple aptitude testing and/ or adaptive treatments, such as individualized training, are likely to be more useful in correcting social inequities than statistical manipulations of test scores, cutoffs, or regression formulas.

COMPREHENSIVE REVIEW

STUDY QUESTIONS:

1. List and describe the factors that should be considered when evaluating a published validity coefficient.

2. Explain the meaning of the standard error of estimate and discuss its role in the evaluation of the validity of a test.

3. Describe the basic approach of decision theory in the evaluation of the usefulness of a selection procedure.

4. Define incremental validity and explain how it is gauged.

5. Explain how the validity of a test can be used to estimate changes in productivity.

6. Discuss the role of values in determining the relative utility of a selection procedure.

7. Describe how the expected utility (EU) of a selection strategy can be calculated.

8. Describe and contrast sequential versus terminal decision-making strategies.

9. Define the concept of a moderator variable and cite an example of one.

10. Compare and contrast the use of multiple regression equations versus multiple cutoff scores in combining information from a test battery.

11. Define and differentiate selection, placement, and classification decisions.

12. Explain slope and intercept biases and cite examples of how each of them might be manifested.

EXERCISES: Statistical Aspects of Validity

1. Calculate the term $\sqrt{1 - r_{xy}^2}$ for the following validity coefficients and explain the meaning of the resulting values.

   Validity Coefficients: .10 .30 .50 .70 .90

2. The standard deviation for the criterion measure to be predicted by a test with a validity coefficient of .60 is 8. What is the standard error of estimate for the predicted criterion scores?

3. If you wished to calculate the predicted criterion score (Y') for a specific individual who took the test mentioned in the previous exercise, you would need to know the individual's score on the test and the coefficients of the regression equation, which would be calculated from the bivariate data on test and criterion scores. However, without any further information, you can calculate the limits within which any given obtained criterion score (Y) is likely to deviate from the criterion score (Y') predicted with the use of the test. Using the Table of Areas under the Normal Curve in the Appendix of this guide and the

standard error (SE) of estimate obtained in Exercise 2, calculate those limits for the 95% and 99% levels of confidence.

4. Sixty percent of the applicants hired for a particular job in a large factory are usually successful on the job. Use of a predictive test with a validity of .60 is instituted. The top 30% of the applicants who take the test are hired. What would be the new expected percentage of successful employees selected by using the test? (See Table 7-1 of the textbook.)

5. Determine the expected increase in productivity for the example in Exercise 4, with the use of Table 7-2 of the textbook.

6. The following multiple regression equation was developed for the purpose of predicting performance in Calculus, based on the Numerical (N) and Reasoning (R) portions of an aptitude test:

Calculus score = Y' = .31N + .20R + 1.50

Assume that a student has a stanine score of 7 on Numerical aptitude and a stanine score of 5 on Reasoning aptitude. What is the student's predicted stanine score in Calculus (Y')?

7. The four scatter diagrams in Figure 5 represent four sets of bivariate data. In each case, as is customary, the scores on the test or predictor are on the X axis and the scores on the criterion are on the Y axis. Inspect each of the diagrams to determine which one of the distributions is homoscedastic. Then, for the remaining distributions, explain the relationship that exists between test scores and the criteria.

Figure 5 – Scatter diagrams of different degrees of variability

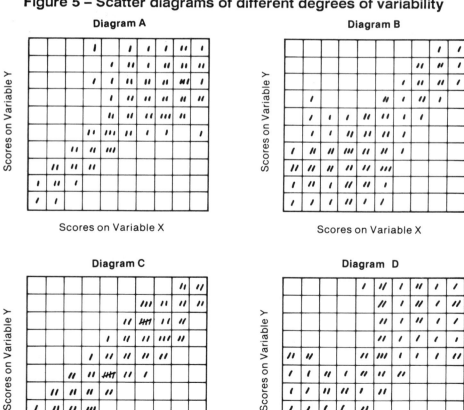

8. Look at Figure 7-1 on page 170 of the textbook and recompute the number of valid and false acceptances as well as valid and false rejections that would result if the cutoff score *on the test* were lowered by one of the units represented in the graph. Then, look at the computations on pp. 179-180 of the textbook and calculate the expected utility (EU) for the modified decision strategy, assuming that the cost of testing remains at .10 on the utility scale.

9. Each of the schematic drawings in Figure 6 represents a hypothetical scatter diagram of the bivariate distributions of data on a predictor, Test X, and a criterion (Y) for samples of whites and blacks. For each of the diagrams, determine whether the test appears to be a valid predictor for each of the racial groups and what would happen if each test were used as a selection device.

Figure 6 Hypothetical scatter diagrams [1]

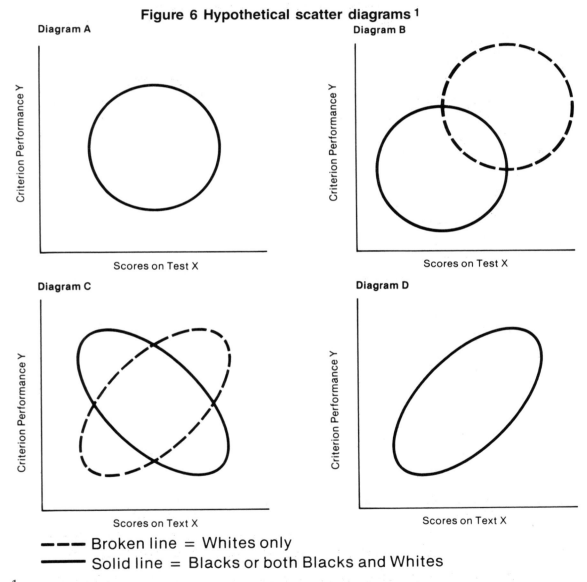

[1] Adapted from R. S. Barrett's "How to Improve Selection While Hiring Minorities and Women." Paper presented at the 1976 American Psychological Association convention.

ANSWERS TO EXERCISES: (Statistical Aspects of Validity)

1.

Validity Coefficients	$\sqrt{1-r_{xy}^2}$
.10	.99
.30	.95
.50	.87
.70	.71
.90	.44

Explanation: By using a test with a validity coefficient of .50, for example, the error in prediction would be 87% as large as the error that would result by chance. The use of such a test would allow us to predict criterion performance with a 13% smaller margin of error than what would result from a mere guess.

2. Standard error of estimate = 6.4

3. Chances are 95 out of 100 that any obtained criterion score would fall between ± (1.96) (6.4) or ± 12.54 of the criterion score predicted by the test in question. Chances are 99 out of 100 that any obtained criterion score would fall between ± (2.58) (6.4) or ± 16.51 of the predicted criterion score.

4. Base rate = .60 Validity = .60 Selection ratio = .30

   The new percentage of successful employees would be 87%; the incremental validity would be the difference between a success rate of 60% and a success rate of 87%.

5. The mean criterion performance of the group selected with the use of the test would be .69 standard deviation units above the expected base performance mean of applicants selected without the use of the test.

6. $Y' = .31 (7) + .20 (5) + 1.50 = 4.67$ or stanine 5

7. The data in scatter diagram C is homoscedastic. Diagram A shows greater variability at the top of the range. Diagram B shows greater variability at the bottom of the range. Diagram D shows greater variability at the top *and* bottom of the range than in the middle.

8. Valid acceptances = 38 + 10 = 48
   False acceptances = 7 + 11 = 18
   Valid rejections = 33 – 11 = 22
   False rejections = 22 – 10 = 12

   $EU = (.48)(1.00) + (.18)(-1.00) + (.22)(0) + (.12)(-0.50) -.10$

   $EU = + .14$

9. *Diagram A*: There is no relationship between X and Y for either group; therefore the test, although technically "culture fair," would be useless as a selection device.

   Diagram B: There is no relationship between X and Y for either group, but whites, as a group, perform better than blacks on both. If the results had not been separated by race, the test might appear to be valid for the combined racial groups. This test, if used, would be unfair in that even though it is not valid, the vast majority of individuals selected by it would be white.

Diagram C: This diagram suggests that the test is an equally valid predictor of Y for both groups (same slope) but in opposite directions. Use of this test would require a different strategy for each racial group, i.e., the selection of high-scoring whites and low-scoring blacks, a practice that would be difficult, if not impossible, to justify.

Diagram D: The test appears to be a fairly good and equally valid predictor of Y for both blacks and whites and could, therefore, be used properly as a selection device.

FILL IN THE BLANKS: Key Terms and Concepts

1. The effect of greater __ __ __ __ __ __ __ __ __ __ __ __ __ __ __ __ __ __ __ __ or variability on correlation coefficients is to increase the magnitude of the obtained correlation.

2. The use of the __ __ __ __ __ __ __ __ __ __ __ __ __ of __ __ __ __ __ __ __ __ to evaluate the predictive efficiency of a test is unrealistically stringent, unless one needs to predict an individual's exact position on the criterion distribution.

3. The Pearson product-moment correlation coefficient is only applicable when both variables are __ __ __ __ __ __ __ __ __ __ __ and when their relationship is __ __ __ __ __ __ and __ __ __ __ __ __ __ throughout the range.

4. In personnel selection, the term that corresponds to the "false positive" of clinical evaluations is __ __ __ __ __ __ __ __ __ __ __ __ __ __ __.

5. In decision theory terminology the __ __ __ __ __ __ __ __ __ __ __ __ __ __ refers to the proportion of applicants who must be accepted.

6. An alternative to terminal decisions that might lead to improved decision-making is the use of __ __ __ __ __ __ __ __ __ __ strategies.

7. The collective name for several especially selected tests that are used together to predict a single criterion is a(n) __ __ __ __ __ __ __ __ __ __ __.

8. When a battery of tests is cross-validated on a second sample, the multiple correlation (R) between the criterion and the battery can be expected to show some

   __ __ __ __ __ __ __ __ __.

9. The strongest argument in favor of using multiple cutoffs rather than a multiple regression equation centers around the issue of __ __ __ __ __ __ __ __ __ __ __ __ __ qualifications.

10. A(n) __ __ __ __ __ __ __ __ __ __ variable is one that appears in the regression equation with a negative weight for the purpose of eliminating the irrelevant variance introduced by another test in the battery.

11. **Screening** is a term that refers either to the earlier stages of selection or to any rough or rapid selection process.

12. When individuals are assigned to two or more specific jobs or treatments on the basis of multiple predictors, the decision-making process is one of
_ _ _ _ _ _ _ _ _ _ _ _ _ _ _. When the assignment to a specific treatment is based on a single score, the decision involved is one of _ _ _ _ _ _ _ _ _.

13. The _ function is a mathematical procedure for determining how closely a person's scores on a set of predictors approximate the scores typical of the members of a certain group.

14. In the statistical sense, the term **test bias** refers to a constant or systematic error, as opposed to chance error, inherent in the use of the test with certain groups.

15. In the context of test bias, the term "differential validity" is used to designate differences in the _ _ _ _ _ _ of the regression lines obtained from two groups.

16. When the point at which the regression line intersects the vertical or Y axis is different for two groups, the resulting problem is called _ _ _ _ _ _ _ _ _ bias.

ANSWERS TO FILL-IN-THE-BLANKS: (Key Terms and Concepts)

1. sample heterogeneity
2. standard error (of) estimate
3. continuous/linear/uniform
4. false rejection
5. selection ratio
6. sequential (strategies)
7. test battery
8. shrinkage
9. compensatory (qualifications)
10. suppressor (variable)
11. screening
12. classification/placement
13. multiple discriminant (function)
14. test bias
15. slope
16. intercept (bias)

MULTIPLE CHOICE: TEST YOURSELF

1. Tests designed to predict success in college show a moderate correlation with actual success as measured by academic grades. It has been argued that many students who would not have succeeded in college anyway choose not to take those tests or attempt college-level work, thus engaging in a form of self-selection. What would be the effect on validity coefficients if every high school senior took a predictor test and attempted one year of college? _____.
   a. Validity coefficients would increase markedly
   b. Validity coefficients would decrease
   c. There would be no effect on validity coefficients
   d. It is impossible to tell what would happen

2. A situation wherein low-scoring and high-scoring applicants who take a selection test show more variability than middle-scoring applicants in terms of job performance would produce an example of _____.
   a. an invalid test
   b. an unfair test
   c. homoscedasticity
   d. heteroscedasticity

3. When the predictive validity coefficient for a test is recomputed on a new sample that is more homogeneous than the sample on which it was originally found, the coefficient will be _____ but the predictions based on the test

   _____.
   a. lower/will be more accurate
   b. higher/will be less accurate
   c. lower/may be just as accurate
   d. higher/may be just as accurate

4. The purpose of a regression equation is to _____

   _____.
   a. establish validity for a test
   b. adjust test validity for criterion factors
   c. predict criterion performance
   d. determine test reliability

5. The standard deviation of a criterion measure to be predicted by a test is 2. The validity coefficient of the test is .60. What is the standard error of estimate for the criterion scores?

   _____
   a. .36
   b. 16
   c. 1.6
   d. none of the above

6. When a test has a validity of zero for a particular use, the standard error of estimate will be

   _____.

   a. zero
   b. the same as the standard deviation of the criterion
   c. infinity
   d. indefinite

7. All other things being equal, the incremental validity resulting from the use of a selection

   test would be highest with a selection ratio of _____.

   a. .05
   b. .50
   c. .90
   d. 1.00

8. All other things being equal, the incremental validity resulting from the use of a test would

   be highest with a base rate of _____.

   a. zero
   b. 5%
   c. 50%
   d. 95%

9. Moderator variables _____.

   a. if present, would result in slope bias
   b. can be assumed to affect validity in most cases
   c. are limited to sex and socioeconomic level
   d. have been shown to improve prediction substantially

10. A test that is uncorrelated with the criterion but has a high correlation with another test in

    the battery may improve prediction when it is incorporated into a multiple regression

    equation. Such a test would be called a _____.

    a. suppressor variable
    b. moderator variable
    c. cutoff factor
    d. regression weight

11. The multiple cutoff procedure would be more appropriate than the use of multiple

    regression equations for _____

    _____.

    a. counseling an individual who has no clear occupational pattern or plans
    b. selecting sonar operators, for whom auditory discrimination is of critical importance
    c. assigning clinical patients to particular types of therapy
    d. planning a remedial program for a child with a reading disability

12. A general intelligence test correlates .45 with success in a particular college. To improve the predictive accuracy, the applicants are also given three other intelligence tests, all of which correlate very highly with each other and the first test. What will be the effect of adding scores from the three additional tests to the regression equation? _____

    _____ .

    a. Predictive accuracy will improve dramatically
    b. Only a very small improvement will occur
    c. Predictive accuracy will decrease
    d. One cannot tell from the information provided

13. Assume the military drafts 1000 people. They are all tested to determine their best roles in the service. Which of the following types of decisions are being made? _____

    _____ .

    a. Selection
    b. Placement
    c. Classification
    d. Positioning

14. Multiple discriminant functions are a statistical technique for _____

    _____ .

    a. predicting job success
    b. classifiying examinees in the group whose scores they most closely resemble
    c. organizing test scores into multiple regression equations
    d. establishing a formula for determining multiple cutoff scores

15. Critical analyses of studies reporting validity coefficients for black and white employment samples have found that _____

    _____ .

    a. discrepancies in the validities for blacks and whites are large and statistically significant
    b. intercept bias in favor of whites is quite common
    c. there is no significant evidence of slope or intercept bias that would penalize blacks
    d. there is significant evidence of both slope and intercept bias that penalizes blacks

16. After a decade of intensive research into test bias with minorities, the current movement is toward _____ .

    a. virtual elimination of any test shown to have any bias
    b. the design of culture-free tests
    c. better selection strategies for fair test usage with minorities
    d. development of special tests for minorities

MINIPROJECTS/SUGGESTED OUTREACH ACTIVITIES:

1. The concept of statistical prediction and its accuracy is at the heart of the material in Chapter 7 and both correlation and regression are, in turn, central to that topic. Therefore, once again, a review of a good textbook in statistics is strongly recommended especially, at

this point, with reference to regression equations, regression coefficients, regression lines, and how each of these is used in prediction.

2. Miniproject 2 for the previous chapter suggested a review of the literature on the validity of academic admission tests. A very appropriate follow-up to that project would be to obtain some local validity data by correlating the admission test scores and final grade point averages (GPAs) for at least 20 students who have already graduated from your school. You might be able to obtain the test scores and GPAs from the Registrar's office, provided that no names are attached to the data. Otherwise, you could gather the data directly by asking alumni for it or even by asking students who are nearing graduation for their test scores and latest GPAs. In any event, you should be aware that you will be dealing with a preselected sample and that the correlation you obtain would be affected by this factor as well as by the size of the sample of data that you gather.

3. Select an "intermediate" and an "ultimate" criterion of success in the field which you are currently studying. The intermediate criterion could consist of some index of academic success, such as graduation with honors. The ultimate criterion should be an index of success appropriate to the profession or field you are preparing to enter. Describe how you would proceed if you had to predict your eventual standing and that of your classmates on each of these two criteria. What data would you select to predict each criterion? How would you combine the data?

4. The "Uniform Guidelines on Employee Selection Procedures" (*Federal Register,* 1978, Vol. 43, No. 166, pp. 38296-38309) are of major importance in the realm of personnel selection practices. A review of this document is certain to increase your understanding of many of the practical issues of test validation and fairness (see especially sections 5 to 14).

ANSWERS TO MULTIPLE CHOICE/TEST YOURSELF ITEMS:

1. a	5. c	9. a	13. c
2. d	6. b	10. a	14. b
3. c	7. a	11. b	15. c
4. c	8. c	12. b	16. c

Chapter 8
ITEM ANALYSIS

CHAPTER OUTLINE

CHAPTER SUMMARY

The validity and reliability of a test depend on the characteristics of its items. Test items, therefore, need to be analyzed both qualitatively and quantitatively throughout the process of test development. The two main aspects of quantitative item analysis are the measurement of item difficulty and item discrimination.

A determination of the difficulty of items is essential to the development and evaluation of ability tests. The most basic measure of item difficulty is the percentage (P) or proportion (p) of persons who answer it correctly. This ordinal measure can be expressed directly or it can be transformed into an equal-unit interval scale by reference to a table of normal curve frequencies and then transformed further into convenient units, such as those of the *delta* scale which has a mean of 13 and a standard deviation of 4. Item difficulty can also be translated into a uniform scale, applicable to two or more groups, by means of the absolute scaling procedure developed by Thurstone. In any event, measures of item difficulty allow the test developer to select those items that will produce, most efficiently and appropriately, the type of discrimination sought, whether that consists of the maximum differentiation among individuals at all levels, or of the selection of a certain segment of test takers.

Item discrimination indices evaluate the degree to which each item differentiates correctly among test takers with regard to the behavior that the test is designed to measure. Item discrimination can be evaluated on the basis of a criterion external to the test or by using the total score on the test itself as the criterion, as well as by a combination of both procedures, depending on the nature and purpose of the test. The procedures for gauging item discrimination typically involve the use of contrasting criterion groups and the computation of the difference between them, such as in the D index, or the use of a correlational method, such as the *phi* coefficient, to assess the relationship between item responses and standing on the criterion.

Item-test regression graphs allow for the simultaneous representation of item difficulty and item discrimination and provide a picture of the relationship between item performance and total score. Item-score regression techniques have served as the basis for the development of a sophisticated form of item analysis, variously designated as item response theory (IRT), latent trait theory, or item characteristic curve (ICC) theory. This approach uses mathematically derived functions to plot curves that represent various item parameters, including difficulty, discrimination, and the probability of guessing the correct responses. Item response theory also allows for the computation of item information functions that can serve to select the most reliable items for a test. In addition, IRT parameters computed on groups of varying abilities are sample-free or invariant and can thus provide a uniform scale of measurement for use with different groups. Although many methodological problems still remain in the application of IRT procedures in different situations, their use is accelerating, especially in the realm of computerized adaptive testing for which they seem particularly appropriate.

The item analysis of speeded tests poses a number of problems due to the fact that both item difficulty and item discrimination measures are significantly affected when only a portion of the people taking a test attempt a given item. Some empirical and statistical procedures have been developed to deal with those difficulties but item analysis data from speeded tests still need to be carefully scrutinized on both technical and logical grounds.

Another critical issue in test development concerns the need for cross-validation, which is the determination of test validity on a different sample of people from that used to select the items. The validity coefficient of a test, as established through an initial sample, can shrink dramatically and even approach zero when the test is cross-validated. This is most likely to happen when the initial pool of items is large and assembled without a previously formulated rationale and when the validation sample and the proportion of items retained are small.

The analysis of test items with regard to their potential cultural bias requires a combination of statistical and judgmental procedures. Statistical analyses attempt to establish whether individuals of equal ability from different cultural groups have different probabilities of success on an item. This can be accomplished by the traditional method of determining the proportions of people in each group who pass the item or through a more comprehensive approach, based on item response theory, that allows item difficulty to be determined independently of other item parameters. Judgmental analysis of cultural bias in item content can be useful at the initial stage of test construction and, even more so, in the final stage when it can aid in the evaluation and interpretation of statistically deviant items.

The greatly expanded use of computers in recent years has stimulated interest in new and much more sophisticated approaches to item design. In addition, the techniques of cognitive psychology offer test developers the possibility of incorporating item specifications that are far more refined than those of the past. Both of these developments, together, hold a great deal of potential to improve and facilitate test construction techniques.

COMPREHENSIVE REVIEW

STUDY QUESTIONS:

1. Explain how the process of item analysis can result in a shortened test that is more valid and reliable than the original longer test.

2. Describe how the difficulty of an item is determined and explain the relationship between the difficulty level of an item and the differentiations it makes.

3. Explain how item difficulty can be expressed on an equal-unit interval scale and describe how those values can be transformed further.

4. Describe the procedure for absolute scaling of item difficulty developed by Thurstone and explain its uses.

5. Describe the cumulative effect of inappropriate levels of difficulty of test items on test scores, conceptually and graphically.

6. Relate item difficulty to selection ratio and to other testing goals.

7. Define item discrimination and explain how it relates to test homogeneity.

8. Discuss the roles of external validation and internal consistency in test construction.

9. Explain the use of extreme groups in the analysis of item discrimination through an example dealing with a teacher-made classroom test.

10. Define the index of discrimination and explain its purpose.

11. Describe and compare the phi coefficient and the biserial correlation.

12. Describe the basic approach of item response theory to the analysis of items and contrast it with other approaches.

13. Discuss the problems inherent in the item analysis of speeded tests.

14. Explain the use of cross-validation in test construction, as well as its importance to that process.

15. Define the concept of item bias and describe the ways in which it can be assessed.

EXERCISES: Item Analysis Statistics

1. Out of 35 students, 26 got item number 20 correct on an exam. Calculate the percentage (P) and the proportion (p) passing for that item.

2. Exactly 16 percent of the students got item number 10 correct. If we assume that the trait measured by the item is normally distributed, what is the delta value for item 10? (You will need to look at the Table of Areas under the Normal Curve in the Appendix of this guide to solve this problem.)

3. Figure 7 represents a hypothetical distribution of total scores for a standardized test of ability. Describe the problem that this score distribution suggests, as far as the difficulty level of the test is concerned, and how the test might be modified in order to correct the problem.

Figure 7 – Hypothetical distribution of total scores for a standardized test of ability

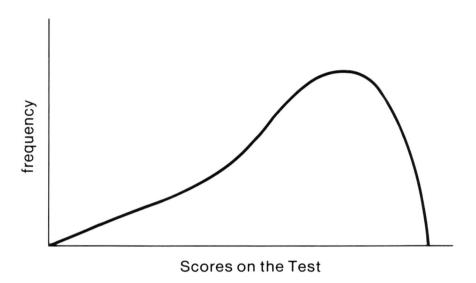

4. For the following item analysis data, which are given in terms of frequencies, compute the item difficulty and discriminative values, in frequencies, for each item; identify the items that appear questionable and explain why they do.

Item	U (N = 25)	M (N = 25)	L (N = 25)
1	22	17	8
2	5	10	15
3	4	0	1
4	15	14	15
5	24	12	0

5. For the same data used in the previous exercise, compute the index of discrimination (D) for each of the five items.

6. What are the minimum values that a phi coefficient computed on a sample of 64 cases must have in order for it to be significant at the .05 and .01 levels? (See p. 218 of the text.)

7. Plot an item-test regression graph for the following hypothetical data on two items from a ten-item test. Use Figure 8-5 in the textbook as a model and identify which of the two items is more difficult and which one discriminates better and why.

	Proportion Correct	
Total Score	Item 1	Item 2
10	1.00	.95
9	.55	.90
8	.80	.70
7	.65	.50
6	.70	.45
5	.85	.30
4	.60	.00
3	.50	.00
2	.20	.00
1	.25	.00

ANSWERS TO EXERCISES: (Item Analysis Statistics)

1. $P = 74\%$ and $p = .74$

2. According to the Table of Areas under the Normal Curve, the z value for $p = .16$ is $+1.00$, therefore the delta value for the item is $13 + 4z = 17$

3. The score distribution is skewed in such a way as to suggest an insufficient test ceiling, meaning that for the group that was tested many items were "too easy" and therefore there is a piling of scores at the upper end of the scale. One way to correct the problem would be to add more difficult items to the test; another way, which could lower reliability, among other things, would be to eliminate a good portion of the easiest items.

4.

Item	Difficulty U + M + L	Discrimination U - L
1	47	14
2	30	−10 *
3	5	3 *
4	44	0 *
5	36	24

* These items appear to be problematic: Item 2 has a negative discriminative value which means that the highest scoring subjects are failing it more frequently than the lowest scoring subjects. Item 3 was passed by a very small number of subjects and, thus, may be too difficult. Item 4 does not discriminate among the extreme groups at all and, thus, may be "dead weight" on the test, depending on its purpose.

5.

Percentage Passing

Item	Upper Group	Lower Group	D
1	88	32	56
2	20	60	− 40
3	16	4	12
4	60	60	0
5	96	0	96

6. In order for the phi coefficient to be significant at the .05 level, it has to have a value of:

$$\Phi_{.05} = \frac{1.96}{\sqrt{64}} = \frac{1.96}{8} = .245$$

To reach the .01 level of significance, the phi coefficient has to have a value of:

$$\Phi_{.01} = \frac{2.58}{\sqrt{64}} = \frac{2.58}{8} = .323$$

Note: This time, maybe you did not even have to look up the z values corresponding to p = .05 and p = .01 in the Table of Areas under the Normal Curve, as they are given in the textbook and they have been used before, but in case you are puzzled by those values, inspection of that Table should clarify them.

7. (See Figure 8.) Item 2 is more difficult than Item 1 because its 50% threshold is higher. Item 2 also discriminates better than Item 1, which can be deduced from the fact that its curve is steeper than that of Item 1, among other things.

Figure 8 – Item-test regression for items 1 and 2

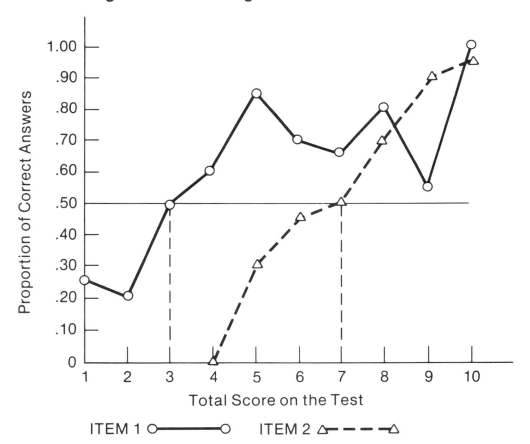

ITEM 1 ○——○   ITEM 2 △– – –△

TRUE/FALSE and WHY?

1. When a test is shortened by the purposeful elimination of items that are shown to be least satisfactory, through item analysis, the shorter version of the test may be more valid and reliable than the original. (T/F) Why? _____

   _____

2. A test item that is passed by everyone would always have to be considered as excess baggage on the test. (T/F) Why? _____

   _____

3. A piling of test scores at the low end of the score distribution would suggest that the test has too many easy items for the group that was tested. (T/F) Why? _____

   _____

4. When test items are selected on the basis of their correlation with a complex external criterion, the internal consistency of the test will most likely be lowered. (T/F) Why? _____

   _____

5. Item discrimination indices for items which occur late in a speeded test are likely to overestimate the discriminative power of those items. (T/F) Why? _____

   _____

6. If persons from different cultural groups have different probabilities of success on certain test items, those items fit the psychometric definition of bias. (T/F) Why? _____

   _____

7. The analysis of item bias that is based on item response theory is becoming the method of choice for such analyses. (T/F) Why? _____

   _____

ANSWERS TO TRUE/FALSE:

1. True	3. False	5. True	7. True
2. False	4. True	6. False	

LIST OF KEY TERMS AND CONCEPTS:

Use the following list of key terms and concepts from Chapter 8 as a review tool to make sure you can define/identify each of them in your own words. The textbook page or pages given after each term are those which contain the definition or explanation of the term.

1. item analysis (p. 202)

2. item difficulty (p. 203)

3. percentage passing (p. 203)

4. delta scale (p. 205)

5. Thurstone absolute scaling (p. 206)

6. skewness (p. 207)

7. item discrimination (p. 210)

8. index of discrimination (D) (p. 216)

9. phi coefficient (p. 218)

10. biserial correlation (pp. 218-219)

11. item-test regression (pp. 219-220)

12. item response theory (IRT)/latent trait theory/item characteristic curve (ICC) theory (p. 221)

13. theta (p. 221)

14. item information function (pp. 222-223)

15. unidimensionality (p. 223)

16. cross-validation (p. 226)

17. validity shrinkage (p. 227)

18. item bias (p. 228)

MULTIPLE CHOICE: TEST YOURSELF

1. The principal role of item analysis is to _____

   _____.

   a. identify test items that may be faulty or superfluous
   b. determine the discrimination index for a test
   c. shorten a test
   d. calculate the validity coefficient for each item on the test

2. Item difficulty is customarily defined as the _____

   _____.

   a. percentage of examinees who fail an item
   b. percentage of examinees who pass an item
   c. biserial correlation for an item
   d. correlation of the item with the criterion

3. The ideal value for item difficulty is _____.

    a. less than 50%
    b. about 50%
    c. greater than 70%
    d. dependent on many factors

4. An item is passed by 84% of the students who take it. The delta value for the item is _____.

    a. 9
    b. 12
    c. 13
    d. 14

5. A test item with a delta value of 2 can be improved by _____

_____.

    a. adding more distractors
    b. changing the distractors no one chooses into more plausible distractors
    c. removing possible cues for the correct answer
    d. all of the above

6. A test is given to a fifth grade class primarily to identify the bottom third of the class for special instruction. The average difficulty (p) for the test items should be approximately

_____.

    a. .30
    b. .50
    c. .70
    d. the same as for any other test

7. Item discrimination means _____

_____.

    a. the extent to which an item correctly discriminates against some examinees
    b. the extent to which an item correctly differentiates among examinees on the appropriate behavior
    c. the amount of reliability in an item
    d. none of the above

8. If all items for a test are chosen on the basis of their correlation with a total test score, the result will yield _____

_____.

    a. maximum test homogeneity
    b. a reduction of test-retest reliability
    c. an increase in validity against external criteria
    d. unpredictable changes

9. In determining item discrimination, it is customary to look at the upper and lower 27% of the examinees as the extreme groups. This percentage was chosen to _____.

   a. simplify the calculations
   b. obtain reliable results and sufficient differentiation
   c. maintain tradition
   d. increase discrimination to a maximum value

10. The D value in item analysis represents _____.

    a. the reliability of the item
    b. the biserial correlation coefficient
    c. the difference in p between the upper and lower groups
    d. absolute item quality

11. The biserial correlation is applied when _____.

    a. the item response and the criterion are genuine dichotomies
    b. the item response and the criterion are continuous variables
    c. a continuous and normally distributed trait underlies the dichotomous item response and the criterion
    d. the item-criterion relationship is not independent of item difficulty

12. Item response theory models are _____.

    a. completely replacing traditional item analysis procedures
    b. less accurate than item discrimination
    c. still under development
    d. increasing test unidimensionality

13. Indices of item difficulty and item discrimination from a speeded test typically _____.

    a. are just as meaningful as those from unspeeded tests
    b. reflect the item's position in the test
    c. will be artificially high
    d. cannot be computed

14. If validity is figured on a test without cross-validation, the coefficient is likely to be _____.

    a. too high
    b. too low
    c. unpredictable
    d. too low by as much as the standard deviation of the test

15. In order to keep shrinkage of a test's validity to a minimum upon cross-validation, it would

    be best to _____ .

    a. use small samples
    b. start with a large initial pool of items
    c. make sure there is no rationale for the items
    d. none of the above

MINIPROJECTS/SUGGESTED OUTREACH ACTIVITIES:

1. A review of the statistical techniques traditionally used in item analysis is strongly recommended at this point. In particular, it would be desirable to investigate the special correlational methods used in item analysis, such as the point-biserial and the tetrachoric correlation coefficients, in addition to the phi coefficient and the biserial correlation discussed in the textbook. Any good basic textbook in statistics for psychology would cover these and would provide further information on item analytic procedures in general. See, for example, *Fundamental Statistics in Psychology and Education* (6th edition) by J. P. Guilford and B. Fruchter (New York: McGraw-Hill, 1978), especially pp. 304-318 and pp. 457-469.

2. The material presented in Chapters 4 through 8 has undoubtedly given you a greater understanding of the process of test development. Chapter 8, in particular, points out in some detail the laboriousness of the process of generating suitable test items. In light of this information, your attitudes toward standardized testing, as well as teacher-made tests, might well have changed considerably. Identify and list any such attitudinal changes you may have had and discuss them with your classmates. One of the areas you might consider would be your perception of the desirability of legislatively mandating the release of items from tests such as the SAT and GRE and their answers. Another relevant area about which your attitudes and perceptions might have changed concerns the need for and role of item analysis in classroom testing.

3. Prepare and, if possible, carry out a plan for replicating a demonstration of the need for cross-validation similar to the one conducted by Cureton and described in page 227 of the textbook. You will need to select a criterion and a way of generating item responses randomly, in order to obtain "test" scores. You will also need to decide on an index of item discrimination for use in your item analysis that is suitable to the criterion and item responses (see Miniproject # 1). Finally, you should be able to establish the "validity" of your entire "test" by correlating the original criterion measures with the scores obtained on the test. In planning this replication, keep in mind the factors that affect validity shrinkage.

4. Miniproject # 1 for Chapter 6 consisted of constructing a short achievement test covering a specific segment of this course. If you did that, you now have an opportunity to do an item analysis of that brief instrument, provided you give it to a few more people in order to generate data for your analysis. The best model to follow for a simple analysis is the one described in the textbook (pp. 214-218). If you did not do the first miniproject in Chapter 6, this would be a good time to try it and follow up with the analysis suggested here.

ANSWERS TO MULTIPLE CHOICE/TEST YOURSELF ITEMS:

1. a	4. a	7. b	10. c	13. b
2. b	5. d	8. a	11. c	14. a
3. d	6. c	9. b	12. c	15. d

Chapter 9
INDIVIDUAL TESTS

CHAPTER OUTLINE

Stanford-Binet Intelligence Scale
    Evolution of the Scales
    The Fourth Edition Stanford-Binet: General Description
    Administration and Scoring
    Standardization and Norms
    Reliability
    Validity

The Wechsler Scales
    The Wechsler Adult Intelligence Scale
        Antecedents of the Wechsler Intelligence Scales
        The WAIS-R: Description
        Norms and Scoring
        Reliability
        Validity

    Wechsler Intelligence Scale for Children
        Description
        Norms and Scoring
        Reliability
        Validity

    Wechsler Preschool and Primary Scale of Intelligence
        Description
        Norms and Scoring
        Reliability
        Validity

    Concluding Remarks on the Wechsler Scales

Assessment of Competence
    Intelligence Tests in the Context of Individual Assessment
    System of Multicultural Pluralistic Assessment

Kaufman Assessment Battery for Children
    Nature and Development
    Norms and Scoring
    Reliability and Validity
    General Evaluation

CHAPTER SUMMARY

The Stanford-Binet Intelligence Scale: Fourth Edition (SB4) is the current version of the scale published in 1916 by Terman and his associates which, in turn, was a revision of the original Binet-Simon scales published in France between 1905 and 1911. The SB4 is an individually administered instrument that retains the adaptive testing procedure and many of the item types from earlier forms but goes beyond them in content coverage and reflects recent developments in the conceptualization of intellectual functioning and in test construction methodology. The current SB extends the verbal focus of earlier editions to include more coverage of quantitative, spatial, and short-term memory tasks. The SB4's items are grouped according to type instead of into age levels, as in the earlier editions, and thus can provide separate scores for up to 15 tests and four major cognitive areas in addition to the composite score for performance on the entire scale. In addition, the current scale, which was standardized on a larger sample than ever before, has been subjected to a greater variety of validation procedures from the outset. While keeping the same units as the traditional deviation IQs of earlier SB editions, the SB4 uses the term "Standard Age Scores" (SAS) rather than "IQ" to designate its scores.

The Wechsler intelligence scales encompass a series of instruments designed for three age levels, from adults to preschool children. The first of these, known as the Wechsler-Bellevue Intelligence Scale, was devised by David Wechsler and published in 1939, with the express purpose of providing an intelligence test suitable for adults both in content and normative procedures. The current version of the adult scale is the Wechsler Adult Intelligence Scale-Revised (WAIS-R). It consists of six verbal and five performance subtests and provides separate standard scores in each of them as well as Verbal, Performance, and Full Scale deviation IQs which are based, respectively, on the verbal subtests, the performance subtests and the entire scale. This format allows for a number of intertest comparisons and probably accounts for much of the popularity of the WAIS and the other Weschler scales, which have followed the same pattern with some variations to accommodate the needs of younger test takers. The Wechsler Intelligence Scale for Children-Revised (WISC-R), for example, has a performance subtest (Mazes) which does not appear in the adult scale and the Wechsler Preschool and Primary Scale of Intelligence (WPPSI) has a verbal subtest (Sentences) and two performance subtests (Animal House and Geometric Design) which differ in content from those of the WISC-R.

All of the Wechsler scales of intelligence are periodically revised to update norms and content. Their standardization samples are typically large and representative of the population of the United States. In addition, their manuals address the issue of reliability and error of measurement rather well and thus provide information that is critical to evaluating the significance of the differences obtained between their various scores. However, none of the scales' manuals provide much data on validity although many studies that have a bearing on this issue, especially from the point of view of factorial composition and correlations with similar scales, are available in the literature.

The Stanford-Binet and the Wechsler scales are among the best instruments currently available, in terms of test development and technical quality. However, in order for them to be properly applied in individual assessment, they require users who are not only fully trained in their administration and scoring, but also sufficiently knowledgeable in psychology to be able to interpret test results in light of appropriate observational and background data. One example of an attempt to formally and deliberately include a variety of data sources in the assessment of children from diverse backgrounds is the System of Multicultural Pluralistic Assessment

(SOMPA) developed by Mercer. This system provides a means for generating data on health and perceptual-motor development, adaptive behavior in the family and community, as well as scholastic abilities. Data on the latter, obtained through the use of the age-appropriate Wechsler scale, are then interpreted in light of the child's ethnic background and sociocultural context.

The Kaufman Assessment Battery for Children (K-ABC) is a new and promising instrument, developed in the 1980s, which attempts to assess the intellectual functioning of children (aged 2.5 to 12.5) from an information processing viewpoint. The K-ABC incorporates some of the recent developments in cognitive psychology as well as a more comprehensive approach to validation than the older Stanford-Binet and Wechsler scales. The design of the K-ABC and its global scores for Sequential Processing, Simultaneous Processing, and Achievement represent an attempt to focus on the tasks of hypothesis generation and hypothesis testing and to get away from the simple labelling that has become associated with traditional tests of intelligence. The justification of the theoretical orientation used in the K-ABC must await the accumulation of empirical data on the effectiveness of the battery. The K-ABC's overall impact on testing practices will, to a large extent, depend on how knowledgeably it is used in practical situations.

COMPREHENSIVE REVIEW

STUDY QUESTIONS:

1. Describe the major landmarks in the history of the Binet scales in terms of their content and standardization.

2. Describe the main administration and scoring features of the Stanford-Binet: Fourth Edition (SB4).

3. Discuss the role of individual intelligence tests, such as the SB4, in clinical assessment from the point of view of their usefulness versus their cost.

4. Describe the validation procedures that have been applied to the SB4.

5. Discuss the history of the development of the Wechsler intelligence scales.

6. Describe the salient features of the current versions of each of the three Wechsler intelligence scales and compare them to each other in terms of their range of applicability.

7. Discuss the strengths and weaknesses of the Wechsler scales.

8. Explain the context in which the System of Multicultural Pluralistic Assessment (SOMPA) developed and describe its components.

9. Discuss the SOMPA's Estimated Learning Potential (ELP) score and its meaning.

10. Describe the major features of the Kaufman Assessment Battery for Children (K-ABC) as well as its strengths and weaknesses.

EXERCISES: Statistics in Individual Intelligence Testing

1. The Standard Age Scores (SAS) for the 15 separate tests of the SB4 have a mean of 50 and a standard deviation of 8. Using the Table of Areas under the Normal Curve in the Appendix, find the z scores and percentile rank equivalents for the following SAS values for SB4 tests:

74   64   54   48   38   28

2. Express each of the percentile ranks you obtained in the previous item in terms of their SB4 area or composite SAS values.

3. The test-retest reliability coefficient for the composite SAS for five-year-olds tested with the SB4 after intervals of between two and eight months is .91. Suppose that you had tested Sally on her fifth birthday and retested her after six months and that her SB4 composite SAS values were 95 and 110, respectively.

   A. Would the difference between Sally's scores on the two occasions be statistically significant and, if so, at what level of significance?

   B. What other factors, if any, would you need to consider in interpreting the obtained difference?

4. Locate the manuals for the WISC-R and WPPSI and study the information each of them provides on stability coefficients which can be found in Table 11 (pp. 32-33) of the WISC-R manual and Table 18 (p. 33) of the WPPSI manual. In light of what you have learned about reliability, what are some of the relevant pieces of information you should notice in evaluating these data?

ANSWERS TO EXERCISES: (Statistics in Individual Intelligence Testing)

1. and 2.

SAS (Tests)	z scores	Percentiles	SAS (Area or Composites)
74	+ 3.00	99.87th	148
64	+ 1.75	96th	128
54	+ 0.50	69th	108
48	− 0.25	40th	96
38	−1.50	7th	76
28	−2.75	0.30th	56

Note that, because of the numerical relationship between the test and the area or composite SAS units, the latter are exactly twice the value of the former. If you have access to the Technical Manual for the SB4, you can look up these and other SAS values and their corresponding percentile ranks directly in Table D.1 (p. 129) of that manual.

3. A. The 15-point difference between Sally's scores on the two occasions would be significant at $p = .0018$ because the SE of measurement $= 16 \sqrt{1 - .91} = 4.8$ and the z value for that difference would be 3.13 (15 divided by 4.8).

   B. The interpretation of the difference between Sally's scores on the two occasions would have to take into account the fact that the scores obtained by preschool children are typically less reliable than those of older children (although this is to some extent mitigated by the use of the appropriate reliability coefficient for that age group.) Of greater significance would be the possible influence of practice effects. In addition, because of the rather large size of the difference, one would also want to learn more about any specific situational factors that might have been at play during the two administrations, e.g., Sally's health at both times, examiner influences, settings in which the administrations were conducted, etc. Finally, an examination of the extent and pattern of the differences between Sally's scores on the separate tests of the SB4 on each administration would probably be helpful in interpreting her score gains.

4. One should note the size and age of the samples used in each case, the intervals between test and retest, the differences between means and standard deviations from the first and the second testing, as well as the patterns of the stability coefficients across subtests and across age groups.

FILL IN THE BLANKS: Individual Intelligence Tests

1. _Intelligence_ tests are the direct descendants of the original Binet scales and are designed for use in a wide variety of situations and validated against relatively broad criteria.

2. The chronological series 1905, 1908, and 1911 would, for the person who is well-versed in individual intelligence testing, immediately call up the sequence of revisions of the _ _ _ _ _ _-_ _ _ _ _ scales.

3. The fourth edition of the _ _ _ _ _ _ _ _ _-_ _ _ _ _
_ _ _ _ _ _ _ _ _ _ _ _ Scale is the current version of the scale that was published by Terman in 1916.

4. In contrast with earlier editions, the current Stanford-Binet has largely discarded the concept of mental ages and the use of IQs in favor of _ _ _ _ _ _ _ _ _ _ _ _ _
_ _ _ _ _ _ (SAS) for separate tests, for areas, and for the entire scale.

5. The first form of the Wechsler scales was the
_ _ _ _ _ _ _ _ _-_ Scale, published in 1939, specifically as an intelligence test for adults.

6. The current version of the scale mentioned in the preceding item is the _Weschler adult intelligence scale-revised_ (WAIS-R), published in 1981.

7. The current downward extension of the WAIS-R, published in 1974 and appropriate for individuals between the ages of 6.5 and 16.5 years, is called the _Wechsler Intelligence Scale for Children-revised_ (WISC-R).

8. The formal name of the "baby" of the Wechsler series of intelligence scales is the _Weschler pre-school and primary Scale of intelligence_ (WPPSI), a revision of which is expected before 1990.

9. The __ __ __ __ __ __   __ __   __ (SOMPA) is a comprehensive program, suitable for ages 5 to 11, that specifically attempts to address the problems of assessing children from culturally and linguistically diverse backgrounds.

10. The __ __ __ __ __ __ __   __ __ __ __ __ __ __ __ __ __ __   __ __ __ __ __ __ __ for __ __ __ __ __ __ __ __ (K-ABC) is an individually administered clinical instrument, developed in the 1980s and suitable for the ages of 2.5 to 12.5 years, whose focus is on the assessment of information processing.

ANSWERS TO FILL-IN-THE-BLANKS: (Individual Intelligence Tests)

1. intelligence (tests)
2. Binet-Simon (scales)
3. Stanford-Binet Intelligence (Scale)
4. Standard Age Scores (SAS)
5. Wechsler-Bellevue Intelligence (Scale)
6. Wechsler Adult Intelligence Scale-Revised (WAIS-R)
7. Wechsler Intelligence Scale (for) Children-Revised (WISC-R)
8. Wechsler Preschool (and) Primary Scale (of) Intelligence (WPPSI)
9. System of Multicultural Pluralistic Assessment (SOMPA)
10. Kaufman Assessment Battery (for) Children (K-ABC)

MATCHING: Key Terms and Concepts—(One letter per number)

___ 1. Starting point for the SB4 tests, selected on the basis of the examinee's chronological age and Vocabulary test score;

___ 2. On the SB4, the point at which four items on two consecutive levels are passed;

___ 3. On the SB4, the point at which three out of four or all four items on two consecutive levels are failed; *ceiling*

___ 4. Shorter versions of a test battery, such as the SB4 or Wechsler scales, used for special or screening purposes;

___ 5. Group factor identified with the Wechsler's Information, Vocabulary, Comprehension and Similarities subtests;

___ 6. Group factor identified with the Wechsler's Block Design and Object Assembly subtests;

___ 7. Group factor usually identified with the Wechsler's Arithmetic, Digit Span, and Coding or Digit Symbol subtests;

___ 8. K-ABC scale for subtests that require synthesis and organization of spatial and visuo-perceptual content that can be surveyed as a whole;

___ 9. K-ABC scale for subtests that require serial or temporal arrangements of verbal, numerical, and visuo-perceptual content;

___ 10. K-ABC scale that assesses ability in reading, arithmetic, word knowledge, and general information;

A. Entry level

B. Achievement Scale

C. Perceptual Organization factor

D. Sequential Processing Scale

E. Abbreviated scales

F. Ceiling level

G. Basal level

H. Freedom from Distractibility factor

I. Verbal Comprehension factor

J. Simultaneous Processing Scale

ANSWERS:

1 - A;   2- G;   3 - F;   4 - E;   5 - I;   6 - C;   7 - H;   8 - J;   9 - D;   10 - B.

MULTIPLE CHOICE: TEST YOURSELF

1. Intelligence tests are usually validated against _____

   _____ .

   a. personality tests
   b. tests of problem-solving skills
   c. individual success in life
   d. scholastic success

2. The 1960 revision of the Stanford-Binet _____

   _____ .

   a. combined Forms L and M
   b. utilized totally new norms
   c. introduced no new content
   d. items a and c above

3. Compared with the norms of the 1930s and 1940s, the 1970's norms for the Binet and other

   intelligence tests have been _____ .

   a. about the same
   b. higher
   c. lower
   d. going up until a reversal began in 1970

4. The administration of the Stanford-Binet requires a highly trained examiner because _____
   _____.

   a. scoring is difficult
   b. rapport must be established
   c. clinical information should also be gathered
   d. all of the above

5. The basal level of the SB4 is _____
   _____.

   a. reached when four items on two consecutive levels are passed
   b. the minimal performance level for passing
   c. reached at the first level when all items are failed
   d. a minimum score required for one's mental level

6. The major innovation in the 1972 edition of the Stanford-Binet was _____
   _____.

   a. new norms
   b. extensive content revision
   c. a change in the scoring
   d. all of the above

7. In the SB4, normative tables are used to convert raw scores to _____
   _____.

   a. an improved ratio IQ
   b. standard age scores
   c. mental age over chronological age
   d. a mean of 500 and a standard deviation of 50

8. A person obtains an overall composite SAS score of 118 on the SB4. Considering the standard error of measurement of the scale, which is approximately 2.5, there is a 95% chance that the person's true score differs by _____ points from his or her obtained score.

   a. ± 2.5
   b. ± 5.0
   c. ± 7.5
   d. ± 10.0

9. As an examinee becomes older, the scores on the Stanford-Binet become _____
   _____.

   a. more reliable
   b. less reliable
   c. less valid
   d. cannot say without more information

10. The major difference between the Wechsler-Bellevue and the Stanford-Binet of the same period was _____

   _____.

   a. the Binet still used ratio IQs while the Wechsler introduced deviation IQs
   b. the Wechsler tested verbal and performance skills separately
   c. the Wechsler-Bellevue was better suited for adults
   d. all of the above

11. The major scores provided by the Wechsler scales are _____

   _____.

   a. a global IQ and general factor scores
   b. verbal, performance and full scale deviation IQs
   c. ratio IQs
   d. standard age scores

12. Norms for the WAIS-R extend over which of the following age ranges?

   a. 16 - 30
   b. 12 - 16
   c. 16 - 74
   d. 18 - 75

13. The WISC was revised in order to _____

   _____.

   a. improve face validity
   b. update norms
   c. increase the length of some subtests
   d. all of the above

14. The SOMPA battery was designed primarily to _____

   _____.

   a. get more accurate assessments of adult intelligence
   b. measure personality characteristics along with intelligence
   c. assess children in light of their sociocultural context
   d. none of the above

15. The primary focus of the K-ABC is on _____

   _____.

   a. information processing
   b. factual knowledge acquired in school
   c. information derived from an interview with the subject's parents
   d. determining IQ level

MINIPROJECTS/SUGGESTED OUTREACH ACTIVITIES:

1. The relationship between scores on intelligence tests and educational attainment is so strong that several people have suggested that, if IQs are needed for comparative purposes but are not available, one way to estimate them is to use the years of education completed by a subject as the basis for a regression formula. Although such a practice is not

unanimously endorsed, it is interesting to examine the data that form the empirical basis for it. A good way to do that, and to review some of the issues discussed in Chapter 9, would be to look at some of the studies on the subject, such as Matarazzo and Herman's "Relationship of education and IQ in the WAIS-R standardization sample" (*Journal of Consulting and Clinical Psychology,* 1984, *52,* 631-634).

2. A careful selection of readings from some of the sources mentioned in the textbook would be extremely helpful in rounding out your knowledge about a number of testing issues and procedures discussed in the text. Three specific recommendations, selected from sources cited in Chapter 9, are:

   A. The *System of Multicultural Pluralistic Assessment* (SOMPA): *Technical Manual* by J.R. Mercer (San Antonio, TX: Psychological Corporation, 1979) which, as Anastasi mentions, includes a description of a specific procedure for developing local norms for that instrument (pp. 144-145) that may be of interest.

   B. A.S. Kaufman's *Intelligent Testing with the WISC-R* (New York: Wiley, 1979) provides many good examples of the use of the WISC-R in the process of generating hypothesis in clinical assessment (see especially Chapters 5 and 6).

   C. Another good source on the hypothesis generation/testing process, with reference to the K-ABC, is the *Interpretive Manual* for that battery, written by A.S. and N.L. Kaufman (Circle Pines, MN: American Guidance Service, 1983).

3. Many psychologists have pointed out that one of the major problems in validating intelligence tests is rooted in the difficulty of defining the construct of intelligence. In particular, an early definition, proposed by E.G. Boring, which essentially stated that intelligence is what intelligence tests measure, is cited frequently as the epitome of that problem. Although the redundancy of that definition was clear to virtually everyone, in practice, the idea really took hold as shown by the fact that even the best intelligence tests, such as the Stanford-Binet and the Wechsler scales, rely very heavily on their high correlations with each other and with other similar tests for evidence of validity. An enlightening and interesting discussion of the history and the problem of defining intelligence can be found in the first chapter of R.J. Sternberg's *Intelligence Applied: Understanding and Increasing Your Intellectual Skills* (San Diego, CA: Harcourt Brace Jovanovich, 1986). This particular reference, by the way, would also be very appropriate as a follow-up to Chapter 12 of the textbook.

ANSWERS TO MULTIPLE CHOICE/TEST YOURSELF ITEMS:

1. d	4. d	7. b	10. d	13. d
2. d	5. a	8. b	11. b	14. c
3. b	6. a	9. a	12. c	15. a

Chapter 10
TESTS FOR SPECIAL POPULATIONS

CHAPTER OUTLINE

Infant and Preschool Testing
  Gesell Developmental Schedules
  Bayley Scales of Infant Development
  McCarthy Scales of Children's Abilities
  Piagetian Scales

Comprehensive Assessment of the Mentally Retarded

Testing the Physically Handicapped
  Hearing Impairments
  Visual Impairments
  Motor Impairments

Cross-Cultural Testing
  The Problem
  Typical Instruments
  Approaches to Cross-Cultural Testing

CHAPTER SUMMARY

Individuals who cannot be properly examined with traditional instruments, due to handicapping conditions, inadequate oral or written language skills, or some other reason, are usually tested with instruments that are especially designed or modified to accommodate their needs. Such instruments may fall under the categories of performance tests, which involve manipulation of objects and minimal use of paper and pencil, nonlanguage tests, which can be administered and taken without the use of oral or written language, or nonverbal tests, which do not require reading. The present chapter deals with such specialized tests for infant and preschool children, for the mentally retarded, for people with sensory and motor handicaps, and for use across cultures and subcultures, as well as with some of the problems involved in testing those populations.

Tests designed for infants and preschool children are all individually administered and are mostly performance or oral tests that either do not require use of paper and pencil or, if so, involve their use only in a rudimentary way. The testing of infants typically places a heavy emphasis on sensorimotor development and consists mainly of standardized procedures for observing and evaluating their behavioral development to assess current status rather than to predict future ability levels. The Gesell Developmental Schedules, for example, are a refinement and elaboration of the qualitative observations made by pediatricians and are based on longitudinal studies of the normal course of development from the age of 4 weeks to 5 years. The Bayley Scales of Infant Development and the McCarthy Scales of Children's Abilities are two additional outstanding examples of tests especially designed for the infant and preschool levels, respectively. In addition to these prototypical instruments, the assessment of children has been enriched by the development of several experimental scales especially designed to investigate the cognitive developmental stages postulated by Jean Piaget. These instruments are typically more flexible and open to qualitative interpretation than others and they exemplify the ordinal approach to norms and the use of age differentiation as a validating criterion. Examples of Piagetian scales include the Concept Assessment Kit—Conservation and the Ordinal Scales of Psychological Development, among others.

The comprehensive assessment of the mentally retarded has undergone a spurt of growth as a result of legislation aimed at assuring that their special educational needs will be recognized and met. Assessment programs for the mentally retarded use traditional intelligence tests to identify levels of retardation from the normative viewpoint. In addition, they usually include an examination of motor development, with instruments such as the Bruininks-Oseretsky Test of Motor Proficiency, and a measure of adaptive behavior in everday-life situations, such as the Vineland Adaptive Behavior Scales.

The problems of testing handicapped persons have also received special attention as a result of legislative mandates aimed at extending their rights and opportunities. Testing the physically handicapped poses special problems in terms of both test administration and interpretation. Typically, these difficulties are handled by modifying existing tests or by including non-test data, such as biographical history, in an attempt to individualize the assessment process. In addition, some efforts have been, and continue to be, made to establish separate norms on various instruments for persons with specific handicaps. For the hearing impaired, for example, the WISC-R Performance Scale was standardized separately and the Hiskey-Nebraska Test of Learning Aptitude was developed and standardized on deaf and hard-of-hearing children. Tests for the blind, which usually have to rely on oral presentation, include modifications of the Binet and Wechsler scales and adaptations of some group tests such as the Scholastic Aptitude Test and the Progressive Matrices. Testing people with motor handicaps poses yet another set of problems in that, depending on the severity of the disorder, such individuals may be unable to respond either orally or in writing. Efforts to accommodate the needs of these individuals include the use of special adaptations of the Leiter International Performance Scale and the Porteus Mazes as well as the use of picture vocabulary tests, such as the Peabody Picture Vocabulary Test, or pictorial classification tests, such as the Columbia Mental Maturity Scale, wherein examinees can respond to the presentation of stimuli by pointing, nodding, or otherwise indicating their choices through whatever communication means they have available.

Cross-cultural testing is a rapidly expanding field that encompasses problems such as the development of educational and occupational selection and placement instruments in different nations and the assessment of culturally diverse populations within a single nation such as the United States. Traditional cross-cultural tests have attempted to rule out the parameters along which cultures differ, such as language, reading skills, and emphasis on speed. In addition, "culture-free" tests, aimed at ruling out test content that is tied to the experiential background specific to certain cultures, have also been tried, without success. Typical instruments in the cross-cultural field include tests such as the Leiter International Performance Scale, the Culture Fair Intelligence Test, Raven's Progressive Matrices, and the Goodenough-Harris Drawing Test. Although cross-cultural tests are needed for research on many important issues, their validation in different cultures has often been neglected or poorly executed and their results have not always been shown to have the same meaning and/or significance in different cultures. Nevertheless, attempts to develop instruments suitable to certain specific cultures or applicable across cultures continue and have already produced some useful additions to the armamentarium of psychologists.

COMPREHENSIVE REVIEW

STUDY QUESTIONS:

1. Define and contrast performance, nonlanguage, and nonverbal tests and cite an example of each type.

2. Discuss the characteristics of tests designed for infants and describe, in detail, the Bayley Scales of Infant Development as an example of those tests.

3. Discuss the characteristics of tests for preschool children and describe, in detail, the McCarthy Scales of Children's Abilities as an example of those tests.

4. Explain the basic approach that underlies the development of Piagetian scales and describe one example of such a scale.

5. Discuss the results of comparative studies using Piagetian scales and list some of the obstacles and advantages that go along with that approach.

6. Describe the procedures involved in the identification and classification of the mentally retarded.

7. Explain the role of adaptive behavior scales in the assessment of the mentally retarded and describe one such scale in detail.

8. Discuss the problems involved in the assessment of the physically handicapped and the major approaches that have been used in that area.

9. List and describe two examples of tests that are used to assess individuals with hearing, visual, or motor impairments.

10. Discuss the problems involved in cross-cultural testing and outline the three major approaches that have been used in that field.

11. List and describe in detail two examples of instruments that are typical of existing tests applicable across cultures.

FILL IN THE BLANKS: Key Terms and Concepts

1. In general, _ _ _ _ _ _ _ _ _ _ _ _ _ tests are those that involve the manipulation of objects with minimal, if any, use of paper and pencil.

2. The Army Beta Examination was a prototype of _ _ _ _ _ _ _ _ _ _ _ _ _ tests, which are those that can be given and taken without the use of oral or written language.

3. Although they frequently measure verbal comprehension, _ _ _ _ _ _ _ _ _ _ _ tests are especially suitable for preschool children and illiterates because they require no reading or writing.

4. The _ (GCI) of the McCarthy Scales of Children's Abilities (MSCA) is a standard score, with a mean of 100 and SD of 16, that is based on 15 out of the 18 tests in the battery.

5. Piaget outlined four stages of cognitive development that span the period from infancy to adolescence and beyond; they are designated as the _ _ _ _ _ _ _ _ _ _ _ _ _ _, the
_ _ _ _ _ _ _ _ _ _ _ _ _ _ _ _, the _ _ _ _ _ _ _ _ _
_ _ _ _ _ _ _ _ _ _ _ _, and the _ _ _ _ _ _ _
_ _ _ _ _ _ _ _ _ _ _ stages.

6. Laurendeau and Pinard have reported detailed information on ten of the tests in their battery of Piagetian tasks; the tests in question are concerned with children's conceptions of _ _ _ _ _ _ _ _ _ _ and _ _ _ _ _ _.

7. In Piagetian terminology, the concept of _ _ _ _ _ _ _ _ _ _ _ _ _ refers to the child's realization that such properties of objects as weight, volume, or number remain unchanged when objects undergo transformations in shape, position, or form.

8. The term _ _ _ _ _ _ _ _ _ is used by Piagetian researchers to describe the phenomenon of inconsistencies between empirical findings and the theoretically postulated sequencing of response patterns.

9. Since the 1977 enactment of the _ _ _ _ _ _ _ _ _ _ for _ _ _ _
_ Act (P.L. 94-142), the testing of children with mental or physical handicaps has undergone conspicuous growth in the United States.

10. The _ on _ _ _ _ _ _ _
_ _ _ _ _ _ _ _ _ _ _ (AAMD) defines _ _ _ _ _ _ _
_ _ _ _ _ _ _ _ _ _ _ _ as "significantly subaverage general intellectual functioning existing concurrently with deficits in adaptive behavior and manifested during the developmental period."

11. Many of the civil rights provisions mandated for other minorities were extended to cover the physically handicapped through Section 504 of the
_ _ _ _ _ _ _ _ _ _ _ _ _ _ _ _ _ _ _ of 1973.

12. The Raven's Progressive Matrices (RPM) test is currently available in three forms which differ in level of difficulty; the names of those forms, in ascending order of difficulty, are the
_ _ _ _ _ _ _ _ Progressive Matrices (CPM), the _ _ _ _ _ _ _ _
Progressive Matrices (SPM), and the _ _ _ _ _ _ _ _ Progressive Matrices (APM).

13. The basic approach of the tests designated as _ _ _ _ _ _ _ _ _-_ _ _ _ is to choose items common to many different cultures and validate the resulting test against local criteria in the respective cultures.

14. Instruments such as the footprint recognition test standardized on aboriginal Australians are really meant to highlight the extent to which the cultural milieu affects the cognitive skills and knowledge acquired by an individual; two additional examples of this type of cross-cultural tests are the __ __ __ __–__–__ __ __ __ Test and the __ of __ __ __ __ __ __ __ __ __ __ __ __ __ __ __ __ __ (BITCH).

ANSWERS TO FILL-IN-THE-BLANKS: (Key Terms and Concepts)

1. performance (tests)
2. nonlanguage (tests)
3. nonverbal (tests)
4. General Cognitive Index (GCI)
5. sensorimotor/preoperational/concrete operational/formal operational
6. causality/space
7. conservation
8. *décalage*
9. (1977) Education (for) All Handicapped Children (Act)
10. American Association (on) Mental Deficiency (AAMD)/mental retardation
11. Rehabilitation Act (of 1973)
12. Coloured/Standard/Advanced (Progressive Matrices) (CPM/SPM/ APM)
13. culture-fair
14. Draw-a-Horse/Black Intelligence Test (of) Cultural Homogeneity (BITCH)

MATCHING: Tests for Special Populations (One letter per number)

___ 1. Standardized procedure for observing and evaluating the behavioral development of children from the age of 4 weeks to 5 years;

___ 2. Published test, based on one of Piaget's best known formulations, which can serve as an indicator of a child's transition from the preoperational to the concrete operational stage of thinking;

___ 3. Current revision of a test series, originally published in Russia, which is useful in testing the mentally retarded and is a prototype of measures of muscle performance;

___ 4. Current revision of a prototypical instrument designed to assess developmental level in terms of one's ability to look after one's own practical needs and take responsibility in daily living;

___ 5. Individual test, developed and standardized on deaf and hard-of-hearing children, which differs from most performance tests in that it eliminates speed and samples a wider variety of intellectual functions;

___ 6. Revision of one of the best known individual intelligence scales that was prepared and adapted for use with blind persons;

___ 7. Current revision of a test, useful in the assessment of people with motor handicaps, wherein the test taker responds by designating one out of four pictures on a plate that best illustrates the meaning of a stimulus word presented orally by the examiner;

___ 8. Test, originally developed for use with cerebral-palsied children, which illustrates the use of pictorial classification in intellectual assessment;

___ 9. Individually administered scale which features the almost complete elimination of instructions, either spoken or pantomime, and was developed through and for use with different ethnic groups;

___ 10. Nonverbal test, used widely in clinics as well as with different cultural and ethnic groups, wherein credit is given for the inclusion of body parts, clothing details, proportion, perspective, and such;

    A. Vineland Adaptive Behavior Scale

    B. Interim Hayes-Binet

    C. Bruininks-Oseretsky Test of Motor Proficiency

    D. Gesell Developmental Schedules

    E. Leiter International Performance Scale

    F. Concept Assessment Kit—Conservation

    G. Columbia Mental Maturity Scale (CMMS)

    H. Goodenough-Harris Drawing Test

    I. Hiskey-Nebraska Test of Learning Aptitude

    J. Peabody Picture Vocabulary Test-Revised (PPVT-R)

ANSWERS:

    1 - D;   2 - F;   3 - C;   4 - A;   5 - I;   6 - B;   7 - J;   8 - G;   9 - E;   10 - H.

TRUE/FALSE and WHY?

1. Infant tests should be used mainly to assess current developmental status rather than to predict subsequent ability levels. (T/F) Why? _True_ _____

_____

2. Piagetian scales are characterized by a rigid and atheoretical framework that focuses on quantitative interpretation. (T/F) Why? _____

_____

3. Research findings suggest that there is a substantial overlap between Piagetian scales, standardized intelligence tests, and school achievement in terms of the overall assessment of children that their measures provide. (T/F) Why? _____

_____

4. According to the "IQ range" definition of levels of mental retardation, the upper limit for profound retardation would correspond to a Wechsler IQ of 25. (T/F) Why? _____

_____

5. The AAMD and most experts in the field of mental retardation agree that an IQ of 70 constitutes the clear dividing line between normality and mental retardation. (T/F) Why?

_____

6. Testing physically handicapped children at an early age is not likely to be productive in ameliorating the effects of their handicaps on their intellectual development. (T/F) Why?

_____

7. Empirical psychometric studies of procedural adaptations of tests such as the College Board's SAT and the GRE General Test suggest that they can provide fair measures for handicapped test takers. (T/F) Why? _____

_____

8. A cultural difference is not likely to become a cultural disadvantage unless individuals have to adjust to and compete in cultures unlike the ones in which they were reared. (T/F) Why? True _____

9. The Leiter International Performance Scale is scored in terms of mental age and ratio IQ, but such an IQ retains the same meaning at different ages. (T/F) Why? _____

_____

10. Investigations that have used the Goodenough Draw-a-Man Test on different cultures and ethnic groups indicate that performance on that test is independent of cultural background. (T/F) Why? _____

_____

ANSWERS TO TRUE/FALSE:

1. True	4. True	7. True	10. False
2. False	5. False	8. True	
3. True	6. False	9. False	

MULTIPLE CHOICE: TEST YOURSELF

1. Performance tests can normally be distinguished by their _____

   _____.

   a. total nonreliance on language
   b. emphasis on object manipulation
   c. nonverbal characteristics
   d. unbiased nature

2. Tests for infants and preschool children usually must be _____

   _____.

   a. nonlanguage
   b. performance
   c. individually administered
   d. none of the above

3. The Gesell Developmental Schedules consist mostly of _____

   _____.

   a. behavioral data gathered through observation
   b. a series of performance tests for children
   c. nonverbal interpretation of pictures
   d. testing infants' aptitudes

4. The Bayley Scales of Infant Development include a(n) _____

   _____.

   a. Mental Scale
   b. Motor Scale
   c. Infant Behavior Record
   d. all of the above

5. Piagetian scales assume _____

   _____.

   a. minimum language development
   b. uniform developmental sequences
   c. motor coordination
   d. operational causality

6. Assessment of the mentally retarded in the United States has _____

   _____.

   a. improved very little in the past 25 years
   b. gotten increased attention, especially since 1977
   c. been replaced by subjective evaluation
   d. turned to nonlanguage performance tests

7. The Oseretsky tests are designed to assess mental retardation through _____.

    a. an evaluation of social skills
    b. Piaget's developmental schedules
    c. verbal facility
    d. an evaluation of motor development

8. The ability to take responsibility for one's behavior and to take care of one's own needs can be evaluated by the _____.

    a Gesell scale
    b. Lincoln-Oseretsky Developmental Scale
    c. Vineland scale
    d. Interim Hayes-Binet

9. Tests used with handicapped individuals _____.

    a. always require special procedural alterations
    b. cannot involve manipulation of objects
    c. usually require reconsideration of reliability and norms
    d. should not be altered in any way that will affect the established norms

10. The testing of hearing impaired children is complicated by the fact that _____.

    a. they are usually handicapped on verbal tests
    b. one cannot assume that the norms of standard tests apply
    c. the idea of speed is hard to convey to them
    d. all of the above

11. Testing of the blind usually entails _____.

    a. performance items
    b. the use of braille
    c. oral or tape-recorded presentation of stimuli
    d. a lowering of norms compared with those of seeing people even when tests have been suitably adapted

12. Tests for the severely orthopedically handicapped should be _____.

    a. individually modified in whatever way is necessary to meet the needs of the test taker, without regard to norms
    b. free of all performance items
    c. presented only through visual means
    d. presented so the test taker only has to point or nod at the correct answer

13. Tests that are designed to minimize cultural influences emphasize _____
    _____.

    a. speed of response rather than content
    b. questions not specific to any given culture
    c. performance-type responses
    d. questions relating to minority subcultures

14. Research on the Goodenough Draw-a-Man Test shows that it _____
    _____.

    a. provides an accurate measure of intelligence in all cultures
    b. serves as an excellent measure of personality
    c. depends heavily on artistic skills
    d. is also culturally dependent, as are other tests

15. The current general consensus among experts in cross-cultural testing is that _____
    _____.

    a. we will see dramatic improvements in cross-cultural testing in the next few years
    b. we will never produce a truly culture-free intelligence test
    c. current cross-cultural tests are quite adequate
    d. more money must be spent on research

MINIPROJECTS/SUGGESTED OUTREACH ACTIVITIES:

1. Each of the special populations discussed in Chapter 10 presents unique problems in assessment which require familiarity with the instruments available as well as with the characteristics of the populations involved. With this in mind, you may wish to become better informed about the area(s) that are of greatest interest to you by reading one or more of the following:

    A. Part III (Standards for Particular Applications) of the *Standards for Educational and Psychological Testing* (see references in p. 22 of the textbook and elsewhere), which contains two brief but informative chapters on "Testing Linguistic Minorities" and "Testing People Who Have Handicapping Conditions."

    B. *Educational Measurement,* Third edition, edited by Robert L. Linn (New York: American Council on Education/Macmillan, 1989), which contains expanded treatments of the topics of "Identification of Mild Handicaps," in Chapter 17 by Lorrie Shepard, and "Testing of Linguistic Minorities," in Chapter 18 by Richard Duran.

    C. Jerome Sattler's *Assessment of Children* (San Diego, CA: Sattler, 1988), which provides one of the best and most comprehensive overviews on the subject of testing children. See especially Chapters 5, 12, 14, and 15, which deal with the issues and tests discussed in Chapter 10 of your textbook.

    D. R.W. Brislin's article on "Cross-cultural Research in Psychology" (*Annual Review of Psychology,* 1983, *34,* 363-400), which gives a good overview of the areas of cross-cultural research, in general, and of cross-cultural testing, in particular.

2. In order to gain further insight into the various fields of testing, there is no substitute for a direct examination of the tests themselves. Depending on what is available to you and what your interests are, you may want to examine the manuals and test kits of one or more of the

instruments discussed in Chapter 10. For example, you could review and compare the manuals and kits for the Bayley Scales of Infant Development and for the McCarthy Scales of Children's Abilities (MSCA) with special regard to the directions for administration of these two scales. Such a review would highlight the difference between testing infants and testing older children quite clearly, as the range of applicability of the MSCA starts exactly where that of the Bayley Scales ends, at 2.5 years. You would thus be able to notice the overlap between the easiest items of the MSCA and the most difficult ones of the Bayley Scales, as well as the large differences in the range of behaviors that can be sampled in the age groups covered by each of the scales.

3. Two additional ways in which you can round out your knowledge of the tests discussed in Chapter 10, or in most of the chapters that follow, are to:

A. Prepare a written Test Evaluation according to the Suggested Outline in Appendix B of the textbook. This format will require you to evaluate the test materials themselves, to read the appropriate sections of the *Standards for Educational and Psychological Testing,* and to look up the *Mental Measurements Yearbook*'s reviews on the test you choose. You could also locate reviews in other sources as well as studies that have been done using the test in question.

B. Conduct a survey in your community to find out who is using the test(s) that interest you and their reasons for selecting those instruments. You could contact counselors or psychologists at elementary schools and high schools, mental health agencies, personnel departments, college counseling and/or testing centers, and state or local agencies involved in rehabilitation, among others, as appropriate. Before contacting the individuals concerned, you should decide exactly what you will ask, based on a prior review of the specific area of testing in question.

ANSWERS TO MULTIPLE CHOICE/TEST YOURSELF ITEMS:

1. b	4. d	7. d	10. d	13. b
2. c	5. b	8. c	11. c	14. d
3. a	6. b	9. c	12. d	15. b

Chapter 11
GROUP TESTING

CHAPTER OUTLINE

CHAPTER SUMMARY

Group testing began during World War I, with the development of the Army Alpha and Army Beta examinations, and has grown enormously since then because of its usefulness to the educational system, industry, and government services, as well as to the armed forces. Group tests, which are suitable for mass testing programs of many sorts, differ from individual tests in the form of their items and in how items are arranged. The typical group test uses multiple-choice items, as opposed to open-ended questions, and presents items of similar content in increasing order of difficulty within separately timed subtests so that each test taker may be exposed to each type of item and have a chance to complete the easier ones first. Some tests utilize special arrangements of items, such as the spiral omnibus format, to ensure that items of each type are attempted within each successive level of difficulty.

Group tests have not only made it possible to conduct large-scale testing programs economically but, because they minimize the roles of the examiner and the scorer, they can be given under more uniform conditions and scored more objectively than individual tests. In addition, the relative ease and speed with which group test data can be gathered have made it possible to accumulate far larger and more representative standardization samples than those obtained for even the best individual tests. On the other hand, group tests provide less opportunity for establishing rapport, or for detecting unusual conditions in the test taker that could influence test performance, than do individual tests. Group tests have also been criticized because of the restrictions they impose on responses, which may occasionally penalize creative test takers, and because their utilization of testing time is not as effective as it can be in individualized testing.

Adaptive testing procedures that are individually tailored to the responses of test takers are now being explored increasingly in an effort to combine the flexibility of individual tests with the advantages of group tests. These techniques, which lend themselves best to computerized test administration, may use a two-stage testing process to route the test taker to the most appropriate one of a set of measures at different levels of difficulty or may start with an item of intermediate difficulty and route the examinee upward or downward after each response, depending on its correctness. More complex sequential testing models, which use ability estimates for each item as the basis for scoring and item information functions for deciding when to stop testing, are also under development. Research findings with these methods indicate that they can be as reliable and valid as conventional tests in spite of their smaller number of items and shorter testing times. Computerized adaptive testing strategies offer great potential not only in circumventing the limitations of traditional group tests but also in terms of expanding the range of item types and response options available to test takers and thus providing a better linkage between testing and remedial interventions.

The Multidimensional Aptitude Battery (MAB) is an example of another approach to combining the features of individual and group tests. The MAB is designed to assess the same skills as the Wechsler Adult Intelligence Scale-Revised (WAIS-R) through a group-administered, paper-and-pencil format that dispenses with the use of a highly trained examiner. The scores on the battery, which is being standardized in almost the same fashion as the WAIS-R, correlate very highly with those of the WAIS-R and show consistently high reliabilities as well.

Multilevel batteries, designed to measure intellectual development over a broad range of age groups in a manner that will produce comparable scores over several years, constitute another type of group test and one that is especially suitable for use in schools. The main function of these batteries is to assess readiness for school learning at each stage in the educational process. Therefore, these batteries typically consist of separate combinations of tests for the primary, elementary school, and high school levels. The Otis-Lennon School Ability Test (OLSAT), the Cognitive Abilities Test (CogAT), and the School and College Ability Tests (SCAT) are three prime examples of multilevel batteries selected for discussion in the textbook because of their generally high quality and the recency of their latest revisions.

The Scholastic Aptitude Test (SAT) of the College Board is an outstanding example of tests that are used in the admission, placement, and counseling of college students. The SAT has undergone continuous development and extensive research since 1926, when it was incorporated into the College Board testing program. SAT scores show fairly high correlations with college grades and are even better predictors of the latter when used in combination with high school grade point average (GPA). The American College Testing Program (ACT) is another widely used test for college admissions although, technically, it is not up to the standards set by the SAT.

Graduate and professional schools also use tests to aid in the selection of applicants. The Graduate Record Examinations (GRE) are a well-known example of this type of test. The GRE program includes a General Test, with Verbal, Quantitative, and Analytical Ability sections, and Subject Tests for many fields of study. The scores on the GRE have been anchored to a fixed reference group of college seniors tested in 1952, but they can also be interpreted normatively by reference to the current scores for specific fields or institutions. The GRE scores are fairly good predictors of graduate school performance, especially when they are used in combination with college grades. The Miller Analogies Test is another instrument that is widely used for graduate school admissions and also in evaluating personnel for high-level jobs in industries. The Miller Analogies Test has a very high ceiling and provides norms for students in several fields as well as for groups of industrial employees and job applicants.

COMPREHENSIVE REVIEW

STUDY QUESTIONS:

1. Describe the major differences in the design of group versus individual tests.

2. List and explain the advantages of group testing over individual testing.

3. List and explain the disadvantages of group testing compared to individual testing.

4. Discuss the aims of individually tailored tests and describe two examples of strategies that can be used in devising such tests.

5. Discuss the role computers can play in adaptive testing and in increasing the versatility of tests.

6. Describe the Multidimensional Aptitude Battery (MAB) and the approach to group testing that it represents.

7. Discuss the role of multilevel batteries and describe their major features in terms of content coverage and organization.

8. List and briefly describe three examples of representative multilevel batteries.

9. Describe the Scholastic Aptitude Test (SAT) of the College Board and cite specific information that can be used to support its role in the college admissions process.

10. Describe the Graduate Record Examinations (GRE) in terms of their coverage, scores, and usefulness in selecting graduate school applicants.

FILL IN THE BLANKS: Key Terms and Concepts

1. *Group* tests are instruments designed primarily for mass testing, whose chief advantages usually include objectivity, low cost, and large norms and whose main limitations center on their impersonal nature and lack of flexibility.

2. In the __ __ __ __ __ __ __ __ __ __ __ __ format of testing, the easiest items of each type are presented first, followed by the next easiest of each type, and so on, until the most difficult items in the test are presented.

3. Individually tailored tests, also designated as __ __ __ __ __ __ __ __,

   __ __ __ __ __ __ __ __ __, __ __ __ __ __ __ __ __, __ __ __ __ __ __ __ __ __ __,

   __ __ __ __ __ __ __, or __ __ __ __ __ __ __ __ – __ __ __ __ __ __ __ __ __ __ testing are techniques that aim to combine some of the advantages of individual and group testing and are particularly suited to computerized administration.

4. In the _ _ _ _ _ _ _ _ _ _ testing model, all test takers start with an item of intermediate difficulty and are routed upward or downward depending on the correctness of their responses to that item and to subsequent ones.

5. _ testing (CAT) procedures can utilize items drawn from a pool assembled through item response theory (IRT) techniques in flexible sequences that are individualized so as to maximize the efficiency of measurement.

6. In CAT, each item in the pool has a(n) _ _ _ _ _ _ _ _ _ _ _ _ _ _ _ _ _ which is used for scoring and which reflects the difficulty level, discriminative value, and probability of guessing the correct response that are associated with the item.

7. In CAT, the _ _ _ _ _ _ _ _ _ _ _ _ _ _ _ _ _ function indicates the precision of measurement and, summed across all of the items attempted, constitutes the _ _ _ _ _ _ _ _ _ _ _ _ _ _ _ function which serves the same purpose as the traditional standard error of measurement.

8. _ have been devised in order to provide comparable measures of intellectual development over a broad range of age groups and/or grade levels.

9. In the most recently developed or revised multilevel batteries the term _ _ _ _ _ _ _ _ _ _ _ _ _ has been replaced by more specific designations that reflect their function in assessing readiness for school learning.

10. The College Board's publications repeatedly emphasize that, in spite of its name, the SAT measures _ _ _ _ _ _ _ _ _ _ _ _ _ _ _ _ _ _ acquired through the individual's experience both in and out of school.

ANSWERS TO FILL-IN-THE-BLANKS: (Key Terms and Concepts)

1. group (tests)
2. spiral omnibus (format)
3. adaptive/sequential/branched/programmed/dynamic/response-contingent (testing)
4. pyramidal (testing model)
5. computerized adaptive (testing) (CAT)
6. ability estimate
7. item information (function)/test information (function)
8. multilevel batteries

9. intelligence

10. developed abilities

MATCHING: Group Tests (One letter per number)

___ 1. Screening instrument, developed in the armed services, that provided a single score based on an equal number of vocabulary, arithmetic, spatial relations, and mechanical ability items;

___ 2. Composite instrument, currently used for selection and classification in all the armed services, that is being revised into a computerized adaptive testing format;

___ 3. Paper-and-pencil measure that has already shown very high correlations with, and was designed to assess the same functions as, the WAIS-R;

___ 4. Multilevel battery, for grades 1 to 12, that was normed jointly with the Metropolitan Achievement Test and the Stanford Achievement Test;

___ 5. Multilevel battery, for grades K through 12, that was normed jointly with the Iowa Tests of Basic Skills and the Tests of Achievement and Proficiency;

___ 6. Multilevel battery, for grades 3.5 to 12.9, that was normed jointly with the Sequential Tests of Educational Progress (STEP) and explicitly acknowledges the impact of schooling on its scores;

___ 7. College Board test, used in the admission, placement, and counseling of college students, that emphasizes measurement of developed abilities in the Verbal and Mathematical areas;

___ 8. Shorter, comparable form of the SAT taken prior to the senior year of high school and used for counseling and for the evaluation of fellowship candidates;

___ 9. Test battery, originally developed for the admission and placement of students in state universities, whose tests include English and Mathematics Usage as well as Social Studies and Natural Sciences Reading;

___ 10. Testing program conducted by the Educational Testing Service, which is used by universities in the admission of post-baccalaureate students and includes a General Test and Subject Tests in various fields;

___ 11. Instrument used in the selection of graduate students and in the evaluation of high-level job applicants, which features an unusually high ceiling and subject matter drawn from many academic fields;

       A. School and College Ability Tests (SCAT)

       B. Scholastic Aptitude Test (SAT)

       C. Armed Services Vocational Aptitude Battery (ASVAB)

       D. Otis-Lennon School Ability Test (OLSAT)

       E. American College Testing Program (ACT)

       F. Preliminary SAT

       G. Multidimensional Aptitude Battery (MAB)

       H. Miller Analogies Test

I. Graduate Record Examinations (GRE)

J. Armed Forces Qualification Test (AFQT)

K. Cognitive Abilities Test (CogAT)

ANSWERS:

1 - J;   2 - C;   3 - G;   4 - D;   5 - K;   6 - A;   7 - B;   8 - F;   9 - E;   10 - I;   11 - H.

MULTIPLE CHOICE: TEST YOURSELF

1. Compared to individual tests, group tests, on the whole, have the following advantage(s): _____ .

   a. more broadly based norms
   b. more objective scoring procedures
   c. the examiner's role is simplified
   d. all of the above

2. Most group tests use the _____ type of test items.

   a. completion
   b. multiple choice
   c. free-response
   d. omnibus

3. The "spiral-omnibus" format used in some group tests means that _____ _____ .

   a. the tests include a built-in key for easy scoring
   b. examinees take only the most difficult items for their level of performance
   c. items of each type are presented successively at increasing levels of difficulty
   d. multilevel items of the same type are presented all at once

4. Group tests are often correctly criticized because _____ _____ .

   a. they are too short
   b. their norms are based on inadequate samples
   c. examiners often give incorrect instructions
   d. little attention can be given to rapport with the test taker

5. Some people have claimed that group tests do not allow the test taker enough room for original thinking. Current research about this issue indicates that _____ _____ .

   a. the restriction caused by multiple-choice items results in serious problems in evaluation
   b. the multiple-choice format is totally inappropriate
   c. response restrictions have not been found to be a significant problem
   d. no investigations have been done on response restrictions

6. The use of a computer to alter the sequencing of item presentation as a result of

   performance on previous items is called _____ testing.

   a. computer
   b. adaptive
   c. alternative-response
   d. CRT

7. Response-contingent testing is most appropriate in _____

   _____.

   a. large college lecture courses
   b. private schools
   c. individualized educational programs
   d. elementary school social studies

8. The principal purpose of multilevel batteries is to _____

   _____.

   a. identify the underachiever
   b. indicate students' readiness for learning at each stage
   c. serve as a basis for advancing students to the next grade
   d. all of the above

9. Group tests that presuppose functional literacy are typically not administered to children

   below the _____ level.

   a. fourth-grade
   b. sixth-grade
   c. eighth-grade
   d. high school

10. The Kuder-Richardson reliabilities for well-prepared multilevel batteries are usually _____

    _____.

    a. .80 or above
    b. .70 to .79
    c. .60 to .69
    d. under .60

11. The multilevel battery that is described in the textbook as an example of what is available at

    the elementary school level and that consists of verbal, quantitative, and nonverbal subtests

    is the _____.

    a. Scholastic Aptitude Test
    b. Miller Analogies Test
    c. Cognitive Abilities Test
    d. Multidimensional Aptitude Battery

12. The SCAT yields scores for _____ .

   a. verbal abilities, quantitative abilities, and the total battery
   b. children between 6 and 12 years of age
   c. innate capacity independent of experience
   d. visual-spatial and manipulative abilities

13. Compared to the most widely used college admission tests, high school grades _____ .

   a. cannot predict college grades as well
   b. can predict college grades as well or slightly better
   c. can predict college grades much better
   d. are used to a much lesser extent

14. Compared with the SAT, the ACT _____ .

   a. is a better test of math skills, but inferior as far as verbal skills are concerned
   b. places more emphasis on subject matter areas
   c. shows much higher validity
   d. is an older test, developed for use in public schools

15. The Miller Analogies Test _____ .

   a. is gradually replacing the GRE for predicting academic success
   b. shows vastly different performance norms for different groups
   c. is designed for predicting success in college
   d. is a high-level speed test for English majors

MINIPROJECTS/SUGGESTED OUTREACH ACTIVITIES:

1. Some of the most exciting and potentially revolutionary advances currently being made in psychological testing stem from the techniques that are made possible by the use of computers. For a brief overview of some of the possibilities and dangers that technological innovations can bring to testing, read Isaac Bejar's chapter on "Speculations on the Future of Test Design" in *Test Design: Developments in Psychology and Psychometrics,* edited by Susan Embretson (Orlando, FL: Academic Press, 1985).

2. During the course of your education you have probably been exposed to at least one of the tests discussed in Chapter 11, as a test taker. If this is so, chances are that you did not pay much attention to the specific procedures of test administration as you were most likely preoccupied with taking the test. One way to supplement whatever first-hand knowledge you have of group tests is to make your services available as a proctor for an examination session with one of those tests. Although elementary and secondary schools typically use their own personnel for such exams, universities and community colleges usually hire students as proctors or test supervisors for the testing programs they conduct, as long as the students are well recommended and are no longer in the position of having to take the test in question again. In addition, group testing in other institutions, such as military bases, often requires the hiring of supervisory personnel to help with test administration. The testing center in your school or your instructor are probably the best sources of information

on how to participate in this activity. Its benefits include the fact that you will almost surely go through an informative test orientation session *and* be paid for your time.

3. If you want to investigate the meaning of the term "high ceiling" directly, and/or if you subscribe to the notion that a humbling experience is good for one's character, find out the nearest location where the Miller Analogies Test is given and register to take it. This project would cost you some money, but it is likely to be quite enjoyable if you like to take tests that are challenging, especially since no dire consequences would follow from taking it simply for the experience of it. Another "high ceiling" test, designed for gifted adults, is the Concept Mastery Test (CMT). Unfortunately, The Psychological Corporation has stopped printing the CMT, but you may find a copy of it available for you to take at a testing center or through your instructor.

4. Miniproject # 2 for Chapter 6 suggested that you investigate the references cited in Chapter 11 in connection with the validity data for tests for the college level and beyond. If you did not follow up on that suggestion then, it would be just as appropriate to do it at this point. See, in particular, the technical handbook edited by T.F. Donlon (New York: CEEB, 1984) on the SAT and/or the most recent *Guide to the Use of the Graduate Record Examination Program* published by the Educational Testing Service of Princeton, N.J.

ANSWERS TO MULTIPLE CHOICE/TEST YOURSELF ITEMS:

1. d	4. d	7. c	10. a	13. b
2. b	5. c	8. b	11. c	14. b
3. c	6. b	9. a	12. a	15. b

Chapter 12

PSYCHOLOGICAL ISSUES IN INTELLIGENCE TESTING

CHAPTER OUTLINE

Longitudinal Studies of Children's Intelligence
   Stability of the IQ
   Instability of the IQ

Intelligence in Early Childhood
   Predictive Validity of Infant and Preschool Tests
   Nature of Early Childhood Intelligence
   Implications for Intervention Programs

Problems in the Testing of Adult Intelligence
   Age Decrement
   Nature of Adult Intelligence

Population Changes in Intelligence Test Performance
   Rising Scores
   Declining Scores

Problems in Cross-Cultural Testing
   Levels of Cultural Differentials
   Cultural Differences and Cultural Handicap
   Language in Transcultural Testing

Nature of Intelligence
   Meaning of an IQ
   Heritability and Modifiability
   Motivation and Intelligence

CHAPTER SUMMARY

Psychological tests are tools whose interpretation requires knowledge of human behavior. Unless test users possess the psychological information necessary to interpret tests properly, tests are likely to be misused and misinterpreted, regardless of how technically sophisticated the tests themselves may be.

An important contribution that psychological research has made to the understanding of the construct of "intelligence" comes from longitudinal studies of the same individuals over long periods of time. These studies have shown that intelligence is both complex and dynamic, rather than unitary and constant. Although group studies demonstrate that intelligence test performance is quite stable over the elementary, high school, and college periods, studies of individuals reveal that people can undergo large shifts in IQ as a consequence of environmental influences and personality characteristics.

Assessing the intelligence of people who have not yet started, or who have already discontinued, their schooling presents a unique difficulty because of the diversity of their activities, in contrast to the relative uniformity of experience of school-age individuals. For infants, this problem is compounded by the fact that their intelligence appears to be qualitatively different from that of school-age children and, thus, the test results of infants have little, if any, validity for predicting later performance unless they are markedly atypical. For older preschoolers, intelligence test scores do have moderate predictive validity. Moreover, attempts to define and evaluate "social competency" in early childhood have led to a realization that personality variables must be taken into account and that both remedial interventions and assessment should be aimed at specific skills rather than at broad developmental indexes such as the IQ.

Cross-sectional studies of adult intelligence have typically shown a peak during the early adulthood years followed by a steady decline in older age groups, while longitudinal studies, as a rule, have shown continuing improvement or stability in several abilities. This difference is most likely attributable to methodological artifacts of the two types of research designs. Cross-sectional studies usually compare older and less educated adults with younger and better educated ones while longitudinal comparisons frequently use intellectually superior individuals or otherwise confound the effects of aging on intelligence test performance. The results of better designed studies of adult intelligence, using the cross-sequential method of comparisons, indicate that genuine ability decrements are not likely to be shown until well over the age of 60 and that the changes that do occur vary with the individual, as a function of health status, "academic" involvement, and the maintenance of a flexible and intellectually stimulating lifestyle.

As far as the general population is concerned, there has been a rise in the mean intelligence test performance over the past several decades which is probably attributable to increasing literacy, higher educational levels, and other cultural changes. However, this rise is by no means uniform in all segments of the population or across all time periods. One of the clear exceptions to the secular rise in tested intelligence is the highly publicized decline in Scholastic Aptitude Test (SAT) scores between 1963 and 1977, which has been commonly attributed to specific changes in the composition of the college-bound segment of the population and to subsequent curricular adjustments to those changes. In any event, the proven influence of cultural conditions on intelligence test results underscores the need for frequent updating of norms and for interpreting scores in light of experiential variables.

Differences across cultures may be so specific that they affect only test responses or so broad that they influence the entire behavior domains that tests assess. Moreover, the effects of the environment on cognitive functioning can be either direct or indirect and can range from mild and/or easily changed to severe and/or irreversible. The pervasiveness of cultural influences on all behavior, and the fact that hereditary and environmental factors, and their effects, are inextricably intertwined, make it impossible to devise a "culture-free" test. In fact, since each culture encourages certain abilities and ways of behaving, the very notion of what is an asset or a handicap may differ across cultures and makes it difficult to devise a test that will be "fair" to more than one cultural group, especially when cultures differ significantly from one another. The traditional cross-cultural approach to testing, which has relied heavily on nonverbal content, does not seem to be an adequate solution to the problem of devising culture-fair instruments because it cannot be assumed that nonverbal tests measure the same functions as verbal tests and because nonlanguage tests, in fact, may be even more culturally loaded than verbal tests. One possible solution to this dilemma is to use translated versions of a common set of anchor items to equate tests across cultures in terms of their difficulty and discriminative value.

Intelligence test scores, such as IQs, should be regarded as descriptive and should be used to help in understanding individuals, rather than to label them. These principles need to be followed not only because intelligence tests do not provide an explanation of the reasons why people perform as they do, but also because such tests do not assess "intelligence" in all of its various meanings and complexity. An additional source of confusion with regard to intelligence tests has arisen from the practice of computing heritability indexes for intelligence on the basis of questionable empirical data on family resemblance on intelligence test scores. Heritability indexes, in general, have serious limitations in that they apply only to the populations on which they were found and not to individuals or to other populations. In addition, no matter how large the heritability index for a given trait is, it should not be taken to imply that the contribution of the environment to that trait is unimportant. There is, in fact, a large and growing body of evidence that intellectual abilities are quite amenable to environmental interventions. Furthermore, although intelligence tests are often considered in isolation, it is widely recognized that personality and intellect coexist within the individual and have reciprocal effects on one another that actually cannot be separated.

COMPREHENSIVE REVIEW

STUDY QUESTIONS:

1. Discuss the relationship that exists between psychological testing and psychological science, as well as why and how that relationship needs to change.

2. Describe the major findings of longitudinal studies of children's intelligence.

3. List and discuss three conditions that have been cited as explanations for the stability of IQs during the course of human development.

4. Discuss the major conditions that have been found to be associated with significant increments and decrements in IQ as far as young people are concerned.

5. Describe the differences that exist in the results of tests of intelligence for infants and for older preschoolers and discuss the major reasons for those differences.

6. Relate the findings of studies of intelligence in early childhood to the planning and evaluation of compensatory educational programs for preschoolers.

7. Discuss and explain the typical findings of longitudinal versus cross-sectional studies of adult intelligence.

8. Describe the advantages of the cross-sequential design for studying changes that occur over the lifespan and discuss the major findings of studies using this design in the realm of tested abilities.

9. Cite two major examples of seemingly contradictory findings in the area of population changes in intelligence test performance and explain each of these findings.

10. Discuss levels of cultural differentials in terms of their relevance to intelligence test performance and the severity and/or permanence of their effects.

11. Define what is meant by a "culture-free" and a "culture-fair" test and explain the difficulties inherent in trying to devise these sorts of instruments.

12. Discuss the use of nonverbal tests in cross-cultural testing and explain why they might be less effective than verbal tests.

13. Suppose that you took an intelligence test and obtained an extremely high IQ. What, if any, objections should you have to being labeled as a "genius" on the basis of that result?

14. Define what a heritability index is, describe how it is obtained, and discuss the limitations of the concept of heritability estimates in general.

15. Discuss the relationship that exists between personality and cognitive variables and cite two examples of personality traits that have a special impact on cognitive functioning.

FILL IN THE BLANKS: Key Terms and Concepts

1. Longitudinal studies are those which examine the same group of individuals over long periods of time.

2. The growing consistency of intelligence test performance in individuals has been explained partly by the _ _ _ _ _ _ _ _ hypothesis, which refers to the fact that as age increases, earlier acquisitions constitute a larger proportion of one's total skills and knowledge.

3. Bradway and Robinson's _ _ _ _ _ _ _ _ _ _ index, which was based on parents' education, father's occupation, and the occupations of both grandfathers, was essentially an index of _ and, like other such measures, was significantly correlated to IQ.

4. The extent to which parents deliberately train a child in skills that are not yet essential has been called a(n) _ _ _ _ _ _ _ _ _ _ _ _ _ _ attempt and has been associated with rising IQs.

5. The concept of _ describes the qualitative changes in competence behavior that are appropriate at different ages, such as the infant's progression from discovering that she or he can affect the environment to complex, goal-directed activities.

6. The focus of intervention and evaluation procedures in compensatory educational programs for children from disadvantaged backgrounds has been greatly expanded by the realization that _ _ _ _ _ _ _ _ _ _ _ _ _ _ _ _ _ _ _ includes a number of emotional, motivational, and attitudinal components, in addition to cognitive variables.

7. _ _ _ _ _ _-_ _ _ _ _ _ _ _ _ _ comparisons are those in which persons of different ages are examined at the same time.

8. The _ _ _ _ _ _ _-_ _ _ _ _ _ _ _ _ _ _ design combines data from traditional cross-sectional and longitudinal studies and compares same-age cohorts at different time periods in an attempt to separate the effects of age from those of experiential factors.

9. The present goal in cross-cultural testing is to devise "_ _ _ _ _ _ _ _ _-_ _ _ _ _" tests that presuppose only experiences that are common to different cultures.

10. Cultural _ _ _ _ _ _ _ _ _ _ _ _ become cultural _ _ _ _ _ _ _ _ _ _ only when individuals move out of the culture or subculture in which they were reared and attempt to function, compete, or succeed in a different milieu.

11. According to Feuerstein, cultural deprivation consists of a lack of _ _ _ _ _ _ _ _ _ _ _ _ _ _ _ _ _ _ experiences that foster the establishment of learning sets, orientations, and other behavior patterns that facilitate subsequent learning.

12. The _ _ _ _ _ _ de _ _ _ _ _ _ _ _ _ _ _ _ _ _ _ _ _ _ (PAA), a Spanish version of the Scholastic Aptitude Test (SAT), has been developed by equating the two scales on the basis of the performance of Spanish-speaking and English-speaking samples on a set of anchor items.

13. A _ is a number that is calculated on the basis of measures of familial resemblance in a given trait and that shows the proportional contribution of genetic factors to the total variance of the trait in a given population under existing conditions.

14. In the comprehensive schema that Atkinson formulated to represent the interrelationships between abilities, motivation, and environmental variables, the concept of _ _ _ _ _ - _ _ - _ _ _ _, or time devoted to an activity, is a critical variable which, combined with level of performance, determines final achievement.

15. _ _ _ _ _ _ _ _ _ _ learning takes place as a result of the fact that even if people are exposed to the same immediate situation, what they attend to, as well as how deeply and for how long they attend to it, plays a pivotal role in learning.

16. The _ _ _ _ _-_ _ _ _ _ _ _, which may be construed as a sort of private self-fulfilling prophecy, is a pointed example of the interrelationship between aptitude and personality traits in that it can at once be a product of and an influence in a person's achievement history.

17. The _ _ _ _ _ _ _ _ _ _ _ _ _ _ _ _ _-_ _ _ _ _ _ _ motive, which can be gauged in infants by the extent and quality of their observation, exploration, and manipulation of the environment, is a prime contributor to cognitive development and a good predictor of later intellectual competence.

ANSWERS TO FILL-IN-THE-BLANKS: (Key Terms and Concepts)

1. longitudinal (studies)
2. overlap (hypothesis)

3. ancestral (index)/(index of) socioeconomic status

4. acceleration (attempt)

5. developmental transformations

6. social competency

7. cross-sectional (comparisons)

8. cross-sequential (design)

9. "culture-fair" (tests)

10. (cultural) differences/(cultural) handicaps

11. mediated learning (experiences)

12. *Prueba (de) Aptitud Académica* (PAA)

13. heritability index

14. time-on-task

15. selective (learning)

16. self-concept

17. environmental-mastery (motive)

TRUE/FALSE and WHY?

1. When the interval between tests is held constant, retest correlations tend to be higher in younger than in older children. (T/F) Why? _False_
   Recall not as good

2. The object of compensatory educational programs is to disrupt the "stability" of IQs that otherwise would have remained low. (T/F) Why? _____

3. Correlational studies of IQ at various stages of childhood provide actuarial data that are applicable to group predictions but not necessarily to the prediction of an individual's future IQ. (T/F) Why? _True_

4. Emotional dependency on parents appears to be a condition that is associated with large IQ gains during the preschool years. (T/F) Why? _____

5. The conclusion that emerges from longitudinal studies of infant intelligence test performance is that tests administered during the first year of life have little or no long-term predictive value. (T/F) Why? _____

6. Infant tests are more helpful in predicting subsequent development within clinical, nonnormal populations than within normal populations. (T/F) Why? _____True_____

_____

7. In general, the findings of research on the nature of early childhood intelligence support the conception of a developmentally unitary intellectual ability in infancy. (T/F) Why? _____

_____

8. Longitudinal studies of tested intelligence in average or below average adults have shown the same age-related decrements found in cross-sectional comparisons. (T/F) Why? _____

_____

9. Intensive studies of persons in their 70s, 80s, and 90s suggest that their intellectual functioning is more closely related to health status than to chronological age. (T/F) Why? _

_____

10. Whether the test scores of a given population rise, fall, or remain stable over time depends primarily on the time period covered. (T/F) Why? _____

_____

11. Empirical evidence, as well as logic, indicates that every test tends to favor persons from the culture in which it was developed. (T/F) Why? _____

_____

12. The assumption that tests which employ nonverbal content provide a more culture-fair measure of intellectual functions than verbal tests has been thoroughly justified. (T/F) Why? _____False_____

_____

13. When intelligence tests have been accurately translated, they can be assumed to be comparable to the original version as far as reliability and validity are concerned. (T/F) Why? _____False_____

_____

14. By and large, existing intelligence tests manage to measure the vast majority of the psychological functions that determine individual achievement. (T/F) Why? _____

_____

15. The primary function of heritability indexes for intellectual traits is to establish the degree to which those traits are subject to modifications. (T/F) Why? _____

_____

16. Studies of the effects of planned compensatory educational programs with school-age children suggest that significant improvement in academic achievement and test performance can be realized. (T/F) Why? _____

_____

ANSWERS TO TRUE/FALSE:

1. False	5. True	9. True	13. False
2. True	6. True	10. True	14. False
3. True	7. False	11. True	15. False
4. False	8. False	12. False	16. True

MULTIPLE CHOICE: TEST YOURSELF

1. In general, studies of the stability of intelligence test performance in elementary, high school, and college students over periods of from 1 to 10 years show test-retest correlations of approximately _____.
   a. .80 or higher
   b. .50 to .80
   c. .20 to .50
   d. these correlations can vary widely

2. Research has shown that IQs are most reliable when they are obtained at ages _____
   _____.
   a. 0 to 18 months
   b. 18 months to 2 years
   c. 3 to 10 years
   d. 10 to 25 years

3. Which of the following is *not* a major factor in increasing the stability of the IQ in older children? _____

   _____.
   a. Environmental stability
   b. The idea behind the overlap hypothesis
   c. The role of prerequisite learning skills
   d. An acceleration attempt by parents

4. A major reason, cited in the textbook, for the apparent failure of compensatory educational programs, such as Head Start, was _____

   _____.
   a. insufficient government funding
   b. evaluation techniques that were too global
   c. lack of close cooperation with parents
   d. inexperienced teachers who were unable to communicate with the children

5. Which of the following is the *least likely* reason for the apparent decline in intelligence test performance in adults over 40? _____

    _____.

    a. Age, per se
    b. The fact that younger adults have had more education
    c. Cultural changes
    d. Experiential factors in the lives of adults

6. Which of the following is the *least likely* reason for the decline in SAT scores during the 1960s and 1970s? _____

    _____.

    a. The test was getting harder each year in response to the better preparation of students
    b. A broader range of people considered college and, therefore, took the test
    c. Schools reduced their academic requirements
    d. Social activities became more important to students

7. The most important single influence on a person's performance in an intelligence test is

    _____.

    a. attitude
    b. environment
    c. ethnic background
    d. socioeconomic status

8. The most important problem associated with standardized testing is _____

    _____.

    a. the misuse and misinterpretation of tests
    b. lack of necessary reliability
    c. inconsistent validity estimates
    d. the overuse of tests for decision-making

9. The principal reason for giving an intelligence test to an individual is to _____

    _____.

    a. assess the individual's current strengths and weaknesses in relation to norms
    b. analyze the individual's mental potential
    c. contribute to the self-understanding of the individual
    d. determine the individual's suitability for a particular job

10. Longitudinal studies of test performance _____

    _____.

    a. compare different groups of people at different age levels
    b. are not as effective as cross-sectional studies
    c. follow the performance of the same group of persons over time
    d. emphasize wide-ranging skill areas

11. Which of the following is true about the IQ of people over 60? _____
    _____.

    a. There is a general decrease in IQ level on standard tests
    b. Some 60-year-olds still do better than the average 25-year-olds
    c. Intelligence test performance improves
    d. None of the above are true

12. All other things being equal, if a person were tested with the WAIS at ages 20, 30, 40, and

    50, how would you expect her/his IQ to vary? _____
    _____.

    a. The IQ would rise until age 40 and then drop
    b. The IQ would drop on each successive examination
    c. There would be a slow increase in the IQ
    d. The person's IQ would remain about the same

13. If a test were designed to be totally culture-free, it _____
    _____.

    a. could be used with anyone of any background
    b. would be unbiased
    c. would measure only nonverbal content
    d. would probably not measure anything of value

14. What is the effect of continuing lifelong education on IQ? _____
    _____.

    a. IQ may actually increase
    b. There will be no effect on IQ
    c. The effect will be impossible to predict
    d. IQ will still decrease after age 40

15. Heritability indexes _____
    _____.

    a. are widely applicable once they have been determined
    b. constitute a good way to gauge the modifiability of a trait
    c. have frequently been based on studies of twins
    d. refer to an individual's hereditary make-up

MINIPROJECTS/SUGGESTED OUTREACH ACTIVITIES:

1. You may have noticed that the summary for Chapter 12 is one of the longest ones in this guide. This is not a coincidence. It is, rather, a by-product of the fact that Chapter 12 is, in itself, a masterful distillation of a wide-ranging spectrum of psychological research and knowledge. A short summary cannot really do justice to the chapter's depth and breadth of coverage. Moreover, the ideas discussed in Chapter 12 are central not only to psychological testing but also to the fields of differential and developmental psychology as well as to research methods in psychology. They are also at the heart of the body of work that Anne Anastasi has produced during her distinguished career. For these reasons, you would be well advised to study this chapter very carefully and to incorporate as much of it as possible into your working knowledge of the field. An ideal way to supplement your insight into the

issues discussed in Chapter 12 would be to read some of Anastasi's major articles on these topics, such as the now classic "Heredity, Environment, and the Question 'How?'" (*Psychological Review,* 1958, *65,* 197-208) or the more recent "Experiential Structuring of Psychological Traits" (*Developmental Review,* 1986, *6,* 181-202), among others. In addition, you might make a mental note that if you ever need to prepare for a comprehensive examination in psychology, such as the GRE Subject Test or a licensure exam, a review of this chapter of the textbook prior to that exam should prove exceedingly worthwhile.

2. Read Chapter 1 of the *Manual for the WISC-R* (San Antonio, TX: The Psychological Corporation, 1974) for a brief introduction to David Wechsler's rationale for that scale. The chapter also contains some of the views that this important pioneer in testing postulated with regard to the concept of intelligence and its measurement.

3. Locate the *WAIS-R Manual,* also by David Wechsler (The Psychological Corporation, 1981), and examine Table 20 (IQ Equivalents of Sums of Scaled Scores), noticing the differences in the test scores needed to obtain a certain IQ, e.g., 100 or 120, at various age levels. For an even more detailed view of the "age decrements" mentioned in the textbook, look at Table 21 (Scaled Score Equivalents of Raw Scores) and contrast the raw scores needed to obtain a given scaled score, e.g., 10 or 8, on some of the WAIS-R subtests, e.g., Vocabulary and Block Design, at various age levels.

4. Review Chapter 12 of the textbook again. Then, based on the research findings that are described, prepare a "prescription" to be followed if one wanted to maximize a person's intelligence test performance from infancy to old age.

5. If the idea of improving your intellectual skills appeals to you, read *Intelligence Applied: Understanding and Increasing Your Intellectual Skills* by Robert J. Sternberg (New York: Harcourt Brace Jovanovich, 1986). This book, which was also mentioned in connection with Miniproject # 3 for Chapter 9, contains many suggestions, as well as practice problems, that should prove useful and enlightening.

ANSWERS TO MULTIPLE CHOICE/TEST YOURSELF ITEMS:

1. b	4. b	7. b	10. c	13. d
2. d	5. a	8. a	11. b	14. a
3. d	6. a	9. a	12. d	15. c

Chapter 13

MEASURING MULTIPLE APTITUDES

CHAPTER OUTLINE

Factor Analysis
    The Factor Matrix
    The Reference Axes
    Interpretation of Factors
    Factorial Composition of a Test
    Factor Loadings and Correlation
    Oblique Axes and Second-Order Factors

Theories of Trait Organization
    The Two-Factor Theory
    Multiple-Factor Theories
    Structure-of-Intellect Model
    Hierarchical Theories
    Nature and Development of Factors

Multiple Aptitude Batteries
    Batteries for General Use
    Batteries for Special Programs

Measurement of Creativity
    Research on Creative Talent
    Tests of Creative Aptitudes
    Creative Achievement

CHAPTER SUMMARY

The impetus to develop multiple aptitude batteries arose from the recognition that, because of the way they were designed, intelligence tests could not capture intraindividual variations in performance reliably, except in the broad categories of verbal and nonverbal skills. In addition, the growing involvement of psychologists in career counseling, and in the selection and placement of personnel, required the construction of specialized measures of performance in vocational areas, such as clerical and mechanical abilities, that would supplement the information derived from intelligence tests. The application of factor analytic techniques provided the theoretical and procedural bases that were needed to identify, sort, and define different abilities and, thus, develop multiple aptitude batteries.

Factor analysis is a statistical technique which serves to explore and understand behavioral data by reducing the number of dimensions needed to describe them, without sacrificing essential information. Although there are several methods that can be used for analyzing a set of variables into common factors, all of them begin with a complete table of intercorrelations among the variables and all of them end with a factor matrix which shows the weight or loading of each factor in each variable. When a set of tests is subjected to factor analysis, the resulting factor loadings represent the correlation between each test and each factor or the factorial validity of the tests. The square of that correlation represents the proportion of common variance between a test and the factor in question which, together with the variance that is specific to the test *and* its error variance, add up to the total variance of the test. The nature of a given factor is deduced from an examination of the tests which have high loadings on that factor and from a psychologically informed interpretation of what those tests have in common. When the axes that best fit the test clusters are oblique, rather than orthogonal, the factors that emerge from an analysis are themselves correlated. Their intercorrelations can, in turn, be analyzed to arrive at second-order factors which then account for the variance that is common to the factors and further reduce the number of dimensions needed to describe the original test data.

Factor analytic techniques have given rise to a variety of different theories about how intellectual traits are organized. In general, British psychologists begin with a single general factor, to which they attribute the major portion of the common variance, and then turn to group factors to account for the remaining intercorrelations, whereas American factor analysts usually account for as much of the common variance as possible through group factors and only postulate a general factor if the data justify it. Spearman's so-called "two-factor theory," with its single "g" factor which accounts for most of the variance in intellectual activities, is a prime example of the British approach, while Thurstone's multiple-factor theory, with its 7 to 12 "primary mental abilities," exemplifies the American approach. In addition, there are alternative schemas, such as Guilford's structure-of-intellect (SI) model, which organizes all intellectual traits along the dimensions of operations, contents, and products for a total of at least 120 distinct possible factors. The hierarchical approaches postulated by Vernon and Humphreys, among others, constitute still another type of schema that has been used in organizing factors.

The proliferation of models of trait organization is understandable when we consider that the traits identified through factor analysis are simply categories that describe the correlation among a set of behavioral measures. Moreover, the factorial composition of a given task may, and frequently does, differ among individuals with diverse experiential backgrounds and can also change within individuals over time, as their cognitive strategies evolve. Thus, the factors extracted from performance on intellectual tasks cannot be viewed as static underlying entities, any more than cognitive skills can be seen as representing fixed or innate properties of the organism.

The Differential Aptitude Tests (DAT) are one of the most widely used of about a dozen or so multiple aptitude batteries that have been developed for general use in educational testing, counseling, and personnel classification. In spite of their longevity, and exemplary norms and method of reporting scores, the DAT, like other such batteries, are disappointing with regard to differential validity, which is precisely the area in which they, and other classification instruments, should excel.

The General Aptitude Test Battery (GATB) of the United States Employment Service (USES) is another major example of a multiple aptitude battery based on factor analytic research. The GATB is used regularly by state employment agencies, and other nonprofit organizations, in the counseling and job referral of a large number of persons. Although a vast body of data has been accumulated on the GATB, and a promising research program to convert it to more sophisticated uses is in progress, the battery has several limitations in its coverage. Moreover, the exclusive reliance on a multiple-cutoff strategy as a procedure for combining the GATB's scores has undoubtedly reduced its effectiveness as a classification tool.

Some of the most exciting developments in the construction and evaluation of instruments for personnel selection and classification are those which are taking place as part of a long-term research program with the Armed Services Vocational Aptitude Battery (ASVAB). This program, which is designated as "Project A," is aimed at reevaluating the ASVAB against a wider, and more precisely assessed, range of criteria and at expanding the coverage of predictors to include personality and interest inventories. Another major project involves the development of a computerized adaptive testing (CAT) version of the ASVAB.

A significant development in psychological testing stems from the attempts to devise measures of creative talent. These attempts came about as a result of the upsurge in research on the nature and cultivation of creativity since midcentury. The two major series of standardized tests of creative aptitudes, all of which are still in experimental form, are the Aptitude Research Project (ARP) tests of divergent thinking, developed by Guilford and his colleagues, and the Torrance Tests of Creative Thinking. The ARP tests evolved from the same long-term factor analytic research that led to Guilford's development of the structure-of-intellect (SI) model. The formulation of the category of divergent thinking, prominent in creative activity, as one of five operations in the SI model, was one of the most productive outcomes of that project and stimulated a great deal of subsequent research on creativity. However, the assessment of creativity is complicated by the fact that creative achievement requires a variety of cognitive and evaluative aptitudes, as well as certain personality traits, appropriate to each field of endeavor, in addition to divergent-production capabilities.

COMPREHENSIVE REVIEW

STUDY QUESTIONS:

1. Discuss the reasons for the development of differential aptitude testing.

2. Explain the purpose of factor analysis and describe the basic elements that are common to all factor analytic techniques.

3. Describe Thurstone's criteria of positive manifold and simple structure and explain why it is useful to rotate reference axes in accordance to those criteria.

4. Discuss how the results of a factor analysis are interpreted.

5. Describe and explain the two basic theorems of factor analysis.

6. Define second-order factors and explain how they are derived.

7. Compare the typical approaches of British and American psychologists to factor analysis and cite examples of two theories of trait organization that are representative of those approaches.

8. Discuss how general, group, and specific factors are related and explain why factorial research has produced such a multiplicity of factors.

9. Describe Guilford's structure-of-intellect (SI) model.

10. Describe the basic features of hierarchical theories of trait organization.

11. Explain the nature of the traits that are identified through factor analysis as well as how and why the factorial composition of a given task may differ across and within individuals.

12. Describe the strengths and weaknesses of the Differential Aptitude Tests (DAT) as an example of a multiple aptitude battery for general use.

13. Discuss the background and limitations of the General Aptitude Test Battery (GATB) of the United States Employment Service (USES).

14. Discuss the developments that are currently taking place with regard to the Armed Services Vocational Aptitude Battery (ASVAB) and explain why they could result in a vastly improved classification instrument.

15. Discuss the background and current status of measures of creative aptitudes and describe two major test series in that area.

EXERCISES: Factor Analysis

1. Reconstruct the original correlation matrix for Tests 1 through 10 from the hypothetical factor matrix presented in Table 13-1 (p. 375) of the textbook. This exercise will require you to go "backwards" from the usual order of steps in factor analysis wherein one *starts* with a correlation matrix and *ends* with a factor matrix. However, the calculations you will be doing are actually done in practice as a final step in factor analysis, just to check on the computational accuracy of the analysis. In order to do this exercise you will need to apply the basic factor analytic theorem that the correlation between any two variables is equal to the sum of the cross-products of their common-factor loadings (see p. 380 of the textbook) and assume that Table 13-1 gives *all* the common-factor loadings between the tests in question.

2. For each of the four tests in Table 7, calculate the proportional contributions of each factor, the error variance, and the specificity of the test. Refer to the textbook (pp. 378-380) for the procedure you will need to follow.

Table 7   FACTOR LOADINGS AND RELIABILITIES FOR FOUR TESTS

FACTORS*

TESTS	V	R	N	P	Reliability Coefficient
Vocabulary	.70	.21	.16	.04	.95
Analogies	.31	.60	.20	.06	.90
Arithmetic	.03	.17	.82	.23	.92
Perceptual Speed	−.02	.00	.10	.65	.88

* V = Verbal;   R = Reasoning;   N = Numerical;   P = Perceptual.

ANSWERS TO EXERCISES: (Factor Analysis)

1.

CORRELATION MATRIX FOR TESTS 1 TO 10

Tests

Tests	1	2	3	4	5	6	7	8	9	10
1		.68	.74	.36	.79	−.11	.03	.13	.12	.10
2			.60	.29	.64	−.06	.06	.15	.13	.11
3				.32	.69	−.07	.06	.15	.13	.11
4					.34	−.05	.01	.06	.05	.04
5						−.10	.03	.12	.12	.10
6							.34	.36	.28	.20
7								.45	.36	.25
8									.40	.29
9										.23

Note the relatively high and uniformly positive correlations of Tests 1 through 5 (within the solid triangle) with each other and of Tests 6 through 10 (within the broken triangle) with each other. Notice also that the correlations that are outside of the triangles, i.e., those between Tests 1 to 5 and Tests 6 to 10 are either negative or very low. This hypothetical example presents a relatively simple factor analysis that resulted in two distinct and unambiguous factors. Therefore, in this case, an inspection of the original correlation matrix, which you reproduced in this exercise, probably would have led to similar conclusions about the data as the factor matrix does. In practice, however, correlation matrices are not always that clear-cut and factor analysis can reveal patterns that are not obvious in the correlation matrix. In any case, factor analysis does simplify the description of data by reducing the number of dimensions needed to present them.

2.

SOURCES OF VARIANCE OF TEST SCORES

Proportional Contributions

Tests	V	R	N	P	Specific	Error
Vocabulary	.49	.04	.03	.00	.39	.05
Analogies	.10	.36	.04	.00	.40	.10
Arithmetic	.00	.03	.67	.05	.17	.08
Percept. Speed	.00	.00	.01	.42	.45	.12

FILL IN THE BLANKS: Key Terms and Concepts

1. _____   _____ batteries were developed primarily as a result of the need to assess intraindividual variations in performance on separate abilities for counseling and placement purposes.

2. The technique of _____   _____, whose principal aim is to simplify the description of data by reducing the number of variables, was instrumental in providing the theoretical basis for constructing multiple aptitude batteries.

3. All factor analyses begin with a(n) __ __ __ __ __ __ __ __ __ __ __ __ __ __ __ __,
which is a table that shows the interrelationships among a set of variables, and end with
a(n) __ __ __ __ __ __ __ __ __ __ __ __, which is a table that shows the weight or loading
of each factor in each variable.

4. In factor analysis, it is customary to represent factors geometrically as
__ __ __ __ __ __ __ __ __ __ __ __ __ __ in terms of which each test can be plotted.

5. The rotation of reference axes in factor analysis is customarily carried out in accordance
with the criterion of __ __ __ __ __ __ __ __ __ __ __ __ __ __ __ __ __, which requires
rotation to such a position as to eliminate all significant negative weights, and the criterion
of __ __ __ __ __ __ __ __ __ __ __ __ __ __ __ __, which means that each test should have
loadings on as few factors as possible.

6. When an orthogonal rotation of axes is applied in the factor analysis of test data, the factor
loadings represent the correlation of each test with the factor, which is the
__ __ __ __ __ __ __ __ __ __ __ __ __ __ __ __ of the test.

7. One of the basic theorems of factor analysis states that the total variance of a test is the
sum of the variances contributed by the __ __ __ __ __ __ __ __ factors (those shared with other
tests), the __ __ __ __ __ __ __ __ __ factors (those occurring in that test alone,) and the
__ __ __ __ __ __ variance.

8. The __ __ __ __ __ __ __ __ __ __ __ __ __ of a test is that portion of its "true" variance it does
not share with any other test with which it was factor analyzed.

9. Another basic theorem of factor analysis states that the correlation between any two
variables is equal to the sum of the __ __ __ __ __ __ __-__ __ __ __ __ __ __ __ __ of their
__ __ __ __ __ __ __-__ __ __ __ __ __ loadings.

10. Reference axes that are at right angles to each other are called
__ __ __ __ __ __ __ __ __ __ __ axes, and represent factors that are uncorrelated, whereas
axes that are not at right angles are called __ __ __ __ __ __ __ __ axes, and represent factors
that are correlated to each other.

11. When the factors that result from an analysis are themselves correlated, it is possible to
"factorize the factors" and derive __ __ __ __ __ __ __ __-__ __ __ __ __ __ factors.

12. Spearman's two-factor theory maintained that all intellectual activities share a single
common factor, called the __ __ __ __ __ __ __ __ factor or "g"; in addition, the theory
postulated many __ __ __ __ __ __ __ __ __ __ or "s" factors, unique to each activity.

13. The postulation of factors such as verbal comprehension, associative memory, and perceptual speed is typical of __ __ __ __ __ __ __ __ __–__ __ __ __ __ __ theories such as Thurstone's, which included about a dozen __ __ __ __ __ factors.

14. Thurstone referred to the group factors he had identified through research on intellectual measures as __ __ __ __ __ __ __ __ __ __ __ __ __ abilities.

15. On the basis of over two decades of factor analytic research, Guilford postulated a boxlike model he called the __ __ __ __ __ __ __ __ __ __–of–__ __ __ __ __ __ __ __ __ __ (SI) model which classifies all intellectual traits along three dimensions and consists of 120 cells.

16. The three dimensions of the SI model are __ __ __ __ __ __ __ __ __ __ __, which consist of what the respondent does, __ __ __ __ __ __ __ __ __, which concern the nature of the information used, and __ __ __ __ __ __ __ __ __, or the form in which the information is processed.

17. Spearman's two-factor theory, Thurstone's multiple-factor theory, and Guilford's SI model are examples of three different theories of __ __ __ __ __ __ __ __ __ __ __ __ __ __ __ __ __ __ __.

18. Another schema that has been used to organize factors, in addition to the ones mentioned in the previous item, is the __ __ __ __ __ __ __ __ __ __ __ __ __ __ __ model, proposed by P.E. Vernon, among others, which starts with the "g" factor at the top and progresses downward to increasingly narrower factors.

19. __ __ __ __ __ __ __ __ are descriptive categories that reflect the changing interrelationships of performance in a variety of situations and are the products of the individual's cumulative experiential history.

20. The __ of the same objective task may differ among individuals with diverse experiential backgrounds and may change within individuals depending on their choice of strategies.

21. The emergence of certain factors may be mediated by the establishment of __ __ __ __ __ __ __ __ __ __ __ __ __ __ __, which enable a person to learn more efficiently the "second time around," as well as by __ __ __ __ __ __ __ __ __ of __ __ __ __ __ __ __ __ __ __, which allows a person to apply acquired skills to the solution of new problems.

22. The critical psychometric property necessary for multiple aptitude batteries to make the distinctive contribution for which they were designed is _ _ _ _ _ _ _ _ _ _ _ _ _ validity, yet, most of the batteries that have been developed are disappointing in precisely this regard.

23. Two of the categories which Guilford devised in the operational dimension of his SI model were _ _ _ _ _ _ _ _ _ _ thinking, which leads to a single correct solution determined by the given facts, and _ _ _ _ _ _ _ _ _ thinking, which "goes off in all directions."

24. The _ _ _ _ _ _ _-_ _ _ _ _ _ _ _ nature of creativity in different fields refers to the notion that creative achievement in any field requires a complex pattern of aptitudes and personality traits appropriate to the field in question.

ANSWERS TO FILL-IN-THE-BLANKS: (Key Terms and Concepts)

1. multiple aptitude (batteries)
2. factor analysis
3. correlation matrix/factor matrix
4. reference axes
5. (criterion of) positive manifold/(criterion of) simple structure
6. factorial validity
7. common (factors)/specific (factors)/error (variance)
8. specificity (of a test)
9. (sum of the) cross-products/common-factor (loadings)
10. orthogonal (axes)/oblique (axes)
11. second-order (factors)
12. general (factor or "g")/specifics (or "s" factors)
13. multiple-factor (theories)/group (factors)
14. primary mental (abilities)
15. structure-(of)-intellect (SI) (model)
16. operations/contents/products
17. (theories of) trait organization
18. hierarchical (model)
19. factors
20. factorial composition
21. learning sets/transfer (of) training

22. differential (validity)

23. convergent (thinking)/divergent (thinking)

24. domain-specific (nature of creativity)

MATCHING: Multiple Aptitude Batteries and Other Tests (One letter per number)

___ 1. Multiple aptitude battery that was the result of the first systematic effort to construct such an instrument;

___ 2. Multiple aptitude battery, first published in 1947, that was designed mainly for educational and career counseling of students in Grades 8 to 12;

___ 3. DAT score which consists of the sum of the raw scores for Verbal Reasoning and Numerical Ability and correlates in the .70s and .80s with academic achievement;

___ 4. Test series developed by the United States Employment Service (USES) for use by counselors in state employment service offices;

___ 5. USES designation for the aptitudes, and their cutoff scores, chosen for a specific occupation;

___ 6. Instrument which is undergoing an intensive long-term research program, designated as Project A, that represents an effort to make the "textbook go operational";

___ 7. Experimental series of tests for the measurement of creative aptitudes, at the high school level and above, that resulted from Guilford's research;

___ 8. Experimental series of tests for the assessment of creative aptitudes, at the elementary school level, that resulted from Guilford's research;

___ 9. Experimental series of tests for the assessment of creative aptitudes, at various educational levels, that resulted from research aimed at fostering creativity;

___ 10. Test designed to assess several aspects of effective reasoning, at the high school, college, and adult levels, through items dealing with inferences, deduction, interpretation, and such;

        A. Armed Services Vocational Aptitude Battery (ASVAB)

        B. Index of Scholastic Aptitude

        C. Chicago Tests of Primary Mental Abilities (PMA)

        D. Aptitude Research Project (ARP) Tests of Divergent Thinking

        E. Special Aptitude Test Battery (SATB)

        F. General Aptitude Test Battery (GATB)

        G. Watson-Glaser Critical Thinking Appraisal

        H. Torrance Tests of Creative Thinking

        I. Creativity Tests for Children

        J. Differential Aptitude Tests (DAT)

ANSWERS:

    1 - C;   2 - J;   3 - B;   4 - F;   5 - E;   6 - A;   7 - D;   8 - I;   9 - H;   10 - G.

MULTIPLE CHOICE: TEST YOURSELF

1. Multiple aptitude batteries were created primarily to _____

   _____.

   a. minimize intraindividual variation
   b. classify preschool children into mental-age-level groups
   c. compare the relative abilities of children with different racial backgrounds
   d. gain information about separate abilities

2. Which of the following is best handled by the use of a multiple aptitude test battery? _____

   _____.

   a. Predicting success in medicine for a group of first-year medical students
   b. Selecting candidates for a school of dentistry
   c. Placing a group of high school dropouts in specific job-training programs
   d. Determining the IQ of a group of first-year college students planning to major in science

3. Which of the following is most responsible for the development of differential aptitude

   tests? _____

   _____.

   a. The application of factor analytic methods
   b. Refinements in the measurement of reliability and validity
   c. Increased interest in the IQ
   d. Developments in clinical psychology that led to the creation of a model for the intellect

4. The principal object of any factor analysis is to _____

   _____.

   a. simplify the description of data
   b. generate new ways to explain interindividual variation
   c. reduce the amount of error in psychological measurements
   d. identify new personality traits

5. A factor matrix _____

   _____.

   a. lists the correlation of each variable with every other variable
   b. places the original raw scores in a table for generating factor scores
   c. presents the loadings of each factor in each test
   d. identifies the most valid questions on a test

6. The first step in a factor analysis is _____

   _____.

   a. developing a correlation matrix
   b. determining if tests have sufficient validity and reliability
   c. replacing all raw scores with their z score equivalents
   d. identifying the principal factors

7. The interpretation and naming of factors calls for _____

_____ .

   a. advanced statistical training
   b. psychological insight
   c. intercorrelations between factors
   d. the loading of individual test items

8. A factor loading is a _____

_____ .

   a. measure of the power of each factor
   b. measure of the extent to which a test may be used to predict academic success
   c. correlation between all possible combinations of items found on two or more tables
   d. none of the above

9. The reason for rotating the reference axes, either orthogonally or obliquely, is to _____

_____ .

   a. obtain the factor structure
   b. help interpret and name the factors
   c. determine the specificity of a test
   d. find the second-order factors

10. Based on the following factor matrix, what is the correlation between tests A and B? _____

Factor Matrix

	I	II
Test A	.90	.05
Test B	.40	.20

   a. .37
   b. .20
   c. .84
   d. .56

11. Some of the differences between the British and American views of trait organization are

that _____ .

   a. the British place more emphasis on the importance of a general factor
   b. American psychologists are more likely to seek specific factors
   c. American psychologists usually work with only one or two "s" factors
   d. both a and b

12. Guilford's structure-of-intellect model classifies intellectual traits into _____

_____ .

   a. 146 cells
   b. 3 dimensions
   c. 44 categories
   d. 14 factors

13. Which of the following tests would most likely be used in vocational counseling? _____

_____.

    a. Watson-Glaser Critical Thinking Appraisal
    b. Wechsler Adult Intelligence Scale-Revised
    c. General Aptitude Test Battery
    d. Torrance's tests

14. The consensus among investigators in the area of creativity is that _____

_____.

    a. creativity and intelligence are negatively correlated
    b. both creativity and intelligence are needed for significant innovative work
    c. intelligence is innate, but creativity can be taught
    d. creativity is more important in the arts, while intelligence is more important in the sciences

15. Measures of creativity have been designed primarily to _____

_____.

    a. assess divergent thinking
    b. assess convergent thinking
    c. assess artistic ability
    d. correlate with the better tests of intelligence

MINIPROJECTS/SUGGESTED OUTREACH ACTIVITIES:

1. The sections of factor analysis (pp. 374-381 and pp. 388-390) in the textbook provide one of the clearest and most concise explanations of this important statistical technique that you are ever likely to find. If you study them carefully, you should be able to read and understand much of the psychological literature that is based on factorial research, without delving further into the computational details of factor analysis. However, in order to internalize, and remember, the information you acquire from the textbook, you would do well to read some of the abundant research that utilizes factor analytic techniques. In the context of psychological testing, it would make a great deal of sense to read the manuals of some of the tests that are based on factorial research or have used factor analysis as a way of investigating construct validity. The three suggested references that follow were selected because each one of them represents a different way of using factor analysis:

    A. The Guilford-Zimmerman Aptitude Survey (GZAS), now published by Consulting Psychologists Press, is a multiple aptitude battery that was developed by J.P. Guilford before he devised his SI model. Although it is not nearly as well-normed, nor as widely used, as the batteries discussed in the text, the succinctness of the GZAS manual (which would be undesirable from other standpoints) makes it ideal for a brief first-hand look at instruments of its type.

    B. The Sixteen Personality Factor Questionnaire (16 PF), published by the Institute for Personality and Ability Testing, is an example of a personality test based on extensive factor analytic research done by Raymond B. Cattell over the course of many years. One interesting feature of the 16 PF is that it provides scores on 4 second-order factors, in addition to the 16 "primary source traits" it was designed to assess. A review of the 16 PF manual, with special reference to second-order factors, should help to clarify your understanding of factors and their intercorrelations.

C. The Fourth Edition of the Stanford-Binet Intelligence Scale (SB4) uses the intercorrelations between its tests, and subsequent factor analysis of scores, as one of three principal types of validation procedures. Read Chapter 6 of the *Technical Manual* for the SB4, published by Riverside Publishing Company, for a very clear and succinct presentation of these data, which are typical of the factor analyses done on all the major individual intelligence tests.

2. The difficulties inherent in assessing, and fostering, creativity are one of the most interesting topics covered in Chapter 13. Barron and Harrington's article on "Creativity, intelligence, and personality" (*Annual Review of Psychology,* 1981, *32,* 439-476) provides a good overview of research in the area of creativity.

3. You might also want to investigate either some of the ARP tests of divergent thinking, now published by Consulting Psychologists Press (formerly Sheridan) under various titles (see pp. 683-684 of the textbook), or the Torrance Tests of Creative Thinking, published by the Scholastic Testing Service. A first-hand review of such instruments would illustrate the gap that exists between creative achievement in real life and the sorts of tasks that have been devised to measure creative aptitude. However, if you were to try your hand at developing some items for a creativity test of your own, either before or after you review some of the tests that were mentioned in Chapter 13, you would undoubtedly become acutely aware of just how difficult the task actually is.

ANSWERS TO MULTIPLE CHOICE/TEST YOURSELF ITEMS:

1. d	4. a	7. b	10. a	13. c
2. c	5. c	8. d	11. a	14. b
3. a	6. a	9. b	12. b	15. a

Chapter 14
EDUCATIONAL TESTING

CHAPTER OUTLINE

Achievement Tests: Their Nature and Uses
    Nature
    Uses
    Essay Versus Objective Questions

General Achievement Batteries
    Nature and Scope
    Metropolitan Achievement Tests

Tests of Minimum Competency in Basic Skills

Standardized Tests in Separate Content Areas

Teacher-Made Classroom Tests

Diagnostic and Prognostic Testing
    Diagnostic Tests
    Criterion-Referenced Tests
    Prognostic Testing
    Computer Utilization in Diagnostic Testing

Assessment in Early Childhood Education

CHAPTER SUMMARY

Achievement tests, which are those designed to measure the effects of a specific program of instruction or training, surpass all other types of standardized tests in the frequency of their use. Achievement tests are often contrasted with aptitude tests and do differ from the latter in that they presuppose more uniformity in antecedent experiences and also in that they are usually given as part of a terminal, rather than a predictive, evaluation. However, neither one of the distinctions drawn between aptitude and achievement tests can be rigidly applied because both types of tests can vary in the kind of learning experiences they presuppose as well as in how they are used. In addition, there can be a good deal of overlap in the content of both types of tests and their respective scores are often very highly correlated.

One erroneous assumption that has been made sometimes is that achievement tests measure the effects of learning while aptitude tests measure "innate capacity." In fact, all ability tests measure only *developed abilities,* although they do differ in terms of the specificity of experiential background they presuppose. Another mistaken notion related to aptitude and achievement testing is seen in the practice of labeling children whose achievement test scores are lower or higher than their aptitude test scores as under- or overachievers. As far as this is concerned, the concepts of under- or overachievement do nothing to explain discrepancies between scores on achievement and aptitude tests given to the same individual on separate occasions. When such discrepancies occur, they are likely to be a function of the errors of measurement of the tests, or of their coverage, their susceptibility to attitudinal and motivational factors, and/or of the nature of intervening experiences between the test administrations.

The uses of achievement tests in the educational process are many and varied. Such tests can be used as aids in the assignment of grades, and in the identification of students with academic weaknesses and/or special learning disabilities, as well as in measuring the progress of those students through remedial work. In addition, achievement tests can be used as a basis for planning what is taught and as aids in the evaluation and improvement of teaching and in the formulation of educational goals.

Objective items, rather than essay questions, are used almost exclusively in standardized testing today. This is largely due to the superiority of objective over essay examinations in terms of their breadth of coverage, reliability, validity, and fairness, as well as to the greater speed with which they can be taken and scored. Essay questions can provide useful supplementary data when adequately evaluated, both in standardized and in nonstandardized testing. Essay writing, however, should be encouraged and developed primarily in the context of instruction.

Several batteries are available for measuring achievement in the major areas covered by academic curricula. These general achievement batteries typically cover a wide range of educational levels and permit comparisons of an individual's standing in different areas as well as from grade to grade. Some of the most widely used batteries are normed concurrently with a test of scholastic aptitude and, thus, also permit comparisons across two types of tests. On the whole, general achievement batteries meet high standards of test development in terms of their norms, reliability, and content validation. The Metropolitan Achievement Tests (MAT), which extend from kindergarten to Grade 12 and were last standardized in 1985 with over 250,000 students, are an example of a general achievement battery discussed in the textbook in some detail.

Another type of standardized instrument used in the educational context consists of tests for the assessment of minimum competency in basic skills. The development of these tests received a great deal of impetus from strong societal concerns about the low levels of competence of high school graduates in reading, writing, and arithmetic. Many tests of minimum competency center on the application of basic skills to everyday-life situations; others, such as the outstanding Basic Skills Assessment developed by Educational Testing Service (ETS), concentrate on school-related needs. Still other competency tests in basic skills, such as the United States Employment Service (USES) Basic Occupational Literacy Test (BOLT) and the Adult Basic Learning Examination (ABLE), have been developed for poorly educated adults.

Standardized tests to measure achievement in many specialized areas of the educational curriculum, e.g., American history or physics, have also been devised and are covered quite fully in the *Mental Measurements Yearbook* (MMY) series. The College Board is a leader in the development and administration of many of these tests, some of which, such as the Advanced Placement Program (APP) series, are used for college admission with advanced standing in a subject.

The largest category of tests used in educational settings is made up of classroom examinations prepared by teachers themselves. Although local classroom tests obviously cannot be standardized, they can be greatly improved by the application of proper test construction techniques. Teacher-made classroom tests should be planned and balanced by drawing up test specifications before any items are written. In addition, teachers should be aware of the many practical rules that exist for effective item writing and should analyze the results of their tests to correct any weaknesses.

Diagnostic tests, designed to analyze the individual's strengths and weaknesses within a specific subject-matter domain and to suggest causes for his or her difficulties, constitute another category of testing within the context of education. Diagnostic tests typically deal with reading and mathematics, as well as with such language functions as listening, speaking, or writing. Reading tests are the most numerous in this category because much attention has been given to the diagnosis of reading disabilities. Although most diagnostic tests are norm-referenced, several criterion-referenced tests in reading and mathematics have also been published. The latter evaluate performance in terms of mastery versus nonmastery of a skill. In spite of the technical problems that criterion-referenced tests present, they have certain advantages in that they can be used prescriptively, as well as diagnostically, and offer considerable flexibility, making it possible to tailor a test to local needs. A related category of instruments consists of prognostic tests designed to predict performance in specific academic courses, e.g., algebra or foreign languages. This can be done by gauging the extent to which individuals have acquired the prerequisite knowledge and skills needed for a course or by assessing how well they learn new material similar to that which they will encounter in the course.

The use of computer programs for interpretive scoring of diagnostic tests, and for combining test scores and other data in the formulation of prescriptions for individualized instructional programs, is a relatively recent and promising development. However, users of such programs should be aware of the *Guidelines for Computer-Based Tests and Interpretations* that have been developed to help evaluate these materials.

Research in early cognitive development, along with the growth of preschool education programs and concerns about the effects of cultural handicaps on children's ability to profit from school instruction, have all been influential in the development of educationally oriented tests for young children that has taken place since 1970. The largest category of tests in this area are those designed to assess school readiness, which refers to the attainment of prerequisite skills, knowledge, attitudes, motivations, and other behavioral traits that enable the learner to profit from school instruction. The Metropolitan Readiness Tests (MRT), the Boehm Test of Basic Concepts-Revised (Boehm R), and the CIRCUS series of tests exemplify three different approaches to the assessment of school readiness and are discussed in the textbook in some detail.

COMPREHENSIVE REVIEW

STUDY QUESTIONS:

1. Compare and contrast aptitude and achievement tests.

2. Discuss the problems that have resulted from labeling some instruments as "aptitude" tests and others as "achievement" tests and explain how such problems might be forestalled in the future.

3. List and describe the roles that achievement tests can play in the educational process.

4. Compare and contrast essay and objective questions, listing the advantages and disadvantages of each.

5. Describe the nature and scope of general achievement batteries, in general, and cite three representative examples of such batteries.

6. Describe the background, content, and technical characteristics of the Metropolitan Achievement Tests (MAT).

7. Discuss the history of tests of minimum competency in basic skills and describe two representative examples of such tests.

8. Describe the uses and characteristics of standardized tests in separate content areas.

9. List and describe the steps that a teacher should follow in preparing a classroom test.

10. Describe four specific examples of how objective test items could be improperly written so as to give an advantage to the observant guesser.

11. Discuss the general approach to the detection and treatment of reading disabilities and explain the role that tests can play in the diagnosis of those problems.

12. Discuss the technical difficulties associated with criterion-referenced testing in the area of basic skills as well as the advantages of that approach compared to norm-referenced testing.

13. Discuss the use of prognostic tests in education and cite an example of one such instrument.

14. List the contributions that computer utilization can make to the field of diagnostic testing in education.

15. Describe the background, content, and characteristics of two major tests used in the assessment of school readiness.

FILL IN THE BLANKS: Key Terms and Concepts

1. _achievement_ tests are those that are designed to measure the effects of a specific program of instruction or training.

2. _aptitude_ tests measure the effects of learning under relatively uncontrolled and unknown conditions and include instruments such as general intelligence tests.

3. The most direct way of assessing aptitude tests is through _-_ _ _ _ _ _ _ _ validity, whereas achievement tests are typically evaluated in terms of _ _ _ _ _ _ _ _-_ _ _ _ _ _ _ _ validation procedures.

4. A useful concept that is replacing the traditional categories of aptitude and achievement, in psychometrics, is that of _ _ _ _ _ _ _ _ _ _ _ _ _ _ _ _ _ _ _ _ _ _; this concept reflects the idea that all ability tests presuppose *some* experiential background although that background may be more or less specific.

5. The term _ _ _ _ _ _ question has come to be used broadly to cover all free-response questions, including not only those that demand a lengthy answer, but also those that require the test taker to produce a short answer or solve a mathematical problem.

6. _ _ _ _ _ _ _ _ _ _ questions call for the choice of a correct answer out of several provided for each question and include items such as multiple-choice, true-false, and matching.

7. **General achievement** batteries are those that measure an individual's performance in the major areas covered by academic curricula and typically permit a comparison of the individual's standing in different areas, as well as over time.

8. The use of **minimum competency** tests in basic skills as a basis for awarding a high school diploma arose out of popular concern about the low level of achievement of high school graduates.

9. The basic concept that underlies the development of tests of minimum competency in basic skills is ___ __ __ __ __ __ __ __ __ __   __ __ __ __ __ __ __ __ __ __ or the possession of the reading, writing, speaking, and computational skills needed to meet the demands of practical situations, such as jobs or the management of one's own life in modern society.

10. The largest number of tests covering the content of specific courses or parts of courses are __ __ __ __ __ __ __ __ __ __ tests prepared by instructors for their own use.

11. A table of __ __ __ __   __ __ __ __ __ __ __ __ __ __ __ __ __ __ __ __ __, which should be drawn up before any test items are prepared, provides a way to plan a test so that its coverage of content areas and instructional objectives will be balanced.

12. A test constructor must decide on the most appropriate __ __ __ __   __ __ __ __ __ for the material to be covered by a test on the basis of the relative merits and practicality of essay versus objective questions for a given course.

13. **Diagnostic** tests usually concentrate on highly specific cognitive processes or content knowledge and are designed to analyze an individual's particular strengths and weaknesses within a certain domain and to suggest possible causes for his or her difficulties.

14. **Criterion-Referenced** tests are those in which the individual's performance is judged as indicating mastery or nonmastery of a certain skill.

15. __ __ __ __ __ __ __ __ __ __ __ __ tests function as aptitude tests in that they undertake to predict performance, but they also resemble achievement tests because their content frequently consists of prerequisite knowledge and skills necessary for a specific academic course.

16. __ __ __ __ __ __ __ __   __ __ __ __ __ __ __ __ __ __ __ is an approach to testing that follows a test-teach-test procedure and evaluates learning potential by observing how well an individual can learn in a one-to-one relation with a professional who functions as examiner, instructor, and clinician.

17. __ __ __ __ __ __ __   __ __ __ __ __ __ __ __ __ is a concept that refers to the attainment of prerequisite skills, knowledge, attitudes, motivations and other behavioral traits that enable the young child to profit maximally from schooling.

ANSWERS TO FILL-IN-THE-BLANKS: (Key Terms and Concepts)

1. achievement (tests)
2. aptitude (tests)
3. predictive criterion-related (validity)/content-related (validation)
4. developed abilities
5. essay (question)
6. objective (questions)
7. general achievement (batteries)
8. minimum competency (tests in basic skills)
9. functional competence
10. classroom (tests)
11. test specifications
12. item form
13. diagnostic (tests)
14. criterion-referenced (tests)
15. prognostic (tests)
16. dynamic assessment
17. school readiness

MATCHING: Educational Tests (One letter per number)

___ 1. Example of a representative educational battery which is extensively discussed in the textbook and which consists of a Survey Battery extending from kindergarten to Grade 12 and three diagnostic batteries in Reading, Mathematics, and Language;

___ 2. Test developed by the USES for adult job applicants with poor educational backgrounds;

___ 3. Tests developed by the American Council on Education which are widely administered for high school equivalency certification;

___ 4. College Board test series which is used to facilitate the granting of college credit for education acquired through independent study and other nontraditional procedures;

___ 5. Examples of names of reading tests of the group survey type;

___ 6. Examples of customized services for the development of criterion-referenced diagnostic tests in basic academic skills;

___ 7. Test which assesses school readiness by focusing on the child's understanding of common relational concepts;

___ 8. Educational Testing Service test, originally developed for use with preschool and kindergarten children, which utilizes a pervasive theme that is intrinsically appealing to youngsters;

      A. Nelson-Denny/Gates-MacGinitie

      B. Tests of General Educational Development (GED)

      C. CIRCUS

      D. Boehm Test of Basic Concepts-Revised (Boehm R)

      E. Metropolitan Achievement Tests (MAT)

      F. MULTISCORE/PRISM

      G. College-Level Examination Program (CLEP)

      H. Basic Occupational Literacy Test (BOLT)

ANSWERS:

    1 - E; 2 - H; 3 - B; 4 - G; 5 - A; 6 - F; 7 - D; 8 - C.

TRUE/FALSE and WHY?

1. Most of the distinctions that can be drawn between aptitude and achievement tests cannot be rigidly applied. (T/F) Why? _____

    _____

2. One way in which achievement and aptitude tests *can* be differentiated is that the former measure the effects of learning while the latter measure "innate capacity" independent of learning. (T/F) Why? F_____

    _____

3. The question of under- or overachievement can be more accurately formulated as overprediction or underprediction from one test to a second test. (T/F) Why? _____

    _____

4. Objective tests are not only more reliable than essay tests, in terms of interscorer agreement, but can also be more valid predictors of well-established criteria of writing performance than essay tests. (T/F) Why? _____

    _____

5. One advantage of the typical general achievement battery over independently constructed achievement tests is that the former can provide for horizontal or vertical comparisons or both. (T/F) Why? True_____

    _____

6. Standardized achievement tests in separate content areas, such as physics or American history, lend themselves to normative comparisons across different areas in much the same way as general achievement batteries do. (T/F) Why? _____

_____

7. The techniques and accumulated experience of professional test constructors have very little, if anything, to contribute to the preparation of local classroom tests. (T/F) Why? ____

_____

8. In general, essay questions are easier to prepare and more appropriate than objective questions for teacher-made classroom tests because essays do not require advance planning. (T/F) Why? _____

_____

9. The diagnosis of learning disabilities and the planning of a subsequent remediation program cannot rest solely on the results of a battery of tests. (T/F) Why? *True*

_____

10. Performance on school readiness tests is strongly correlated with socioeconomic level and with performance on intelligence tests. (T/F) Why? *True*

_____

ANSWERS TO TRUE/FALSE:

1. True	4. True	7. False	10. True
2. False	5. True	8. False	
3. True	6. False	9. True	

MULTIPLE CHOICE: TEST YOURSELF

1. Which of the following is the most commonly used type of standardized test? _____

_____.

   a. Achievement
   b. Aptitude
   c. Personality
   d. Interest

2. One distinctive difference between aptitude and achievement tests is that, usually, aptitude

   tests _____ ,

   whereas achievement tests _____

   _____.

   a. measure the effects of standardized sets of past experiences/reflect learning under
      unknown conditions
   b. measure innate learning ability/measure what has been learned
   c. are predominantly nonverbal/are predominantly verbal
   d. are used to predict/are used for terminal evaluation

3. From among the following, the best example of an achievement test is _____

   _____.

   a. a test like the Stanford-Binet or WAIS-R
   b. a final examination in introductory psychology
   c. a vocational assessment test
   d. a performance evaluation based on a total job analysis

4. The results of achievement tests can be used to _____

   _____.

   a. assess an individual's level of accomplishment in a course of study
   b. evaluate the success of an instructional program
   c. diagnose deficiencies in academic preparation
   d. all of the above are legitimate uses

5. Which of the following is *not* an appropriate use of aptitude and achievement tests? _____

   _____.

   a. Aptitude tests can be used to predict performance in advanced programs
   b. Achievement test results can be used to evaluate the overall performance of a class of
      students, or an entire school, compared with other groups
   c. Aptitude and achievement test scores for each student can be compared to identify
      underachievers
   d. All of the above are legitimate uses

6. Objective tests, usually of the multiple-choice variety, have generally replaced essay

   examinations because _____

   _____.

   a. objective tests are easier to score
   b. essay examinations are generally less reliable than objective exams
   c. objective exams are generally fairer to individuals than essay exams
   d. all of the above are true

7. Nationally administered achievement tests, such as the Iowa Tests of Basic Skills or the Stanford Achievement Test, are applied most appropriately when they are used to _____ .

    a. identify teachers whose classes are not performing up to standard
    b. assign grades to students on a more equitable basis than teacher-made tests
    c. locate students who are not performing well so they can receive special help
    d. identify the most advanced school districts in the nation

8. The procedure of norming achievement test batteries concurrently with intelligence tests _____ .

    a. assures the validity of the achievement test batteries
    b. permits direct comparisons of scores on the two tests
    c. removes the biasing effects of IQ from achievement test scores
    d. assures the reliability of both sets of tests

9. Content validity for large-scale achievement tests is established by _____ .

    a. extensively analyzing relevant textbooks and other related materials
    b. subjecting items to review by experts
    c. setting up specification tables
    d. all of the above

10. Tests of minimum competency are being developed largely to _____ .

    a. replace existing tests such as the SAT or ACT for admitting students to college
    b. demonstrate basic differences in the innate ability of various cultural groups
    c. identify the strengths and weaknesses of individual students
    d. screen students in terms of whether they have achieved "functional literacy"

11. The most important, and also the most frequently overlooked, step in creating a good teacher-made test is _____ .

    a. adequate advance planning, using a table of specifications
    b. the inclusion of essay questions
    c. the evaluation of the test after it is given
    d. the development of alternate forms

12. An experienced writer of multiple-choice items probably would _____ .

    a. make the correct alternative longer than the others
    b. reread the items or have them reviewed by another person
    c. give some grammatical cues that would help eliminate one wrong alternative
    d. concentrate on writing items that call for rote memory

13. Tests that are primarily designed to detect problem areas and identify possible causes are
    called _____.
    a. criterion-referenced
    b. diagnostic
    c. standardized
    d. item-referenced

14. A teacher frequently administers professionally prepared tests during the semester.
    Students who show mastery-level performance move on. Those scoring below mastery are
    assigned additional work until they achieve mastery. This teacher is, most likely, using ____
    _____
    tests.
    a. norm-referenced
    b. objective achievement
    c. criterion-referenced
    d. diagnostic

15. The CIRCUS tests were originally designed primarily for _____
    _____.
    a. preschoolers
    b. elementary students
    c. sixth- to eighth-graders
    d. private school students

MINIPROJECTS/SUGGESTED OUTREACH ACTIVITIES:

1. The handbook entitled *Educational Measurement* (3rd ed.), edited by Robert L. Linn (New
   York: American Council on Education/Macmillan, 1989), was already cited in connection
   with two of the topics in Chapter 10 of the textbook. However, many of the other areas
   covered by that handbook are, naturally, very relevant to educational testing and provide
   expanded treatments of the topics in Chapter 14. Depending on your interests, you may
   want to read one or more of the following chapters in *Educational Measurement:*

   A. Chapter 8, "The Specification and Development of Tests of Achievement and Ability,"
      by Jason Millman and Jennifer Greene, which, among other things, contains a section
      on item writing that should prove informative as well as useful to you as a student of
      psychological testing *and* as a test taker (see Miniproject # 3 below).

   B. Chapter 9, "The Four Generations of Computerized Educational Measurement," by C.
      Victor Bunderson *et al.,* which provides an interesting and informative account of the
      history, present status, and future trends in the use of computers for educational
      assessment.

   C. Chapter 14, "Certification of Student Competence," by Richard M. Jaeger, which
      presents a fascinating discussion of the thorny issues involved in competency testing,
      including the problems of setting standards.

2. One of the most important publications that you could review with regard to the topic of
   computer utilization in testing is the pamphlet on *Guidelines for Computer-Based Tests and
   Interpretations* published by the American Psychological Association in 1986. This

document, which was prepared by the Committees on Professional Standards (COPS) and on Psychological Tests and Assessment (CPTA), interprets testing standards as they relate to computer utilization and would help to familiarize you with some of the special issues and professional responsibilities involved in the development and use of computerized techniques for testing and related purposes.

3. As a follow-up to whatever practice you have already had writing test items of the multiple-choice variety and/or to what you have learned about item writing rules from the textbook and elsewhere, locate and review multiple-choice items from several sources. You could, for example, use newspaper or magazine quizzes, study guides (including this one), or old tests you may have in your possession. See if you can spot extraneous cues that give away the answers or help to eliminate incorrect alternatives. Make a list of those, and other weaknesses you can spot, and try to come up with as thorough a list of item writing rules as you can. You could combine this project with the reading suggested in Miniproject # 1 A, for this chapter, by comparing the list you develop with the one that appears in that reference (Table 8.3 "Rules for Writing Multiple-Choice Test Items," p.353 of *Educational Measurement*.)

ANSWERS TO MULTIPLE CHOICE/TEST YOURSELF ITEMS:

1. a	4. d	7. c	10. d	13. b
2. d	5. c	8. b	11. a	14. c
3. b	6. d	9. d	12. b	15. a

Chapter 15

OCCUPATIONAL TESTING

CHAPTER OUTLINE

Validation of Employment Tests
    Local Criterion-Related Validation
    Content-Related Validation: Global Procedures
    Content-Related Validation: Job Element Method
    Bayesian Model for Test Validation

The Role of Academic Intelligence

Special Aptitude Tests
    Psychomotor Skills
    Mechanical Aptitudes
    Clerical Aptitudes
    Computer-Related Aptitudes

Testing in the Professions
    Law School Admission Test
    Certification and Licensure of Psychologists

Career Counseling
    Comprehensive Programs for Career Exploration
    Assessment of Career Maturity

CHAPTER SUMMARY

Psychological tests play a significant role as aids in occupational decisions both at the institutional level, in terms of the selection and classification of personnel, and at the individual level, in terms of vocational counseling or career guidance. Although nearly any test may be useful in making occupational decisions, the instruments most frequently used for that purpose are the multiple aptitude batteries and interest inventories described elsewhere in the textbook and the special aptitude tests that are discussed in this chapter.

The need to ascertain the validity of tests for particular uses is especially urgent in the occupational field because of societal concerns about the possible unfairness of selection devices to disadvantaged minorities and also because of the demonstrated link between productivity and the validity of selection instruments. The traditional view in personnel psychology has been that, ideally, tests should undergo full-scale validation against local criteria of job performance. However, because of the practical difficulties that this process presents, a number of alternatives have been explored. These alternatives include the use of content-related validation procedures through systematic job analyses, as well as the use of global assessment procedures that resemble the job situation, such as probationary appointments, job samples, simulations, and assessment center techniques that include situational tests.

The notion that job analyses should focus on critical job requirements led to the development of the job element method for constructing tests and demonstrating their content validity. This method, which was pioneered by Primoff and his associates, is, in turn, related to the concept of synthetic validation, which consists of using the demonstrated validity of certain tests for separate job elements, in combination with the weights for those elements in a particular job, to predict a complex criterion.

Another alternative to local criterion-related validation of selection tests was developed by Schmidt and Hunter through a special application of Bayesian statistics. This model allows for the use of prior information on the validity of a test, through an analysis of the generalizability of prior findings to the new job in question. Investigations conducted by Schmidt and Hunter, and others, have shown a much wider generalizability of validity across jobs and work settings than was previously recognized.

Tests of academic intelligence or scholastic ability are an important component of many personnel selection programs because the broad verbal, quantitative, and other abstract thinking skills that they assess are relevant to a wide variety of jobs. Several short tests of academic intelligence, such as the Personnel Tests for Industry and the Wonderlic Personnel Test, have been developed for use in industry. Although this type of test contributes substantially to the prediction of job performance, many jobs also require the assessment of more specialized skills and knowledge through special aptitude tests. The principal areas, described in the textbook, for which special aptitude tests have been developed are psychomotor skills, mechanical aptitudes, clerical aptitudes, and, more recently, computer-related aptitudes. Even though several of these areas are now incorporated in some multiple aptitude batteries, special aptitude tests, as a rule, provide more extensive normative and validation data for pertinent occupational samples, and allow greater flexibility in their use, than do multiple aptitude batteries.

Standardized tests are also used in the selection of students for admission to professional training in fields such as medicine, nursing, law, and many others. These special testing programs usually include a scholastic aptitude test and may include one or more achievement tests on preprofessional training. The Law School Admission Test (LSAT) is an example of this sort of examination and is discussed in the textbook in some detail.

Another level at which standardized testing is used in the professions is that of specialty certification and selection of job applicants after the completion of their training. The National Teacher Examinations (NTE) Programs, for example, are used to evaluate the academic preparation of prospective teachers for certification, hiring, and other purposes. Similarly, the Examination for Professional Practice in Psychology (EPPP), which samples common knowledge that is basic to the practice of psychology, is used across the United States as one of the requirements for the certification and/or licensing of psychologists.

As far as career counseling of individuals is concerned, the two types of instruments that are most applicable are multiple aptitude batteries and interest inventories, both of which are discussed in other parts of the textbook. However, two additional kinds of instruments, designed specifically for career counseling, belong in the context of occupational testing, namely, comprehensive programs for career exploration and measures of career maturity. Some career counseling programs, such as the Differential Aptitude Tests (DAT) Career Planning Report, have been developed for use in conjunction with multiple aptitude batteries, whereas others have been developed completely as career exploration systems. An example of the latter approach is the Planning Career Goals (PCG) program which is based on a comprehensive longitudinal study of high school students known as Project TALENT. Another approach to comprehensive career exploration is that represented by the System for Interactive Guidance Information (SIGI-PLUS), which uses an interactive computer program with an extensive database to guide the individual toward effective decision-making. The assessment of career maturity, or mastery of the vocational tasks appropriate to one's age level and effectiveness in coping with such tasks, is still another technique that can be used in career counseling. The Career Development Inventory, prepared by Super, is one example of the instruments that have been designed to assess career maturity.

COMPREHENSIVE REVIEW

STUDY QUESTIONS:

1. List and describe each of the four steps involved in local criterion-related validation.

2. Discuss the advantages and disadvantages of local criterion-related validation.

3. Explain how content-related validation techniques can be applied to personnel selection tests.

4. Describe three different types of global assessment procedures that approximate actual job performance.

5. Discuss the basis for the development of the job element method of content-related validation.

6. Define synthetic validity and describe how it is derived and applied.

7. Discuss the Bayesian model for test validation and describe the major findings that have resulted from the use of that model.

8. Compare and contrast the role of tests of academic intelligence versus special aptitude tests in the selection of personnel.

9. Describe one example of a special aptitude test in each of the following areas: psychomotor skills, mechanical aptitudes, and clerical aptitudes.

10. Discuss the functions of standardized testing in the professions, citing examples of instruments that are representative of those used for each purpose you discuss.

11. If you had to advise a friend about how to find a competent psychologist, what could you tell your friend in terms of the credentials that are available and what those credentials represent?

12. Describe examples of two different types of comprehensive programs for career exploration that are cited in the text.

13. Discuss the concept of career maturity and how that concept may be used in career counseling.

FILL IN THE BLANKS: Key Terms and Concepts

1. The ideal __ __ __ __ __   __ __ __ __ __ __ __ __ __–__ __ __ __ __ __ __ validation procedure would require the hiring of an unselected sample of applicants for a given position and their retention on the job long enough to accumulate adequate data on their performance.

2. A(n) __ __ __ __ __ __ __ __ __ __ __ __ __ __ is a process that involves the identification of the major elements of a job and the specification of the corresponding skills, knowledge, and other worker traits required for the job.

3. One approach to personnel selection consists of using global assessment procedures that resemble the job situation as much as possible, such as __, __ __ __ __ __ __ __ __ __ __, and __ __ __ __ __ __ __ __ __ __ __.

4. The __ __-__ __ __ __ __ test is a simulation technique that has been adapted for testing executives in many contexts and which consists of having the test taker handle a carefully prepared set of incoming letters, memoranda, and such.

5. The __ __ __ __ __ __ __ __ __ __ __ __ __ __ __ approach, first developed for the selection of military personnel during World War II, typically involves the evaluation of a small group of persons, over the course of two or three days, with situational tests and other techniques that simulate the job environment.

6. The concept of __, as used by Flanagan and others, refers to those aspects of job performance that differentiate most sharply between the better and the poorer workers.

7. The __ __ __ __ __ __ __ __ __ __ __ __ __ __ __ __ __ __ technique, proposed by Flanagan as a means of implementing the concept of critical requirements, calls for the description of specific instances of job behavior that are characteristic of satisfactory or unsatisfactory workers.

8. The __ __ __ __ __ __ __ __ __ __ __ method for constructing employment tests and demonstrating their content validity was fully developed by Primoff and others at the U.S. Office of Personnel Management; this method provides for the description of the specific behavioral requirements of a job, from which test items can be drawn.

9. The concept of __ __ __ __ __ __ __ __ __ __ validity can be defined as "the inferring of validity in a specific situation from a systematic analysis of job elements, a determination of test validity for these elements, and a combination of elemental validities into a whole."

10. The __ _-__ __ __ __ __ __ __ __ __ __ is a statistical procedure used by Primoff to compute an estimate of synthetic validity by combining the job element method and multiple regression equations.

11. The _ _ _ _ _ _ _ _ _ model for test validation, developed by Schmidt and Hunter, allows for the use of prior information to assess the validity of a test in a particular situation through an assessment of the degree of generalizability of prior validity findings to the present situation.

12. The cluster of skills and knowledge developed in the course of formal education which has been described as _ _ _ _ _ _ _ _ _ _ _ _ _ _ _ _ _ _ _ _ _ _ consists mainly of verbal comprehension, quantitative reasoning, and other aspects of abstract thinking, and is predictive of performance in a wide range of activiities.

13. _ _ _ _ _ _ _ _ _ _ _ _ _ _ _ _ _ tests were developed in order to fill in the major gaps in the coverage of intelligence tests by providing for the assessment of more specialized and/or practical abilities.

14. Tests of _ _ _ _ _ _ _ _ _ _ _ _ _ _ _ _ _ _ _ are typically apparatus tests concerned with manual dexterity and used principally in the selection of industrial and military personnel.

15. _ _ _ _ _ _ _ _ _ _ _ _ _ _ _ _ _ _ _ _ tests cover a wide variety of functions which may include psychomotor, perceptual, and spatial aptitudes, as well as information about the sorts of tools encountered through everyday experience in an industrialized society.

16. Tests designed to measure _ _ _ _ _ _ _ _ _ _ _ _ _ _ _ _ _ _ _ _ are characterized by an emphasis on perceptual speed and accuracy but may also sample activities such as alphabetizing, coding, and spelling.

17. In the field of psychology it is customary to differentiate between _ _ _ _ _ _ _ _ _ _ _ _ _ _ _, which is concerned with control of the title "psychologist," and _ _ _ _ _ _ _ _ _ _ _, which is designed to control the practice of psychology.

18. The diplomate status that the _ _ _ _ _ _ _ _ _ _ _ _ _ _ of _ _ _ _ _ _ _ _ _ _ _ _ _ _ _ _ _ _ _ _ _ _ _ _ _ (ABPP) provides for psychologists differs from licensing or certification in that it is a higher level of accreditation and takes into account areas of specialization.

19. The Planning Career Goals (PCG) system for career exploration is a product of a longitudinal study of high school students, known as _ _ _ _ _ _ _ _ _ _ _ _ _ _ _ _, which utilized a comprehensive battery of aptitude and achievement tests as well as interest and personality inventories.

20. The concept of __ __ __ __ __ __ __ __ __ __ __ __ __, as postulated by Super and his associates, refers to one's mastery of the vocational tasks appropriate to one's age level and also to one's effectiveness in coping with those tasks.

ANSWERS TO FILL-IN-THE-BLANKS: (Key Terms and Concepts)

1. local criterion-related (validation)
2. job analysis
3. probationary appointments/job samples/simulations
4. in-basket (test)
5. assessment center (approach)
6. critical requirements
7. critical incident (technique)
8. job element (method)
9. synthetic (validity)
10. J-coefficient
11. Bayesian (model for test validation)
12. academic intelligence
13. special aptitude (tests)
14. (tests of) psychomotor skills
15. mechanical aptitude (tests)
16. clerical aptitudes
17. certification/licensing
18. American Board (of) Professional Psychology (ABPP)
19. Project TALENT
20. career maturity

MATCHING: Occupational Tests (One letter per number)

___ 1. Instrument, developed through research with job element techniques, which permits the rating of jobs in terms of common behavioral requirements;

___ 2. Brief general cognitive test, used in industry, which includes a variety of verbal, numerical, and spatial items and yields a single total score;

___ 3. Test of simple manipulative skills that involves the use of tweezers and a screwdriver and is scored in terms of time;

___ 4. Manual dexterity test that measures gross and fine motor activities by having the test takers insert pins in small holes and assemble pins, collars, and washers, without the use of tools;

___ 5. One of the best single measures of spatial aptitude, requiring the examinee to determine how two or more parts fit into a complete figure;

___ 6. Test that assesses perceptual speed and accuracy by means of two separately timed subtests dealing with number and name comparisons;

___ 7. Test that assesses reading comprehension at a high level of complexity, in addition to functions such as deductive reasoning, analysis of conclusions, evaluation of arguments, and writing;

___ 8. Standardized measure prepared by Super to assess, among other things, what a student knows about the world of work, and what the student has done to plan for her or his occupational future;

      A. Crawford Small Parts Dexterity Test

      B. Career Development Inventory

      C. Revised Minnesota Paper Form Board Test

      D. Minnesota Clerical Test

      E. Wonderlic Personnel Test

      F. Purdue Pegboard

      G. Position Analysis Questionnaire (PAQ)

      H. Law School Admission Test (LSAT)

ANSWERS:

    1 - G; 2 - E; 3 - A; 4 - F; 5 - C; 6 - D; 7 - H; 8 - B.

TRUE/FALSE and WHY?

1. A full-scale longitudinal validation study is unrealistic in the large majority of industrial situations. (T/F) Why? _____ .

2. One of the advantages of the assessment center technique is that its validity can be generalized from one center to another. (T/F) Why? _____

_____

3. In spite of the high correlation between performance on tests of academic intelligence and amount of education, the selection of job applicants on the basis of the amount of formal education they have had would not really be fair. (T/F) Why? *True*

_____

4. Special aptitude tests contribute very little or nothing, beyond what most standard multiple aptitude batteries offer, to the process of personnel selection. (T/F) Why? _____

_____

5. Correlational and factor analytic studies of large numbers of motor tests have revealed broad group factors comparable to those found for intellectual functions. (T/F) Why? ____

_____

6. Women generally excel in tests of manual dexterity and perceptual discrimination, whereas men, as a group, are markedly superior in tests of mechanical reasoning or information. (T/F) Why? _____

_____

7. The typical professional school testing program relies exclusively on tests of scholastic aptitude or general academic intelligence. (T/F) Why? _____

_____

8. Law School Admission Test scores have been found to correlate more highly with performance on the bar examination than with law school grades. (T/F) Why? _____

_____

9. Licensing laws constitute a way of assuring the public that psychologists have the highest qualifications required for the proper practice of their specialty. (T/F) Why? _____

_____

10. Students at the junior high school level demonstrate their vocational maturity by the wisdom and consistency of the ultimate career goals they choose. (T/F) Why? _____

_____

ANSWERS TO TRUE/FALSE:

1. True	4. False	7. False	10. False
2. False	5. False	8. True	
3. True	6. True	9. False	

MULTIPLE CHOICE: TEST YOURSELF

1. Which of the following reasons best explains why most occupational tests are hardly ever validated through criterion-related procedures at the local level? _____

_____ .

   a. Trained personnel are not available
   b. Local users are not interested in local validation
   c. It is unrealistic for small concerns to go through local validation
   d. Local validation, even under ideal conditions, offers no advantages

2. Which of the following is *not* one of the four steps in conducting a local criterion-related validation? _____

    _____.

    a. Conducting a job analysis
    b. Selecting or constructing a test
    c. Hiring only those who do well on the selection test
    d. Correlating test results with job performance

3. The job analysis, as a step in content-related validation, should _____

    _____.

    a. list the salary and fringe benefits
    b. identify the particulars that separate the job from any other job
    c. indicate the person(s) who should be hired
    d. all of the above

4. For some higher level positions, candidates are sometimes put through a wide range of tests over as much as a two- or three-day period. This approach, which may include situational tests, role playing, job simulations, personal interviews, and other evaluations, is known as the _____.

    a. multiple aptitude evaluation
    b. job element validation
    c. personnel selection analysis
    d. assessment center technique

5. When job candidates are asked to perform a task that is actually a part of the work to be performed on the job, under uniform working conditions, the method of evaluation being used is called a _____.

    a. job sample
    b. critical activity
    c. personal analysis
    d. selection analysis

6. As part of a job analysis, a job element is a(n) _____

    _____.

    a. aspect of the job that correlates highly with success
    b. specific job behavior that differentiates between good and poor employees
    c. group problem-solving technique
    d. job dimension used in evaluating overall value to the employer

7. Most intelligence tests primarily depend upon _____

    _____.

    a. perceptual speed
    b. academic-type knowledge and skills
    c. psychomotor skills
    d. a combination of performance-type skills

8. A relatively new approach to the validation of personnel selection tests, which allows for the utilization of previously obtained data in assessing the validity of a test in a particular situation, is called the _____.

    a. Y coefficient
    b. multiple regressor system
    c. job element method
    d. Bayesian model

9. Of the following types of job applicants, the ones *least likely* to be given one of the major types of special aptitude tests discussed in the textbook are _____.

    a. clerical workers
    b. drill press operators
    c. sales managers
    d. assembly-line workers

10. Most psychomotor skills tests focus on _____.

    a. manual dexterity
    b. speed of perception
    c. general overall body coordination
    d. spatial relationships

11. The Revised Minnesota Paper Form Board Test is primarily a measure of _____.

    a. spatial aptitude
    b. mechanical aptitude
    c. finger dexterity
    d. coordinated movement

12. The scores on most clerical aptitude tests depend predominantly on _____.

    a. verbal comprehension
    b. perceptual speed
    c. eye-hand coordination
    d. spatial visualization

13. The Computer Aptitude, Literacy, and Interest Profile, for the most part, involves _____.

    a. a series of special computerized games
    b. the identification of good computer programs
    c. a job sample
    d. reasoning applied to visual, nonverbal content

14. The best predictions for success in law school can be made from _____

_____ .

   a. Law School Admission Test results
   b. college grades
   c. general intelligence test scores
   d. both a and b

15. Available measures of an individual's level of career maturity, such as Super's Career

Development Inventory, are particularly useful _____

_____ .

   a. at the elementary school level
   b. at the high school level
   c. in the course of professional school training
   d. when an individual is getting set to retire

MINIPROJECTS/SUGGESTED OUTREACH ACTIVITIES:

1. One appropriate avenue to pursue as a follow-up to the information you have acquired on occupational testing is to conduct a survey of the personnel departments of some of the major employers in your area, with the purpose of finding out what instruments they use in selecting job applicants. If possible, choose companies that employ workers in a variety of jobs or choose several smaller companies that would provide information on a representative range of occupational categories.

2. If you have access to test materials through your instructor or through a testing center or lab, locate one of the tests of academic intelligence especially developed for use in industry, e.g., the Personnel Tests for Industry, or one of the special aptitude tests described in Chapter 15. Study the manual and materials for the test you have selected and prepare a Test Evaluation following the suggested outline in Appendix B of the textbook. Most of the instruments mentioned in Chapter 15 are relatively brief and easy to study compared to the fairly complex and comprehensive batteries that were discussed in the previous two chapters.

3. One of the most important general references in the area of occupational testing is the book, prepared by the Division of Industrial and Organizational Psychology of the American Psychological Association (APA), entitled *Principles for the Validation and Use of Personnel Selection Procedures* (3rd ed., 1987). A review of this publication would help to expand your understanding of what constitutes good practice in the realm of occupational testing.

ANSWERS TO MULTIPLE CHOICE/TEST YOURSELF ITEMS:

1. c	4. d	7. b	10. a	13. d
2. c	5. a	8. d	11. a	14. d
3. b	6. b	9. c	12. b	15. b

Chapter 16
CLINICAL TESTING

CHAPTER OUTLINE

CHAPTER SUMMARY

Clinical psychologists employ a variety of sources of data, such as interviews, case histories, and tests of most types, in their efforts to generate and test hypotheses about the people whom they study intensively in the course of their work. Some of the tests used by clinicians are psychometrically weak and even those whose psychometric properties are sound do not yield sufficiently precise results for individual diagnosis. However, the use of test results as tools to generate leads, in the context of multiple sources of data, provides a safeguard against overgeneralization from isolated test scores.

Individual intelligence tests can provide the clinician with information ranging from the objective level of measurement represented by quantitative scores to the qualitative analysis of irregularities of performance. In addition, many clinicians routinely explore the pattern, or profile, of intelligence test scores for possible indices of psychopathology. Procedures such as the examination of the amount of scatter in test scores, the computation of a deterioration index, and the analysis of score patterns associated with particular clinical syndromes have been used for many years, especially in conjunction with the Wechsler scales. However, decades of research on these forms of pattern analysis have provided little support for their diagnostic value, a fact that is not surprising given the variety and complexity of the methodological considerations that such research entails. Nevertheless, intelligence tests can provide a wealth of information in clinical cases, if the psychometric data are combined with qualitative observations and other sources of data in a sophisticated fashion, such as the approach espoused by Kaufman.

The behavioral effects of brain pathology can vary, in a complex fashion, as a function of the age of the individual, the chronicity, source, extent, and locus of the pathology, and also as a function of experiential factors unique to the affected person. Brain damage encompasses a wide range of disorders with diverse behavioral manifestations, many of which can also stem from factors other than cerebral dysfunction. These facts, which have been increasingly recognized since midcentury, complicate the diagnosis of brain damage to such an extent that no single technique can be considered totally dependable. Therefore, clinical neuropsychologists typically use corroborative information from a variety of sources, such as electroencephalography and computerized axial tomography (CAT) scans. In addition, there is a whole array of behavioral measures that can serve an important function in the assessment of brain damage and in the planning and monitoring of rehabilitation programs.

Some of the most effective single tests that can be used to screen for brain damage are instruments, such as the Benton Visual Retention Test and the Bender Visual Motor Gestalt Test, that concentrate on assessing the perception of spatial relations and memory for newly learned material, both of which are functions which are very likely to be disrupted by brain pathology. Many clinicians use a combination of tests that assess different skills and deficits in a "flexible" battery approach that can be tailored to individual cases. In addition, comprehensive standardized batteries that provide measures of all significant neuropsychological skills have also been devised. The Halstead-Reitan Neuropsychological Test Battery and the Luria-Nebraska Neuropsychological Battery are two major examples of the standardized approach to neuropsychological assessment discussed in the text.

Another problematic area of clinical assessment is the identification of specific learning disabilities. Although educators have become increasingly aware of the high frequency of occurrence of this type of handicap, the diagnosis and remediation of learning disabilities (LD) have been complicated by the looseness with which the designation has been employed. It is now recognized that the LD population is heterogeneous with regard to the behavioral symptoms they manifest and with regard to the etiology of those symptoms. Nevertheless, several LD subgroups have been differentiated in terms of whether the cluster of symptoms presented are primarily academic deficits, hyperactivity/impulsive behavior, or motor disorders. Children with learning disabilities, by definition, show normal or above-average intelligence, in combination with serious difficulties in learning one or more basic education skills. However, the LD syndrome *may* occur at any intellectual level and in combination with a variety of perceptual, language, coordination, memory, and/or attention deficits, as well as with emotional and motivational problems.

The diversity encountered among the LD population, along with the need for highly specific information about the nature and extent of the disabilities in each case, require the use of an assortment of tests and observational procedures for proper diagnosis. Although regular achievement batteries and other group tests may be used as screening devices, individually administered wide-range achievement tests, such as the Kaufman Test of Educational Achievement (K-TEA), are especially suitable for the initial assessment of learning disabilities. Individual intelligence tests and tests prepared especially for children with learning disabilities, such as the Illinois Test of Psycholinguistic Abilities (ITPA) and the Porch Index of Communicative Ability in Children (PICAC), can also be of help in the intensive study of individual cases. In addition, dynamic assessment techniques, which cover a number of procedures that elicit supplementary qualitative data about an individual through a deliberate departure from standardized test administration, have been gaining popularity since the 1970s. The assessment of learning potential, as practiced by Feuerstein and others, is a particularly promising approach that involves a test-teach-test format in which the child is taught to perform a task that he or she was initially unable to carry out. An even more sophisticated dynamic assessment approach is the multidimensional latent trait model for change, recently developed by Embretson, which combines item response theory techniques, cognitive task decomposition, and the use of microcomputers to assess and facilitate learning. This work already constitutes a significant achievement in psychometrics and bodes well for the future of cognitive assessment and remediation.

The application of learning principles to the management of behavior change has been quite significant within clinical psychology, where this approach is designated as behavior therapy. Even though assessment procedures are vital to the definition of the individual's problem, to the selection of appropriate treatments, as well as to the monitoring of their results, behavior therapists initially paid little attention to assessment. Since the mid-1970s, however, the importance of assessment procedures in behavior therapy has been increasingly recognized. Although there are many physiological, observational, and self-report techniques that can be used in behavioral assessment, most of them do not meet the traditional psychometric standards with regard to uniformity, normative data, reliability, and validity. The need for behavioral assessment techniques to meet those standards has been increasingly recognized, as has the fact that alternative statistical procedures to evaluate those techniques may be necessary in many cases.

Clinical assessment differs from other areas in which psychological tests are used in that the individual judgment of the clinician enters into both the data-gathering and the data-synthesis phases of an evaluation to a unique degree. This situation represents at once an advantage and a potential hazard in the process of assessment and has given rise to research comparing predictions made through clinical judgment and those obtained by the application of statistical procedures. Since the objectivity and skill of the individual clinician in making predictions are themselves critical variables in determining the accuracy of those predictions, no definitive answer can be given to the question posed by such comparisons. Nevertheless, it is recognized that the most effective procedures are those which combine clinical and statistical approaches and that the validity of clinical predictions needs to be continuously and systematically investigated whenever feasible.

The final product of most clinical assessments is a written report, wherein the clinician synthesizes the salient aspects of a case. The content of the report should follow directly from the purpose of the assessment and should focus on interpretations and conclusions rather than on specific data. The organization and integration of data, as well as the use of a writing style and vocabulary appropriate to the report reader, are also crucial to the effectiveness of the clinical report as a tool for communicating assessment results.

Although the potential contribution of computers to clinical diagnosis is quite impressive, much of their potential, in areas such as the application of adaptive (CAT) techniques to personality testing and the integration of data from tests and other sources, is still largely unexplored. The applications of computers that are currently available for assessment are confined mostly to the administration, scoring, and narrative interpretation of several traditional tests. Although computerized test interpretations can save time and can be more thorough than an individual clinician, they are also fraught with potential for misuse, especially with regard to the responsibilities and qualifications of users and the availability of information needed to evaluate such services.

COMPREHENSIVE REVIEW

STUDY QUESTIONS:

1. Discuss the role that psychological tests play in the context of a clinician's work.

2. List and describe the three major procedures used in analyzing the pattern of intelligence test scores.

3. Discuss the methodological requirements that must be considered in evaluating research on the various forms of pattern analysis with the Wechsler scales.

4. Describe the types of qualitative information that can be gathered in the course of individual intelligence testing.

5. Describe the major features of Kaufman's approach to the interpretation of test performance.

6. List the characteristics of tests for the assessment of neuropsychological impairment and describe the Bender-Gestalt as an example of those instruments.

7. Discuss the historical origins of the field of neuropsychological assessment and cite the major findings of early research on brain damage.

8. List and discuss the main variables that influence the behavioral effects of brain pathology.

9. Compare and contrast the "flexible" battery approach to neuropsychological assessment with the standardized battery approach.

10. Describe the major features of the Luria-Nebraska Neuropsychological Battery.

11. Discuss the problems associated with the identification of specific learning disabilities.

12. List and briefly describe the types of assessment techniques that can be used to screen and diagnose learning disabilities.

13. Define dynamic assessment, describe its major features as currently practiced, and explain why that approach holds such great promise.

14. Discuss the role of assessment in the context of behavior therapy and describe the three main types of procedures that are used commonly in behavioral assessment.

15. Discuss the main differences between clinical and statistical predictions and cite the major findings of the research that has compared the two methods.

16. Explain the function that the clinical report serves in assessment and describe the features that characterize a good report.

17. Discuss the potential contributions and the potential dangers inherent in the use of computers in clinical assessment.

FILL IN THE BLANKS: Key Terms and Concepts

1. The broad field of clinical psychology has close ties with more narrowly defined specialties that also involve the intensive study of individuals, such as _ _ _ _ _ _ psychology, _ _ _ _ _ _ psychology, and _ _ _ _ _ _ _ _ psychology, which covers the practice of psychology as it pertains to legal matters.

2. The Wechsler scales lend themselves especially well to _PATTeRN_ or _profile_ analyses because the results of all of their subtests are expressed in comparable standard scores.

3. The three major procedures used in analyzing Wechsler scale profiles are the examination of the amount of _ _ _ _ _ _ _, or variation among subtest scores, the computation of the _ _ _ _ _ _ _ _ _ _ _ _ _ _ _ _, based on the difference between "hold" and "don't hold" tests, and the review of the _ _ _ _ _ _ _ _ _ _ _ _ associated with certain clinical syndromes.

4. One of the major sources of leads derived from the use of individual intelligence tests in clinical assessment is the observation and _Qualitative_ analysis of idiosyncracies in a person's performance.

5. _Neuropsychological_ tests are instruments which are designed to assess organicity or brain damage and are generally based on the premise of a differential deficit in different functions.

6. Two of the main variables that shape the behavioral effects of brain damage are the _age_ at which the injury is sustained and the _chronicity_ of a case, which refers to the amount of time elapsed since the injury.

7. Typically, children with _learning disibilities_ show normal or above-normal intelligence in combination with pronounced difficulties in acquiring reading, writing, and/or arithmetical skills.

8. Many LD children show a disturbance in the acquisition of the ability to understand language or to use language meaningfully which is designated as _.

9. The term _ _ _ _ _ _ _ _ _ _ _ _ _ _ _ _ _ _ covers a number of clinical procedures that essentially involve the deliberate departure from standardized test administration in order to elicit additional qualitative data about an individual.

10. One of the earliest dynamic assessment techniques, known as "*testing the limits*," consists of procedures such as giving additional cues or time to the test taker, or asking the test taker how she or he set out to solve a problem and suggesting a different first step.

11. A relatively new approach to dynamic assessment, exemplified by the work of Feuerstein, is designated as *learning-potential* assessment and involves a test-teach-test format in which the examinee is given instruction on broadly applicable learning or problem-solving skills.

12. The techniques known as _ _ _ _ _ _ _ _ _ _ _ _ _ _ _ _ _ represent an application of major learning principles to the management of clinical problems.

13. The process of _ _ _ _ _ _ _ _ _ _ _ _ _ _ _ _ _ _ in behavior therapy involves a full specification of the treatment objective, including a description of the stimuli that elicit the target behavior and an investigation of the conditions that maintain unwanted behavior.

14. The three major types of assessment procedures used in the course of behavior therapy are _ _ _ _ _ _ _ _ _ _ _ _ _ _ measures, _ _ _ _ _ _ _ _ _ _ _ _ _ _ _ _ _ _ of the target behavior, and _ _ _ _ -_ _ _ _ _ _ _ by the client.

15. What a clinician does in assessing a client can be seen as a special case of _ _ _ _ _ _ _ _ _ _ _ _ _ _ _ _ _ _, which is the process through which anyone comes to know and understand another person.

16. A distinguising feature of clinical assessments is their reliance on the judgment of the clinician in both the _ _ _ _ _-_ _ _ _ _ _ _ _ _ _ _ and the _ _ _ _ -_ _ _ _ _ _ _ _ _ _ _ phases of the assessment.

17. By establishing and maintaining rapport, the skillful clinician can elicit from a client the pertinent facts about his or her _ _ _ _ _ _ _ _ _ _ _ _ _ _, which has been described as "an unbiased population of events which is as convincing an operational definition of a person as one can hope for."

18. The finding that an actuarial model of a clinician's own behavior will yield more valid predictions than does the clinician is known as "_ _ _ _ _ _ _ _ _ _ _ _ _ _" and reflects the influence that random procedural errors can have on decision-making.

19. A report that is seen as "remarkably accurate," due to the fact that it contains general, stereotyped statements that apply to most people, serves to demonstrate the influence of the "_ _ _ _ _ _ effect" in a striking fashion.

20. The most sophisticated application of computers to clinical assessment that is currently in wide use is the computerized _ _ _ _ _ _ _ _ _

   _ _ _ _ _ _ _ _ _ _ _ _ _ _ _, which is produced by a program that includes a large library of statements to be attached to specific levels or patterns of scores.

ANSWERS TO FILL-IN-THE-BLANKS: (Key Terms and Concepts)

1. school (psychology)/health (psychology)/forensic (psychology)
2. pattern (or) profile (analyses)
3. scatter/deterioration index/score patterns
4. qualitative (analysis)
5. neuropsychological (tests)
6. age/chronicity
7. learning disabilities
8. developmental aphasia
9. dynamic assessment
10. "testing the limits"
11. learning-potential (assessment)
12. behavior therapy
13. functional analysis
14. physiological (measures)/direct observation/self-report (by the client)
15. person cognition
16. data-gathering/data-synthesis
17. life history
18. "bootstrapping"
19. "Barnum effect"
20. (computerized) narrative interpretation

TRUE/FALSE and WHY?

1. Even if well-designed future investigations should conclusively show a relationship between intelligence test score patterns and diagnostic categories, the results would not apply equally to all individuals. (T/F) Why? _____

   _____

2. Brain damage may produce the opposite behavior pattern in two individuals. (T/F) Why? _

   _____

3. Empirical investigations have repeatedly shown that left-hemisphere lesions tend to be associated with lower Performance than Verbal IQs (P<V) on the Wechsler scales whereas right-hemisphere and diffuse brain damage tend to show the opposite pattern (P>V). (T/F) Why? _____

   _____

4. Available research to date has lent a good deal of support to the traditional concept of minimal brain dysfunction as a distinct childhood syndrome. (T/F) Why? _____

   _____

5. Research on preschool children indicates that, at that age level, the brain-injured are frequently deficient in all intellectual functions. (T/F) Why? _____

   _____

6. Neuropsychological tests that assess one or two major functions are particualrly well-suited for differential diagnosis. (T/F) Why? _____

7. At the present stage, the generalizability and transportability of the learning-potential assessment techniques developed by Feuerstein and others have not been adequately demonstrated. (T/F) Why? _____

   _____

8. The assumption of similarity between oneself and another person can serve the clinician well in the process of making diagnostic and prognostic inferences. (T/F) Why? _____

   _____

9. Meehl demonstrated that, almost without exception, the routine application of statistical procedures yielded as many, or more, correct predictions as did clinical analysis. (T/F) Why? _____

   _____

10. The most desirable format and outline for all clinical reports has become quite standard over the past few decades. (T/F) Why? _____

    _____

ANSWERS TO TRUE/FALSE:

1. True	4. False	7. True	10. False
2. True	5. True	8. False	
3. False	6. False	9. True	

LISTS OF SIGNIFICANT NAMES AND REPRESENTATIVE TESTS

The following lists contain the names of some people whose work in the area of clinical testing is of special significance and the titles of some of the best-known, or most representative, instruments discussed in Chapter 16. The pertinent textbook pages are also listed. You may use these lists as review tools to make sure you can identify the people, in terms of their major contributions, and the tests, in terms of their main features.

Names:

1. Alan Kaufman (pp. 484 and 499)

2. Elizabeth Koppitz (pp. 488-489)

3. Kurt Goldstein (p. 489)

4. Ralph Reitan (pp. 490 and 493)

5. Reuver Feuerstein (pp. 503-504)

6. Susan Embretson (pp. 504-505)

7. Paul Meehl (pp. 513-514)

Tests:

1. Benton Visual Retention Test (pp. 485-486)

2. Bender Visual Motor Gestalt Test (pp. 486-489)

3. Halstead-Reitan Neuropsychological Test Battery (p. 493)

4. Luria-Nebraska Neuropsychological Battery (pp. 493-496)

5. Kaufman Test of Educational Achievement (K-TEA) (p. 499)

6. Illinois Test of Psycholinguistic Abilities (ITPA) (p. 501)

7. Porch Index of Communicative Ability in Children (PICAC) (pp. 501-502)

8. Learning Potential Assessment Device (LPAD) (p. 504)

9. Fear Survey Schedule (p. 508)

10. Conflict Resolution Inventory (p. 508)

MULTIPLE CHOICE: TEST YOURSELF

1. Clinical psychologists use tests primarily _____
   _____.

   a. as a substitute for a lengthy interview
   b. as a primary source of reliable information about their clients
   c. as a source of hypotheses to test further
   d. only when all other techniques fail

2. A clinical psychologist examining a WISC-R profile is usually most interested in _____
   _____.

   a. the pattern of subtest scores
   b. the overall score the individual achieves
   c. the reliability and validity coefficients
   d. comparative results obtained by similar individuals

3. The main problem(s) with pattern analysis is(are) _____
   _____.

   a. score differences may only reflect imperfect subtest reliability
   b. statistically significant differences in subtest scores are often found in the records of normal people
   c. factors that are irrelevant to diagnosis may cause the differences that are obtained
   d. all of the above

4. The single most important aspect of a test that will negate the value of pattern analysis is
   _____.

   a. the type of questions
   b. interitem correlations
   c. lack of subtest reliability
   d. item-score deterioration

5. The major emphasis of the Bender-Gestalt is on _____
   _____.

   a. perceptual-auditory disorders
   b. speed of response
   c. visual perception disorders
   d. retention of verbal passages

6. Unusually poor performance on the Benton or the Bender-Gestalt is frequently associated
   with _____.

   a. mental retardation
   b. anxiety disorders
   c. language problems
   d. brain damage

7. One of the most remarkable aspects of brain damage is the fact that _____
_____.

    a. its symptoms vary widely
    b. it is closely associated with language development
    c. its effects are usually irreversible
    d. it seldom affects short-term memory

8. The Halstead-Reitan and Luria-Nebraska batteries are designed primarily to assess _____
_____.

    a. intelligence
    b. personality characteristics
    c. brain pathology
    d. motor-linguistic problems

9. Learning disabilities are usually viewed as _____
_____.

    a. symptoms of serious brain pathology
    b. irreversible in most cases
    c. a handicap that can possibly be overcome
    d. caused by emotional factors

10. Which of the following tests is(are) designed primarily for the assessment of learning
disorders? _____
_____.

    a. Illinois Test of Psycholinguistic Abilities
    b. Porch Index of Communicative Ability in Children
    c. Frostig Developmental Test of Visual Perception
    d. All of the above are used

11. The learning-potential assessment techniques developed by Feuerstein and others are
characterized by _____
_____.

    a. the fact that they assess abilities that were always present but not overtly shown
    b. their close link between assessment and remediation
    c. the generalizability of their effects to the child's interpersonal functioning
    d. the fact that little or no training is needed to use them

12. Target behavior, graded steps, clear specification of objectives, and subgoals are all aspects
of _____.

    a. the clinical assessment of personality
    b. behavior modification programs
    c. the PICAC technique
    d. none of the above

13. Which of the following procedures are used in the assessment of behavioral change? _____

_____.

   a. Physiological measures
   b. Direct observations of target behavior
   c. Self-reports by the client
   d. All of the above can be used

14. One of the principal problems with behavioral assessment techniques has been _____

_____.

   a. lack of standardization of materials and procedures
   b. that they often yield conflicting results
   c. that they do nothing about the underlying causes of the problem
   d. their inordinate length

15. Given our present state of knowledge, the best overall procedure for synthesizing test data

    about individuals is _____.

   a. the statistical approach
   b. the clinical approach
   c. the physiological approach
   d. a combination of the clinical and statistical approaches

MINIPROJECTS/SUGGESTED OUTREACH ACTIVITIES:

The content of Chapter 16 spans what is surely the most diversified area of assessment, a fact that can be easily surmised from the length and breadth of the chapter (and of its summary in this guide). Moreover, many of the topics in clinical testing are intrinsically interesting to most people and worthy of further pursuit. What follows, then, are only a few out of the many possible suggestions that could be made for follow-up readings and activities to pursue those topics.

1. Silverstein's procedure for evaluating the statistical significance of differences between the Wechsler subtest scores of a given person is described in his 1982 article on "Pattern Analysis as Simultaneous Statistical Inference" (*Journal of Consulting and Clinical Psychology, 50,* 234-240.) This article would be a most appropriate follow-up to the discussion on pattern analysis of test scores because it presents the most satisfactory, and widely used, solution yet devised to the problem of how to use Wechsler subtest score differences in a fashion that is at least partly defensible from a methodological standpoint. In addition, a careful reading of the article would be an excellent way to review and solidify your knowledge about reliability and errors of measurement.

2. The area of neuropsychological assessment is one of the most rapidly growing clinical specialties. Although there is a vast literature that you could sample in order to acquaint yourself better with that field, the *Handbook of Clinical Neuropsychology,* edited by Susan Filskov and Thomas Boll, which now consists of two volumes (New York: Wiley, 1980 and 1986), is probably one of the best places to start.

3. Another vibrant field, which is sure to evolve rapidly and have a dramatic influence in how testing is conducted, is the area of dynamic assessment. The book *Dynamic Assessment: An Interactional Approach to Evaluating Learning Potential,* edited by Carol S. Lidz (New York: Guilford Press, 1987), contains reviews of the theoretical and empirical foundations,

current applications, and major issues and implications of dynamic assessment contributed by its major proponents.

4. In the field of behavioral assessment, one of the outstanding references you could review is the *Handbook of Behavioral Assessment* (2nd ed.), edited by A.R. Ciminero *et al.* (New York: Wiley, 1986). This handbook, like the two preceding references, provides a wide-ranging review of its area from which you might select the readings that interest you most.

5. Report writing is, in most cases, the culmination of the work of the clinical assessor. The best way to become acquainted with what constitutes a good report is to examine some reports directly. If you have access to sample reports from your instructor or elsewhere, provided that confidentiality can be maintained, by all means avail yourself of the opportunity to read them. However, failing that, you might examine one of the books that Anastasi suggests, such as Norman Tallent's *Psychological Report Writing* (Englewood Cliffs, N.J.: Prentice Hall, 1988). This book, now in its third edition, presents not only the desirable features, and pitfalls, of report writing, but also includes several examples of good and poor reports from a variety of settings.

6. *Computerized Psychological Assessment: A Practitioner's Guide,* edited by James Butcher (New York: Basic Books, 1987), is an excellent compendium of the computer applications currently available for use in clinical settings. As the other handbooks mentioned in this section, Butcher's book consists of contributions from distinguished experts, in this case from the field of computer applications *and* from various areas of clinical assessment.

ANSWERS TO MULTIPLE CHOICE/TEST YOURSELF ITEMS:

1. c	4. c	7. a	10. d	13. d
2. a	5. c	8. c	11. b	14. a
3. d	6. d	9. c	12. b	15. d

Chapter 17
SELF-REPORT INVENTORIES

CHAPTER OUTLINE

Content-Related Validation

Empirical Criterion Keying
    Basic Approach
    The Minnesota Multiphasic Personality Inventory
    California Psychological Inventory
    Personality Inventory for Children
    Millon Clinical Multiaxial Inventory

Factor Analysis in Test Development
    The Guilford Inventories
    Comrey Personality Scales
    The Cattell Inventories

Personality Theory in Test Development
    Edwards Personal Preference Schedule
    Personality Research Form and Jackson Personality Inventory

Test-Taking Attitudes and Response Biases
    Faking and Social Desirability
    Forced-Choice Technique
    Response Sets and Response Styles

Traits, States, and Situations
    Interactions of Persons and Situations
    Traits and States

Current Status of Personality Inventories

CHAPTER SUMMARY

In conventional psychometric terminology, instruments for the measurement of emotional, motivational, interpersonal, and attitudinal characteristics are designated as "personality tests." The present chapter deals with personality inventories which, along with the projective techniques discussed in Chapter 19, are the most numerous types of personality tests.

Personality inventories can be developed through a variety of approaches. These approaches are not mutually exclusive; they can be, and recently have increasingly been, combined. The major procedures that are currently used in formulating, assembling, selecting, and grouping personality inventory items are content validation, empirical criterion keying, factor analysis, and the application of personality theory.

Content-related validation was used in the development of the Woodworth Personal Data Sheet, the prototype of self-report inventories designed to screen military personnel during World War I for serious emotional disturbances. This inventory, which was an attempt to standardize a psychiatric interview and adapt it for mass testing, consists of questions that deal directly with deviant or maladaptive behaviors. Among current inventories, the Mooney Problem Check List, which is designed simply to identify problems in several areas of adaptive functioning either for group discussion or for individual counseling, is one of the clearest examples of the use of content validation.

Empirical criterion keying is a procedure that involves the selection of items and the assignment of scoring weights to each response in an inventory on the basis of some external criterion. Unlike content validation, which rests on a literal interpretation of questionnaire items, the empirical criterion keying approach treats responses, regardless of their content or veracity, as symptomatic of the criterion behavior.

The Minnesota Multiphasic Personality Inventory (MMPI) is an outstanding example of criterion keying in personality test construction. The MMPI is the most widely used personality inventory and also one of the most assiduously investigated. It consists of 550 statements to which the test taker gives the responses "True," "False," or "Cannot Say" and, in its basic form, it provides scores on 10 clinical and three "validity" scales. Eight of the clinical scales were keyed on the basis of responses of normal adults versus clinical groups representing traditional psychiatric diagnoses, while the other two were keyed on other contrasted samples. The "validity" scales are essentially checks on carelessness, misunderstanding, malingering, and the operation of special response sets. In addition to the basic scales, over 300 new scales, which vary widely in their content, derivation, and psychometric characteristics, have been developed for use with the MMPI. Several systems for coding MMPI profiles have evolved over the years and a number of reference works that present empirical data about people who show frequently occurring patterns or codes are also available. In spite of these aids and others, like computerized systems for generating reports, proper interpretation and use of the MMPI require considerable psychological sophistication and the consideration of demographic and contextual variables. Since 1983 the MMPI has been undergoing its first revision, and a major restandardization. The revised MMPI includes separate adult and adolescent forms and should be available for operational use by 1990.

The California Psychological Inventory (CPI), the Personality Inventory for Children (PIC), and the Millon Clinical Multiaxial Inventory (MCMI) are three additional examples of major personality inventories, discussed in the textbook, that were developed at least partly through empirical criterion keying. The CPI, which draws almost half of its items from the MMPI, was designed specifically for use with normal adults. The PIC, which like the MMPI was developed at the University of Minnesota, is really an inventory of observed behavior designed to assess personality functioning in children and adolescents through items answered by a knowledgeable adult, usually the mother. The MCMI is an instrument whose development was aimed at meeting the criticisms leveled against the MMPI and cuts across various methodologies. The MCMI was designed specifically for diagnostic screening and its scales are consistent with the classification system used in the third edition of the *Diagnostic and Statistical Manual of Mental Disorders* (DSM-III).

Factor analysis has been used extensively to attempt to classify personality traits and also to develop several personality tests. The Guilford-Zimmerman Temperament Survey, the Comrey Personality Scales, and the Sixteen Personality Factor Questionnaire (16 PF) are three well-known examples of personality inventories developed through factor analytic techniques discussed in the textbook. Although factor analysis is an effective technique for grouping personality inventory items into clusters that are relatively homogeneous and independent, it cannot substitute for empirical validation. Therefore, to the extent that inventories have relied exclusively on factor analytic studies in their development, they are in need of further validation.

A number of personality tests have been constructed within the framework of one or another personality theory. The manifest need system proposed by Murray and his associates at the Harvard Psychological Clinic in 1938 is a theoretical framework that has been used repeatedly in personality test construction. The Edwards Personal Preference Schedule (EPPS) and the Personality Research Form (PRF) are two examples of inventories that used Murray's system as their starting point and are discussed in the textbook at some length.

Self-report inventories are particularly susceptible to malingering or faking. Numerous empirical investigations have demonstrated that respondents are able to create the impression they desire, whether favorable or unfavorable. Therefore, all the major personality inventories include one or more of the procedures that have been developed in an effort to confront the problem of deliberate dissembling by respondents. The forced-choice technique, used by the EPPS among others, is one of those procedures and was developed specifically to counteract the effect of social desirability in questionnaire responses. It requires the respondent to choose between descriptive terms or phrases that appear equally acceptable but differ in validity. However, there is evidence that the forced-choice format does not eliminate the influence of social desirability in inventory responses. Moreover, the procedure is most often applied in such a way, e.g., in the EPPS, that it produces ipsative scores wherein the frame of reference is the individual rather than the normative sample. This, in turn, introduces technical difficulties and eliminates information that may be significant in many testing situations.

Response sets include not only the tendency to choose socially desirable response alternatives, but also propensities toward acquiescence and deviant responding. The voluminous research on these response sets first centered on efforts to rule out their influence because they were regarded as a source of irrelevant variance. Later, response sets came to be viewed by many as important indicators of personality traits and were investigated in their own right and described as "response styles." The controversy over the significance of response styles in personality measurement continues and has stimulated extensive research.

Another long-standing controversy in personality assessment concerns the issue of the generalizability of personality traits versus the situational specificity of behavior. The impetus toward behavioral specificity arose in the 1960s, largely from social learning theorists who were dissatisfied with the early view of traits as fixed, underlying causal entities. The results of subsequent research aimed at assessing the impact of situations on behavior highlighted the extent to which behavior variance depends upon both persons *and* situations, as well as their interaction, and has led to a growing consensus in this area. The differentiation between traits and states, which is exemplified in Spielberger's State-Trait Anxiety Inventory (STAI), is another way to conceptualize the behavior domain assessed by personality tests. It, along with other methodological and theoretical innovations that have arisen from earlier critiques of personality assessment, have had a salutary effect on the field.

COMPREHENSIVE REVIEW

STUDY QUESTIONS:

1. Define personality tests and describe the major areas in which they are used.

2. List and explain each of the four main approaches to the development of self-report personality inventories.

3. Describe the Mooney Problem Check List as an example of an inventory based on content validation.

4. Describe the background and major features of the Minnesota Multiphasic Personality Inventory (MMPI), including its format and basic scales.

5. Discuss the reasons why pattern analysis of MMPI profiles is often more advantageous than the interpretation of isolated scale scores.

6. Discuss the limitations of the MMPI as an instrument for differential diagnosis.

7. Describe the major changes that have been made in the revision of the MMPI that was initiated in the early 1980s.

8. Describe the special characteristics of the California Psychological Inventory (CPI), the Personality Inventory for Children (PIC), and the Millon Clinical Multiaxial Inventory (MCMI), with special reference to how these instruments relate to the MMPI.

9. Discuss the role of factor analysis in the development of Cattell's Sixteen Personality Factor Questionnaire (16 PF).

10. Identify the personality theory that was used as a basis for designing the Edwards Personal Preference Schedule (EPPS) and the Personality Research Form (PRF), and describe the major features of those instruments.

11. Explain what "ipsative scores" are and how they affect the interpretation of test results.

12. Discuss the impact of response biases on personality testing and describe some of the procedures that have been devised to counteract those biases.

13. Describe the forced-choice technique and discuss the findings that relate to its effectiveness in controlling the influence of social desirability in self-report inventories.

14. Discuss the issue of response sets and response styles as it has been conceptualized in personality assessment over time.

15. Discuss the relationships that exist between traits, states, and situations and how they are currently understood to affect behavior.

16. Describe the present status of self-report inventories in personality assessment.

FILL IN THE BLANKS: Key Terms and Concepts

1. In conventional psychometric terminology, _ _ _ _ _ _ _ _ _ _ _ _ _ tests are instruments used for the measurement of emotional, motivational, interpersonal, and attitudinal characteristics, as distinguished from abilities.

2. The major approaches currently used in the development of personality inventories are based on _ _ _ _ _ _ _ validation, _ keying, _ _ _ _ _ _ analysis, and _ _ _ _ _ _ _ _ _ _ _ _ _ theory.

3. Whereas _ _ _ _ _ _ _ _ validation rests essentially on a literal or veridical interpretation of questionnaire items, in _ responses are treated as diagnostic or symptomatic of the criterion behavior with which they are associated.

4. A(n) _ _ _ _ _–_ _ _ _ _ _ inventory is a series of standardized verbal stimuli that is usually presented in a paper-and-pencil format suitable for group administration and is especially subject to malingering or faking.

5. In its original basic form, the MMPI provides scores on ten "_ _ _ _ _ _ _ _ _ scales," such as Hysteria and Paranoia, and on three "_ _ _ _ _ _ _ _ _ scales," which represent checks on carelessness, misunderstanding, and the operation of special response sets.

6. The norms on the original MMPI control sample of approximately 1,500 persons are reported in the form of _ _ _ _ _ _ _ _ _, which are standard scores with a mean of 50 and an SD of 10.

7. The fact that the diagnostic groups used in selecting MMPI items differed from the normal controls in more than one trait and the fact that some of the same traits may occur in more than one scale have resulted in the _ and _ _ _ _ _ _ _ _ of MMPI scales which, in turn, account for some of the advantages of pattern analysis over single scale interpretation.

8. The high intercorrelations among the basic MMPI clinical scales, which might have been avoided if items had been selected by comparing the responses of each clinical group with those of other clinical groups, make their value in _ _ _ _ _ _ _ _ _ _ _ _ _ _ _ _ _ _ diagnosis questionable.

9. The scales of the Millon Clinical Multiaxial Inventory (MCMI) are consistent with the classificatory system followed in the third edition of the _ _ _ _ _ _ _ _ _ _ _ _ _ _ and _ _ _ _ _ _ _ _ _ _ _ _ _ _ _ _ _ _ of _ _ _ _ _ _ _ _ _ _ _ _ _ _ _ _ _ _ (DSM-III).

10. Cattell's factor analytic investigations of the intercorrelations of personality trait ratings assigned to people by their associates led to what he has described as "the ＿＿＿＿＿＿＿＿ ＿＿＿＿＿＿＿ traits of personality" which may, in fact, reflect social stereotypes and judgment errors more than trait organization.

11. When an individual responds by expressing a preference for one item against another, the resulting score is ＿＿＿＿＿＿＿＿＿, which means that the frame of reference for its interpretation has to be the individual rather than the normative sample.

12. A. L. Edwards was the first to investigate the ＿＿＿＿＿＿＿ ＿＿＿＿＿＿＿＿＿＿＿＿ (SD) variable, which he conceptualized primarily as a tendency, of which the respondent is largely unaware, to "put up a good front."

13. The influence of ＿＿＿＿＿＿＿＿＿ ＿＿＿＿＿, such as acquiescence and deviation, in both ability and personality tests was observed by investigators well before massive research into their operation in personality inventories began in midcentury.

14. The ＿＿＿＿＿＿＿–＿＿＿＿＿＿ technique essentially requires the respondent to choose between two descriptive terms or phrases that appear equally acceptable but differ in validity.

15. The use of the forced-choice technique to control for SD requires two types of information about each response alternative, namely, its desirability or "＿＿＿＿＿＿＿＿＿＿＿ index" and its validity or "＿＿＿＿＿＿＿＿＿＿＿＿＿＿＿＿ index."

16. When response sets came to be regarded as indicators of broad and durable personality characteristics that were worth studying in their own right, they began to be commonly described as ＿＿＿＿＿＿＿＿＿ ＿＿＿＿＿＿.

17. The early view of ＿＿＿＿＿＿＿ as fixed, unchanging, underlying entities came under strong criticism in the 1960s, especially from social learning theorists who emphasized the ＿＿＿＿＿＿＿＿＿＿＿＿ ＿＿＿＿＿＿＿＿＿＿＿ of behavior.

ANSWERS TO FILL-IN-THE-BLANKS: (Key Terms and Concepts)

1. personality (tests)
2. content (validation)/empirical criterion (keying)/factor (analysis)/personality (theory)
3. content (validation)/empirical criterion keying
4. self-report (inventory)
5. "clinical (scales)"/"validity (scales)"
6. T scores

7. multidimensionality (and) overlap (of MMPI scales)

8. differential (diagnosis)

9. *Diagnostic (and) Statistical Manual of Mental Disorders* (DSM-III)

10. "(the) primary source (traits of personality)"

11. ipsative

12. social desirability (SD)

13. response sets

14. forced-choice (technique)

15. "preference (index)"/"discriminative (index)"

16. response styles

17. traits/situational specificity

MATCHING: Self-Report Inventories (One letter per number)

___ 1. Prototype of self-report personality inventories developed for use during World War I, in an attempt to standardize a psychiatric interview;

___ 2. Inventory that relies on content validation to identify self-perceived and self-reported sources of difficulty for group discussion or individual counseling;

___ 3. Outstanding example of criterion keying in personality test construction that is the most widely used personality inventory and has generated over 8,000 published references to date;

___ 4. Inventory which draws nearly half of its items from the MMPI but was developed specifically for use with normal adult populations;

___ 5. Instrument for differential diagnosis whose development was deliberately undertaken to meet the criticisms of the MMPI and to apply intervening advances in psychopathology and test construction;

___ 6. Instrument that resulted from a pioneering series of studies aimed at systematically classifying personality traits through factor analysis of intercorrelations among individual items from many personality inventories;

___ 7. The best known of the inventories developed by Cattell to assess his "primary source traits of personality;"

___ 8. Instrument designed to assess the strength of 15 of the needs proposed by Murray through a series of 210 pairs of statements within which test takers must choose one as more characteristic of themselves than the other;

___ 9. Instrument developed by Jackson which, while taking Murray's personality theory as its starting point, incorporates multiple strategies for personality test development and reflects many technical advances in test construction;

___ 10. Instrument developed by Spielberger to differentiate between a transitory emotional condition characterized by feelings of tension and apprehension and a relatively stable tendency to respond to situations as threatening;

      A. Millon Clinical Multiaxial Inventory (MCMI)

   B. Personality Research Form (PRF)

   C. Sixteen Personality Factor Questionnaire (16 PF)

   D. California Psychological Inventory (CPI)

   E. State-Trait Anxiety Inventory (STAI)

   F. Edwards Personal Preference Schedule (EPPS)

   G. Mooney Problem Check List

   H. Woodworth Personal Data Sheet

   I. Minnesota Multiphasic Personality Inventory (MMPI)

   J. Guilford-Zimmerman Temperament Survey

ANSWERS:

1 - H; 2 - G; 3 - I; 4 - D; 5 - A; 6 - J; 7 - C; 8 - F; 9 - B; 10 - E.

TRUE/FALSE and WHY?

1. The major approaches to the development of personality inventories, such as content validation and factor analysis, are mutually exclusive. (T/F) Why? _____
_____

2. The so-called validity scales of the MMPI are not concerned with validity in the technical sense. (T/F) Why? _____
_____

3. A T score of 70 or higher on the MMPI's Schizophrenia scale can be taken as an almost certain indication of the presence of schizophrenia. (T/F) Why? _____
_____

4. The various codebooks and computerized systems now available for interpreting MMPI profiles have freed the overworked clinician from having to participate in the interpretation of the results of that test. (T/F) Why? _____
_____

5. According to its author, the MCMI is *not* a general personality instrument to be used for "normal" populations. (T/F) Why? _____
_____

6. Homogeneity and factorial purity of personality inventory scales are desirable goals in test construction but cannot substitute for empirical validation. (T/F) Why? _____
_____

7. Empirical investigations of instruments such as the EPPS, the PRF, and the TAT indicate that the needs they assess, which were drawn from Murray's personality theory, are essentially equivalent across the various tests. (T/F) Why? _____

_____

8. There is a good deal of evidence that suggests that respondents can dissemble successfully on personality inventories, even to the point of simulating the characteristics that are desirable in specific occupations. (T/F) Why? _____

_____

9. Independent research with the EPPS indicates that the forced-choice technique successfully eliminates the influence of the SD variable and also prevents test takers from faking to create a desired impression for specific purposes. (T/F) Why? _____

_____

10. There is a growing consensus that people differ in the degree of behavioral specificity they display across situations and that situations also differ in the behavioral constraints they impose. (T/F) Why? _____

_____

ANSWERS TO TRUE/FALSE:

1. False	4. False	7. False	10. True
2. True	5. True	8. True	
3. False	6. True	9. False	

MULTIPLE CHOICE: TEST YOURSELF

1. The primary use for self-report inventories is as a tool in _____

_____ .

   a. career decision-making
   b. counseling and diagnosis
   c. self-evaluation of personality
   d. selection of employees

2. Which of the following is *not* one of the basic methods for formulating a self-report inventory? _____

_____ .

   a. Content validation
   b. Differential response analysis
   c. Factor analysis
   d. Empirical criterion keying

3. Which of the following instruments is based on content validation? _____

_____.

  a. Mooney Problem Check List
  b. Minnesota Multiphasic Personality Inventory (MMPI)
  c. Sixteen Personality Factor Questionnaire (16 PF)
  d. Guilford-Zimmerman Temperament Survey

4. The use of contrasting groups to develop a self-report inventory is a procedure followed in

_____.

  a. content validation
  b. factor analysis
  c. the forced-choice technique
  d. empirical criterion keying

5. The lie (L) score on the MMPI is based upon _____

_____.

  a. the consistency of a person's responses across similar items in the inventory
  b. the test taker's tendency to answer key questions in a favorable direction
  c. interscale consistency
  d. none of the above

6. Which of the following is a fundamental technical weakness of the MMPI? _____

_____.

  a. High intercorrelations among the scales
  b. Low split-half reliabilities
  c. Limited size of the normative sample
  d. All of the above are problems

7. As contrasted with the MMPI, the California Psychological Inventory (CPI) _____

_____.

  a. has more items and fewer scales
  b. is more suited for use with normal populations
  c. does not have a validity scale
  d. is specifically designed for children

8. A distinguishing feature of the Personality Inventory for Children (PIC) is _____

_____.

  a. that it is an inventory of observed behavior
  b. that the responses are all given orally
  c. its built-in diagnostic scale
  d. that it has no validity scales

9. Cattell's 16 PF is based upon _____.

  a. factorial research
  b. content validation
  c. multiple regression formulas
  d. empirical criterion keying

10. When using the EPPS, one must be cautious about comparing the scores of two individuals because _____

_____.

    a. the EPPS has very low reliability
    b. the scores are based on percentile ranks
    c. the scores are ipsative
    d. the meaning of the EPPS scales is not very clear

11. The forced-choice technique is used to _____

_____.

    a. increase reliability
    b. reduce faking
    c. counteract the ipsative nature of the items
    d. increase test validity

12. Self-report inventories are especially susceptible to _____

_____.

    a. faking
    b. low scorer reliability
    c. ipsative scoring
    d. criterion contamination

13. Persons who are more likely to answer "True" or "Yes" than "False" or "No" demonstrate a response bias known as _____.

    a. deviation
    b. acquiescence
    c. social desirability
    d. none of the above

14. People often behave quite differently in different settings or situations. Psychologists term this _____.

    a. unreliability
    b. state specificity
    c. situational specificity
    d. trait analysis

15. The current state of self-report inventories can best be described as _____

_____.

    a. neutral, with neither growth nor loss of status
    b. moving into a period of slower growth
    c. grim, since empirical analysis shows the poor validity of these tests
    d. good, with a strong possibility of additional growth and technical improvement

MINIPROJECTS/SUGGESTED OUTREACH ACTIVITIES:

1. The area of personality testing, covered in the last part of the textbook which begins with Chapter 17, is inextricably tied to the field of personality theory, a large subspecialty within psychology. If you have already had a course in Theories of Personality, you will find the

material in this and subsequent chapters easier to grasp because you will be able to place it within that context. If you have not had such a course, you may wish to review a textbook in the area, with special reference to theories, like Murray's need system, which have served as a framework for the development of personality assessment instruments. Two of the best-known textbooks in the area of personality theory are *Theories of Personality* (3rd ed.) by C.S. Hall and G. Lindzey (New York: Wiley, 1978) and *Personality Theories: A Comparative Analysis* (5th ed.) by Salvatore Maddi (Belmont, CA: Wadsworth, 1988).

2. If you are intrigued by the MMPI, and would like a relatively brief but comprehensive introduction to that test, John Graham's book *The MMPI: A Practical Guide* (2nd. ed.), published by Oxford University Press (1987), is probably the best place to start. For a more thorough approach, the two-volume work *An MMPI Handbook* by W.G. Dahlstrom, G.S. Welsh, and L.E. Dahlstrom (University of Minnesota Press, 1972, 1975) is unsurpassed in its depth of coverage of Clinical Interpretation (Volume I) and Research Applications (Volume II) of the MMPI.

3. Over the many years that the MMPI has been in heavy use by both clinicians and academicians, several humorous versions of that instrument have been circulated. The amusement these MMPI parodies provide stems mainly from the fact that many of the real MMPI items are rather awkward in either their wording or content and, therefore, easy to caricature. However, in order to be able to appreciate the humor in the parodies, you first need to familiarize yourself with the original. After you have had a chance to take the MMPI or read through all of its items, you would probably enjoy two very short satirical "revisions" of it that appear in the book entitled *Oral Sadism and the Vegetarian Personality,* edited by G.C. Ellenbogen (New York: Brunner/Mazel, 1986). In spite of its unseemly title, that book contains a number of genuinely funny pieces that take a lighthearted view of various psychological topics, including several related to testing and assessment.

4. Figure 17-2, on p. 544 of the textbook, shows a set of raw scores on each of the 15 needs assessed by the EPPS, and their corresponding percentile scores. Each raw score represents the number of times that the respondent chose a statement of a given need over a statement of another with which it was paired. Raw scores can range from zero to 28. To understand the difference between ipsative and normative scores more clearly, use Figure 17-2 as follows: a) rank each of the 15 needs according to its percentile score; b) rank each need according to its raw score; c) compare the positions of each need on each set of ranks and note the changes that occur (e.g., heterosexuality); d) compare the percentile scores for needs with identical raw scores and note discrepancies (e.g., order vs. exhibition). If you can get a copy of the EPPS, take it yourself. Then, read the manual, score the test, and analyze your own scores as suggested here.

ANSWERS TO MULTIPLE CHOICE/TEST YOURSELF ITEMS:

1. b	4. d	7. b	10. c	13. b
2. b	5. b	8. a	11. b	14. c
3. a	6. d	9. a	12. a	15. d

Chapter 18
MEASURING INTERESTS, VALUES, AND ATTITUDES

CHAPTER OUTLINE

CHAPTER SUMMARY

The present chapter surveys a variety of self-report inventories that evaluate important aspects of personality, such as interests, values, and attitudes, but cannot be rigidly categorized because of their overlap with each other. The assessment of interests received its strongest impetus from educational and career counseling and is carried out primarily in that context. The assessment of opinions and attitudes, on the other hand, originated in social psychological research and is used in that field as well as in applied areas that require the gauging and prediction of public opinion. Other types of self-report inventories discussed in Chapter 18 deal with broad personal orientations and are used mainly in research on different facets of personality.

In the area of career counseling, the use of interest inventories, which are tests designed to assess the individual's interest in different fields of work and/or study, has increased relative to that of ability tests since midcentury. During that time, career counseling itself has undergone major changes which involve an increasing emphasis on self-exploration and on expanding the career options open to all individuals, and especially to women.

The Strong-Campbell Interest Inventory form of the Strong Vocational Interest Blank (SVIB-SCII) is the current version of one of the most widely used interest inventories which was first published in 1927. The Strong inventory introduced empirical criterion keying of items, to which test takers respond primarily by expressing their liking or dislike; the items are scored according to the responses of people in different occupations. The Strong has undergone extensive revisions over the years, including the introduction of a theoretical framework to guide score organization and interpretation, the merging of men's and women's forms and renorming of all occupational scales on both sexes, and a substantial increase in the number of scales for occupations that require less than a college degree for entry. In addition, extensive data have been accumulated about the Strong's reliability and validity through a continuing research program. These data suggest a good deal of stability for occupational scales and occupational group profiles over periods of two to three decades. Concurrent and predictive validity as well as construct validation data for the Strong have also been found quite satisfactory.

Four additional interest inventories, each one illustrating some noteworthy feature, are discussed in the textbook. The Jackson Vocational Interest Survey (JVIS), which contrasts sharply with the SVIB-SCII in its approach, exemplifies sophisticated test construction procedures. Its development started with a definition of the constructs to be measured, i.e., work roles and work styles, and proceeded with exhaustive statistical analyses, including the establishment of an empirical linkage with the occupational data base of the Strong inventory. The Kuder Occupational Interest Survey (KOIS), the Career Assessment Inventory (CAI), and the Self-Directed Search (SDS) are the three additional interest inventories chosen for discussion in the textbook. The major trends apparent in these and other current inventories include the increasing use of Holland's model of general occupational themes as a theoretical basis, the provision of scores on both broad interest scales and specific occupational scales, and the cross-utilization of empirical data banks for interpretive purposes. In addition, the occupational levels that inventories cover are being expanded into the vocational/technical arena and there is a growing recognition that inventories can be viewed as intervention techniques, which will probably lead to greater use of individualized methods in their development, administration, and interpretation.

Instruments designed for the assessment of values and evaluative orientations, which have undergone a resurgence since the 1960s, vary widely in methodology, content, and specific objectives. The Study of Values, by Allport, Vernon, and Lindzey, is an example of a fairly wide-ranging inventory meant to measure the relative strength of six fundamental interests, motives, or evaluative attitudes suggested by Spranger's theory. The Work Values Inventory, developed by Super after some 20 years of research, is a more focused inventory of values specifically designed to explore the sources of satisfaction that individuals seek in their work. Kohlberg's cognitive model of moral development, which postulates six stages of development arranged in a purportedly invariant sequence, has stimulated a great deal of interest in the assessment of moral development. Kohlberg's own Moral Judgment Scale and The Defining Issues Test are two instruments described in the text that have used Kohlberg's theoretical orientation in the evaluation of a person's level of understanding of abstract moral principles.

Attitudes, which are commonly defined as tendencies to react favorably or unfavorably to certain classes of stimuli, cannot be differentiated from opinions in a consistent or defensible fashion. However, in terms of assessment methodology, opinion surveys have traditionally been distinguished from attitude scales. The former are usually concerned with isolated answers to specific questions that are tabulated and analyzed separately, whereas the latter typically yield a total score based on the individual's agreement or disagreement with a series of statements about a given stimulus category. The three major approaches to attitude scale construction commonly encountered in the psychological testing literature are the Thurstone, Guttman, and Likert types of scales. Of these, the Likert-type scales are used more frequently because they are easier to construct than the other two types and yet they yield comparable reliabilities.

The construct of "locus of control," as described by Rotter, has served as the basis for a great deal of research and has led to the development of several scales aimed at assessing it, of which the best known is Rotter's own I-E scale. That instrument, which examines the individual's generalized expectancies for internal versus external control of reinforcement, and other locus of control scales, illustrate a very productive use of psychometric tools in the conduct of investigations on central aspects of personality.

Another illustration of a psychological concept that has been widely used in research and has served as the basis for the development of many self-report inventories is masculinity-femininity (M-F). However, masculinity and femininity have not proven to be effective constructs for categorizing human personality and their conceptualization has changed drastically over the past few decades. One of the changes can be seen in the evolution and popularity of the concept of androgyny, which, in turn, has brought about significant changes in the types of instruments that assess sex-based constructs. Still more recently, there seems to be some movement toward a decreased emphasis on either M-F *or* androgyny both as global traits and in personality measurement.

COMPREHENSIVE REVIEW

STUDY QUESTIONS:

1. Discuss the major changes that have occurred in the area of career counseling and explain how those changes have affected interest inventories.

2. Describe the history and evolution of the Strong interest inventory, including the characteristics that distinguish it from other inventories.

3. Describe the information that can be obtained from the current Strong-Campbell Interest Inventory (SVIB-SCII) and discuss the psychometric features of that instrument.

4. Contrast and compare the SVIB-SCII with the Jackson Vocational Interest Survey (JVIS).

5. Discuss the history of the Kuder interest inventories and compare the current Kuder Occupational Interest Survey (KOIS) with the SVIB-SCII.

6. Describe the Career Assessment Inventory (CAI) in terms of its similarities to, and differences from, other interest inventories.

7. Discuss Holland's general approach to the assessment of vocational interests and how the Self-Directed Search (SDS) fits into that approach.

8. List and describe the significant trends that become apparent from an overview of the current major interest inventories.

9. Describe and compare the Study of Values and the Work Values Inventory.

10. Discuss Kohlberg's theory of moral development and describe one example of the instruments associated with that theory.

11. Compare and contrast opinion surveys with attitude scales.

12. Describe the three major approaches to attitude scale construction discussed in the textbook.

13. Discuss the construct of locus of control and describe how it is assessed.

14. Describe the history and current status of masculinity-femininity (M-F) scales.

FILL IN THE BLANKS: Key Terms, Concepts, and Names

1. The development of __ __ __ __ __ __ __ __ __ __ __ __ __ __ __ __ __ __ __ __ __, which often compare an individual's expressed preferences with those typical of people in various occupations, received its strongest impetus from educational and career counseling.

2. The theoretical model used in most of the current interest inventories discussed in the text is __ __ __ __ __ __ __ __'__ __ __ __ __ __ __ __ __ __ __ model of general occupational themes.

3. The results of many current interest inventories, e.g., the SVIB-SCII and the SDS, are linked with the occupations listed in the __ __ __ __ __ __ __ __ __ __ of __ __ __ __ __ __ __ __ __ __ __ __ __ __ __ __ __ __ __ __ (DOT) and other materials developed by the U.S. Employment Service.

4. The major dimensions or constructs that the JVIS set out to assess were defined in terms of __ __ __ __ __ __ __ __ __, which pertain to what a person does on the job, and __ __ __ __ __ __ __ __ __ __, which refer to the specific kinds of behavior expected in different working environments.

5. When interest inventories serve to support and strengthen existing vocational aspirations or to provide increased self-understanding, they move beyond the realm of assessment and can be viewed as __ __ __ __ __ __ __ __ __ __ __ __ __ techniques.

6. Following a Piagetian orientation, __ __ __ __ __ __ __ __ __ described six stages of __ __ __ __ __ __ __ __ __ __ __ __ __ __ __, ranging from the premoral level to the formulation of self-accepted principles derived by individual reasoning.

7. A(n) __ __ __ __ __ __ __ __ is defined as a tendency to react favorably or unfavorably toward a designated class of stimuli, such as an ethnic group, a custom, or an institution; the key connotation of that concept is one of response __ __ __ __ __ __ __ __ __ __ __ toward certain categories of stimuli.

8. Whereas __ __ __ __ __ __ __ surveys are typically concerned with answers to specific questions that need not be related, __ __ __ __ __ __ __ __ scales usually yield a total score that indicates the direction and intensity of the individual's response to a stimulus category.

9. The development of a(n) __ __ __ __ __ __ __ __ __ __–type scale involves the gathering of statements that express a wide range of attitudes toward an object and the assignment of values to those statements according to how judges classify them.

10. The development of __ __ __ __ __ __ __–type scales, which were originally meant to assess whether a set of attitude statements is unidimensional, involves the identification of a set of items that fall into an ordered sequence in terms of their endorsement by respondents.

11. __ __ __ __ __ __–type scales call for graded responses, usually expressed in terms of five categories ranging from "strongly agree" to "strongly disagree," to each statement in the scale.

12. Rotter's construct of __ __ __ __ __ __ of __ __ __ __ __ __ __ __ refers to whether individuals perceive a causal relationship between their own behavior and a consequent event or whether reinforcement following some action is perceived as being the result of chance, fate, or other external forces.

13. Locus of control can be viewed as one dimension of the broader concept of __ __ __ __ __ __ __ __ __ __ __ __ __ __ __ __ __ __, which also involves the perceived stability and controllability of various conditions that affect the individual.

14. The pioneering instrument for measuring __ __ __ __ __ __ __ __ __ __ __ __– __ __ __ __ __ __ __ __ __ (M-F) was developed by Terman and Miles and involved the selection of items on the basis of the relative frequency of responses given by males and females in the American culture of the time.

15. As currently used in personality research, the term __ __ __ __ __ __ __ __ __ __ characterizes the individual who shows the favorable traits stereotypically associated with both sexes, such as a combination of assertiveness and competence with warmth and compassion.

ANSWERS TO FILL-IN-THE-BLANKS: (Key Terms, Concepts and Names)

1. interest inventories
2. Holland's hexagonal (model of general occupational themes)
3. *Dictionary (of) Occupational Titles* (DOT)
4. work roles/work styles
5. intervention (techniques)

6. Kohlberg/(stages of) moral development

7. attitude/(response) consistency

8. opinion (surveys)/attitude (scales)

9. Thurstone(-type scale)

10. Guttman(-type scales)

11. Likert(-type scales)

12. locus (of) control

13. causal attribution

14. masculinity-femininity (M-F)

15. androgyny

MATCHING: Measures of Interests, Values, and Attitudes (One letter per number)

___ 1. Current version of the pioneering instrument for the assessment of occupational interests, which provides scores on six General Occupational Themes, 23 Basic Interest Scales, 207 Occupational Scales, as well as a set of Administrative Indexes and two Special Scales;

___ 2. Instrument which exemplifies construct validation and a generally sophisticated approach to test construction, at every stage of its development and is one of the newest interest inventories;

___ 3. Current version of one of the oldest interest inventory series, which now provides occupational scale scores expressed in terms of correlations between the test taker's interest pattern and the interest patterns of 126 occupational groups;

___ 4. Recently released inventory that is patterned on the SVIB-SCII but was designed specifically for persons seeking a career that does not require a four-year college degree or advanced professional training;

___ 5. Instrument developed by Holland, which is self-administered, self-scored, and self-interpreted and, though organized around interests, also calls for self-ratings of abilities and reported competencies;

___ 6. Instrument whose latest edition was prepared by Allport, Vernon, and Lindzey and which was originally suggested by Spranger's treatise on *Types of Men;*

___ 7. Inventory that explores the sources of satisfaction that the individual seeks in his or her occupation and was developed by Super for use in academic and career counseling;

___ 8. Instrument that combines Kohlberg's theoretical orientation with sound test construction procedures to generate scores that indicate the person's degree of sophistication in understanding and applying abstract moral principles;

___ 9. Instrument developed by Rotter to assess the individual's generalized expectancies regarding the locus of control of reinforcements;

___10. Instrument developed by Spence and Helmreich, which is one of the principal examples of the third generation of M-F measures;

A. Career Assessment Inventory (CAI)

  B. Self-Directed Search (SDS)

  C. Work Values Inventory

  D. Personal Attributes Questionnaire

  E. The Defining Issues Test

  F. Strong-Campbell Interest Inventory form of the Strong Vocational Interest Blank (SVIB-SCII)

  G. Jackson Vocational Interest Survey (JVIS)

  H. I-E Scale

  I. Kuder Occupational Interest Survey (KOIS)

  J. Study of Values

ANSWERS:

  1 - F; 2 - G; 3 - I; 4 - A; 5 - B; 6 - J; 7 - C; 8 - E; 9 - H; 10 - D.

TRUE/FALSE and WHY?

1. In counseling, the use of interest tests, relative to that of ability tests, has decreased since midcentury. (T/F) Why? _____

_____

2. The fact that interest inventories often compare an individual's expressed interests with those typical of persons in different occupations tends to perpetuate existing group differences. (T/F) Why? _____

_____

3. In Holland's model of occupational themes, each theme characterizes not only a type of person, but also the type of working environment that a person finds most congenial. (T/F) Why? _____

_____

4. The occupational criterion groups used in developing the latest Strong Occupational Scales were made up of persons selected solely on the basis of age and current occupation. (T/F) Why? _____

_____

5. The interrelations among the General Occupational Themes found in the general reference samples of the SVIB-SCII are of special relevance to construct validation. (T/F) Why? _____

_____

6. Super's contention that vocational choice is the implementation of a self-concept has found very little, if any, empirical substantiation. (T/F) Why? _____

_____

7. Kohlberg's argument that stages of moral development unfold in an invariant sequence has consistently been justified by research data. (T/F) Why? _____

_____

8. One of the most extensive applications of attitude measurement is found in research in social psychology. (T/F) Why? _____

_____

9. Various factor analytic studies of Rotter's I-E Scale have found that the construct assessed by that scale may be subdivided into several distinct factors. (T/F) Why? _____

_____

10. The constructs of masculinity and femininity have proven to be quite effective for categorizing human personality and as a basis for test development. (T/F) Why? _____

_____

ANSWERS TO TRUE/FALSE:

1. False	4. False	7. False	10. False
2. True	5. True	8. True	
3. True	6. False	9. True	

MULTIPLE CHOICE: TEST YOURSELF

1. The use of interest inventories is of greatest value in _____

_____.

   a. industrial employment offices
   b. psychological research
   c. individual guidance and counseling
   d. the selection of applicants for a specific job

2. A high score on an Occupational Scale of the SVIB-SCII means that _____

_____.

   a. the individual would be successful in that occupation
   b. the individual is talented in that field of endeavor
   c. the individual shares common interests with people already in that occupation
   d. none of the above

3. The scoring for the SVIB-SCII Occupational Scales was developed by means of _____

   _____ .

   a. criterion keying
   b. content validation
   c. factor analysis
   d. regression equations

4. Studies of the long-term stability of the Strong Occupational Scales, over periods of as long

   as 20 years, yield correlations that fall mostly in the _____ .

   a. .80s and .90s
   b. .60s and .70s
   c. .40s and .50s
   d. .20s and .30s

5. In contrast with the SVIB-SCII, the JVIS _____

   _____ .

   a. focuses on broader interest areas
   b. is more anchored in construct validation
   c. utilizes the forced-choice format
   d. all of the above

6. The Kuder interest inventories have historically provided a set of scores which _____

   _____ .

   a. cover 10 broad interest areas
   b. rely on empirical criterion keying
   c. cover 207 occupational areas
   d. are based on true/false items

7. The Career Assessment Inventory _____

   _____ .

   a. has been in use almost as long as the Strong inventories
   b. concentrates on technical and semiprofessional occupations
   c. requires a higher level of reading skills than most other inventories
   d. is one of the few interest inventories that does not use Holland's general themes

8. Unlike most other interest scales, the SDS is _____

   _____ .

   a. self-administered
   b. self-scored
   c. self-interpreted
   d. all of the above

9. Which of the following is *not* a significant trend among current interest inventories? _____

   _____.

   a. The merging of major theoretical approaches
   b. The cross-utilization of empirical data banks
   c. A reduction in the number and range of occupations covered
   d. A recognition of such inventories as intervention techniques

10. Which of the following is *not* one of the names associated with the three major approaches

    to attitude scale construction? _____.

    a. Thurstone
    b. Guttman
    c. Likert
    d. Lindzey

11. The scale values for a Thurstone-type scale are determined by _____

    _____.

    a. experts in attitude measurement
    b. a panel of judges
    c. statistical analysis from a sample administration
    d. none of the above

12. The simplest scale to construct, and the most often used, is the _____

    _____.

    a. Thurstone-type scale
    b. Guttman-type scale
    c. Likert-type scale
    d. all of the above are equally difficult to construct

13. Which of the following is an example of a Likert-type scale? _____

    _____.

    a. Moral Judgment Scale
    b. Strong-Campbell Interest Inventory
    c. Jackson Vocational Interest Survey
    d. Minnesota School Attitude Survey

14. The Rotter I-E Scale assesses one's expectancies about _____

    _____.

    a. the attitudes of others towards one's own behavior
    b. the locus of control of reinforcement
    c. success in one's chosen occupation
    d. the typical response style of other people

15. As opposed to first- and second-generation M-F scales, third-generation M-F instruments

_____

_____ .

    a. encompass the concept of androgyny
    b. treat M-F as opposite poles of a single bipolar scale
    c. use criterion keying for selecting and scoring items
    d. provide a single global score

MINIPROJECTS/SUGGESTED OUTREACH ACTIVITIES:

1. A review of the *Manual for the SVIB-SCII* or the *User's Guide for the SVIB-SCII* was already suggested in Miniproject # 3 for Chapter 6. If you have not had a chance to take the SVIB-SCII or to review that instrument, this would be a good time to do so. The Strong is an interesting inventory to take, as it requires one to consider and express one's preferences about a wide range of occupations, activities, and pursuits. It is also an excellent instrument to review from a psychometric standpoint because it incorporates so many of the concepts that are central to testing and because its psychometric properties have been investigated continuously and exhaustively. In addition, if you are able to take the inventory yourself, the profile you would receive with the results would provide you with an opportunity to interpret a great number of scores and, in conjunction with the *User's Guide,* would probably be helpful in crystallizing and/or reaffirming your vocational goals.

2. Whether or not you are able to take the Strong inventory, it would also be desirable to take and review either the Self-Directed Search or the Study of Values. If you have the results of the SVIB-SCII, the SDS or the Study of Values would provide you with a good opportunity to make comparisons across instruments that purportedly assess similar constructs. But, even if you have not taken the Strong, you are likely to find a first-hand acquaintance with the SDS or the values study both interesting and productive.

3. In order to investigate the principal conceptual basis that underlies the Strong inventories, conduct structured interviews with samples of students in each of four very different fields of study. The purpose of the interview would be to ascertain their preferences in terms of leisure activities, academic interests, and any other pursuits that you think might differentiate among the groups (e.g., musical tastes, political philosophies, etc.). If you conduct your interviews in a standardized fashion, you would be able to quantify the results, assess the group differences and similarities that you find, and provide feedback to the participants. You might even have a pilot version of a new interest inventory!

4. As you probably have surmised already, the field of attitude measurement is a vast and diverse one. One way to ascertain that diversity quite directly would be to locate and review the second edition of Robinson and Shaver's compendium of *Measures of Social Psychological Attitudes* (Ann Arbor: University of Michigan, Institute for Social Research, 1973). A first-hand look at the instruments contained in that book, which include measures of constructs such as Machiavellianism, helplessness, and self-esteem, is almost guaranteed to stimulate your investigative propensities.

5. The evolution of masculinity and femininity as psychological constructs, and of the measures designed to assess them, is one of the most lively topics discussed in Chapter 18. If you are interested in pursuing that topic, Anne Constantinople's review entitled "Masculinity-Femininity: An Exception to a Famous Dictum?" (*Psychological Review,* 1973,

80, 389-407) is one of the best places to start. For information about subsequent work in that area, including the current conceptualization of androgyny, see one of the reviews cited by Anastasi in page 592 of the textbook (e.g., Bem, 1985, or Spence, 1985).

ANSWERS TO MULTIPLE CHOICE/TEST YOURSELF ITEMS:

1. c	4. b	7. b	10. d	13. d
2. c	5. d	8. d	11. b	14. b
3. a	6. a	9. c	12. c	15. a

Chapter 19
PROJECTIVE TECHNIQUES

CHAPTER OUTLINE

Nature of Projective Techniques

Inkblot Techniques
    The Rorschach
    The Holtzman Inkblot Technique

Thematic Apperception Test and Related Instruments
    Thematic Apperception Test
    Adaptations of the TAT and Related Tests

Other Projective Techniques
    Verbal Techniques
    Pictorial Techniques
    Expressive Techniques

Evaluation of Projective Techniques
    Rapport and Applicability
    Faking
    Examiner and Situational Variables
    Norms
    Reliability
    Validity
    The Projective Hypothesis
    Projective Techniques as Psychometric Instruments
    Projective Techniques as Clinical Tools

CHAPTER SUMMARY

Projective techniques are instruments characterized by the assignment of a relatively unstructured task to test takers, who are often unaware of the type of interpretations that will be made of their responses. These instruments typically represent a global approach to the assessment of personality and are regarded as especially effective in revealing its unconscious or covert aspects. Projective methods originated in the clinical setting, often reflecting the influence of psychoanalytic concepts, and have remained a predominantly clinical tool.

The Rorschach inkblot series, one of the most popular projective techniques, was developed by a Swiss psychiatrist in the early part of this century, on the basis of clinical observations of the differential responses of patients with various psychiatric syndromes. The technique that Rorschach developed involves the sequential presentation of 10 stimulus cards on each of which is printed a bilaterally symmetrical inkblot. The respondent is first asked to tell what each blot could represent and later, during the inquiry phase of the administration, is questioned about the location and other aspects of the associations given for each blot. Several systems for scoring the Rorschach have been developed over the years, most of which include the location, determinants, and content of responses among their main scoring categories. However, individual variability in response productivity (R) on the Rorschach, and the fact that the variability in R may be related to extraneous factors, greatly complicate the study and interpretation of Rorschach scores. In spite of this and other methodological problems, the Rorschach remains very popular in clinical circles. In recent years there have been several efforts to improve the psychometric soundness of the Rorschach, of which the most ambitious is the one undertaken by Exner. In addition, the Holtzman Inkblot Technique (HIT), which is an entirely new instrument modeled after the Rorschach but designed to eliminate its principal technical deficiencies, has been devised as an alternative. Although more data are needed to establish the diagnostic significance and validity of HIT scores, available results on that technique are promising.

The Thematic Apperception Test (TAT) developed by Murray and his associates at the Harvard Psychological Clinic is another well-known projective instrument. In contrast to the inkblot techniques, the TAT uses more highly structured stimuli and requires more complex and meaningfully organized verbal responses. The TAT, which consists of stories made up by the respondent upon presentation of cards containing vague pictures, is usually interpreted on the basis of qualitative content analysis. The analysis of TAT stories is usually done in reference to Murray's list of "needs," such as achievement and affiliation, and "press," which refers to environmental forces that facilitate or interfere with the satisfaction of needs. Although a number of quantitative scoring schemes, and a fair amount of normative information, have been published for use with the TAT, in clinical practice such procedures are seldom used. Many adaptations of the TAT, of varying quality and degrees of resemblance to the original, have also been developed for special purposes. The Children's Apperception Test (CAT), for example, uses cards that substitute animals for people in an effort to stimulate projection in young test takers, but has apparently not been very successful in that regard. There are also some versions, such as the Senior Apperception Technique, that have been developed especially for the aged and feature elderly persons in the stimulus cards.

Some projective techniques, such as word association and sentence completion tests, are wholly verbal in that they use only words in both stimulus materials and responses. Others employ pictorial material in ways that differ from those of the inkblot and TAT techniques. The Rosenzweig Picture-Frustration Study (P-F Study), for example, presents a series of cartoons in which frustrating circumstances are portrayed and requires the respondent to write what the frustrated person would reply under such circumstances. Still another category of projective devices, and one that is rather large and amorphous, is comprised of techniques that call for relatively free self-expression. All of these techniques, which include activities such as drawing and the dramatic use of toys, have been employed as therapeutic as well as diagnostic procedures. A well-known example of these expressive projective techniques is the Machover Draw-a-Person Test (D-A-P), which, because of its highly questionable validity, can probably serve best as part of a clinical interview rather than as a psychometric instrument.

Projective techniques differ widely among themselves, both in their theoretical soundness and in the amount and quality of data available on which to evaluate and interpret them. Nevertheless, certain general observations can be made about most instruments in that category. On the positive side, projective techniques, which are usually intrinsically interesting and nonthreatening, may be quite effective in building rapport and also in testing persons who are verbally limited. Similarly, although it cannot be assumed that projective tests are completely immune to faking, they are less susceptible to it than self-report inventories. On the other hand, most projective techniques are inadequately standardized with respect to both administration and scoring and many of them lack adequate normative data. These and other features typical of projective devices, such as the small number and wide diversity of responses, also make it extremely difficult to gather appropriate data on their reliability. In addition, the large majority of published validation studies on projective techniques are inconclusive due to procedural deficiencies in either experimental controls or statistical analyses, or both. With respect to ascertaining the validity of projective instruments, it should be noted that the methodological problems inherent in their study can sometimes produce spurious evidence of validity, where none exists, and at other times can result in underestimating their validity. The few well-designed validation studies of projective tests that have been done suggest that their validity is largely a function of the experience of the clinicians who use and interpret them and that validity may also vary with different respondents and/or across different techniques.

The fundamental assumptions on which the projective hypothesis is based, namely, that the individual's responses to the ambiguous stimuli presented to her or him reflect significant, often covert, and relatively enduring personality attributes, have not been supported by research. Indeed, there is ample evidence that other explanations may account as well or better for the individual's responses to unstructured test stimuli. Furthermore, there is a truly impressive accumulation of studies that have *failed* to demonstrate any validity for some projective techniques, such as the traditional Rorschach and the D-A-P. In spite of these circumstances, the status of projective techniques remains substantially unchanged, with enthusiastic support for them from clinicians and doubts about them from statisticians.

The seeming contradiction between the largely negative results accumulated over five decades of research with projective techniques and their continued use can be understood if it is recognized that, with a few exceptions, these techniques are not truly tests. Rather, projective devices are coming to be regarded as supplementary qualitative interviewing aids whose value is proportional to the skill of the clinician and whose proper input consists of the suggestion of leads for further exploration.

COMPREHENSIVE REVIEW

STUDY QUESTIONS:

1. List and discuss the major features that distinguish projective techniques from other personality assessment tools.

2. Describe the procedures used to administer and score the Rorschach inkblots.

3. Discuss the methodological problems involved in the use and interpretation of the Rorschach.

4. Describe the efforts that Exner and his associates have made to put the Rorschach on a psychometrically sound basis.

5. Compare and contrast the Holtzman Inkblot Technique (HIT) with the Rorschach.

6. Describe the main features of the Thematic Apperception Test (TAT), including its administration, scoring, and interpretation.

7. Describe the major adaptations of the TAT that have been developed for special populations.

8. Describe the history and present status of word association tests.

9. Discuss sentence completion techniques and describe one example of this type of projective device.

10. Describe the purpose and procedures of the Rosenzweig Picture-Frustration Study (P-F Study).

11. Discuss the major types of expressive techniques used in projective assessment and explain why they might best serve as part of a clinical interview.

12. List and discuss the major advantages of projective techniques as assessment devices.

13. List and discuss the major disadvantages of projective techniques as assessment devices.

14. Discuss how the unique characteristics of projective techniques may lead to overestimating or underestimating their validity.

15. Discuss the current status of the projective hypothesis and of projective techniques.

FILL IN THE BLANKS: Key Terms, Concepts, and Names

1. _ _ _ _ _ _ _ _ _ _   _ _ _ _ _ _ _ _ _ _ _ consist of relatively unstructured tasks whose often disguised purpose is to assess personality, especially its unconscious aspects, in a global fashion.

2. The major varieties of projective instruments discussed in the text are _ _ _ _ _ _ _ _ techniques, such as the Rorschach, _ _ _ _ _ _ _ techniques, such as word association tests, _ _ _ _ _ _ _ _ _ _ techniques, such as the P-F Study, _ _ _ _ _ _ _ _ _ _ _ techniques, such as the D-A-P, and the _ _ _ _ _ _ _ _   _ _ _ _ _ _ _ _ _ _ _ Test (TAT) and related instruments.

3. _ _ _ _ _ _ _ _ _ developed the scoring system that he applied to the innovative diagnostic tool he first described in 1921 on the basis of his clinical observations of the responses typical of various psychiatric groups.

4. The most common scoring categories for the Rorschach include _ _ _ _ _ _ _ _ _, which refers to the part of the blot with which each response is associated, _ _ _ _ _ _ _ _ _ _ _ _ _, such as color and form, and _ _ _ _ _ _ _, which typically includes categories such as human and animal figures. In addition, a _ _ _ _ _ _ _ _ _ score is often found on the basis of the relative frequency of different responses among people in general.

5. A variable that greatly complicates the interpretation of Rorschach scores is the total number of responses, known as _, or R.

6. The most ambitious effort to put the Rorschach on a psychometrically sound basis was undertaken by _ _ _ _ _ _, who developed a _ _ _ _ _ _ _ _ _ _ _ _ _ _ system for administering, scoring, and interpreting that test and proceeded to collect a considerable body of psychometric data on many of its variables.

7. The _ _ _ _ _ _ _ _ _ Rorschach is a special clinical adaptation wherein the inkblots are presented for joint interpretation by married couples and other natural groups.

8. The _ (HIT), which is modeled after the Rorschach, represents a genuine attempt to achieve acceptable psychometric standards and eliminate the main deficiencies of the earlier instrument.

9. TAT stories are typically interpreted by first determining who is the "_ _ _ _ _," or character with whom the respondent has identified, and then analyzing the content of the stories in terms of Murray's list of "_ _ _ _ _ _" and "_ _ _ _ _ _"; the latter refers to the environmental forces that facilitate or interfere with the satisfaction of needs.

10. One of the most extensive research programs utilizing a TAT adaptation is the one conducted by McClelland and his coworkers on the _ _ _ _ _ _ _ _ _ _ _ _ _ _ _ _ (n-Ach).

11. The _ for _ _ _ _ _ _ _ _ _ (RATC) is a recently developed adaptation of the TAT that uses stimulus cards depicting familiar interpersonal situations involving children and represents a serious effort to combine the projective method with good psychometric practices.

12. A verbal technique that antedated the flood of projective tests by more than 50 years is the _ _ _ _ _ _ _ _ _ _ _ _ _ _ _ _ _ test, which was used by early experimental psychologists, such as Wundt and Cattell, and was systematized as a clinical tool by Jung.

13. The _ _ _ _ _-_ _ _ _ _ _ _ _ _ _ Free Association Test, which was designed as a psychiatric screening instrument, used a list of 100 stimulus words and was scored on the basis of the "commonality" of responses given by the examinee.

14. Fill-in-the-blanks items, such as the ones in this segment of your review, are similar in format to a verbal projective technique known as _ _ _ _ _ _ _ _ _ _ _ _ _ _ _ _ _ _ _ tests, although the latter are designed for a different purpose and permit an almost unlimited variety of possible responses.

15. The most prominent proponent of the construct of locus of control, discussed in Chapter 18, is also the author of one of the most widely used sentence completion tests, namely, the _ _ _ _ _ _ Incomplete Sentences Blank.

16. The _ _ _ _ _ _ _ _ _ _ _ _ _ _ _ _ _ _-_ _ _ _ _ _ _ _ _ _ _ _ _ Study (P-F Study) is an ingenious application of pictorial material to projective assessment that consists of a series of cartoons wherein the respondent must project what the frustrated person who is depicted would reply in a given situation.

17. _ _ _ _ _ _ _ _ _ _ _ techniques are a large and amorphous category of projective devices that utilize almost every art medium and type of subject matter and can be used for therapy as well as for diagnosis. The techniques most frequently used in this category are _ _ _ _ _ _ _ _ and dramatic use of _ _ _ _ _.

18. A well-known example of the use of human figure drawings in projective assessment is the _ _ _ _ _ _ _ _ _ _ _ _ _ _-_ _-_ _ _ _ _ _ _ Test (D-A-P), which is interpreted by qualitatively analyzing features of the drawings and preparing a composite personality description based on that analysis.

19. The most common reasons why studies of projective techniques may produce spurious evidence of validity are: a) the _ _ _ _ _ _ _ _ _ _ _ _ _ _ _ of criterion or test data with knowledge acquired by criterion judges or examiners; b) the failure to _ _ _ _ _ _-_ _ _ _ _ _ _ _ _ the signs that differentiate significantly between criterion groups; c) _ _ _ _ _ _ _ _ _ _ _ _ accuracy, which is an example of the "Barnum effect;" and d) _ _ _ _ _ _ _ _ _ validation, which is a special example of the mechanism that underlies the survival of superstitions.

20. Borrowing a concept from information theory, Cronbach and Gleser characterized interviewing and projective techniques as procedures wherein _ _ _ _ _ _ _ _ _ _, or breadth of coverage, is achieved at the expense of lowered _ _ _ _ _ _ _ _ _, or dependability of information.

ANSWERS TO FILL-IN-THE-BLANKS: (Key Terms, Concepts, and Names)

1. projective techniques
2. inkblot (techniques)/verbal (techniques)/pictorial (techniques)/expressive (techniques)/Thematic Apperception (Test) (TAT)
3. Rorschach
4. location/determinants/content/popularity
5. response productivity (or R)

6. Exner/comprehensive (system)

7. consensus (Rorschach)

8. Holtzman Inkblot Technique (HIT)

9. "hero"/"needs"/"press"

10. achievement need (n-Ach)

11. Roberts Apperception Test (for) Children (RATC)

12. word association (test)

13. Kent-Rosanoff (Free Association Test)

14. sentence completion (tests)

15. Rotter (Incomplete Sentences Blank)

16. Rosenzweig Picture-Frustration (Study) (P-F Study)

17. expressive (techniques)/drawing/(dramatic use of) toys

18. Machover Draw-a-Person (Test) (D-A-P)

19. a) contamination (of criterion or test data)/b) (failure to) cross-validate/c) stereotype (accuracy)/d) illusory (validation)

20. bandwidth/fidelity

TRUE/FALSE and WHY?

1. Test takers are usually aware of the type of psychological interpretation that will be made of their responses to projective instruments. (T/F) Why? _____

   _____

2. The use of percentages is a satisfactory and adequate solution to the problem that differential response productivity poses in the interpretation of Rorschach scores. (T/F) Why? _____

   _____

3. The Rorschach appears most promising when it is used either as a measure of cognitive style and perceptual organization, or as a structured interview by a skilled clinician. (T/F) Why? _____

   _____

4. Experimental data suggest that TAT responses are significantly affected by conditions such as hunger, sleep deprivation, and social frustration. (T/F) Why? _____

   _____

5. Several studies with elementary school children have found that they are more likely to produce clinically significant material in response to animal pictures than to human pictures. (T/F) Why? _____

_____

6. Although the Kent-Rosanoff Free Association Test has retained its position as a standard laboratory technique, its diagnostic use has declined. (T/F) Why? _____

_____

7. The interpretive guide for the Machover D-A-P Test abounds in sweeping generalizations for which no substantial evidence is provided. (T/F) Why? _____

_____

8. Basically, projective techniques and self-report inventories differ from each other in degree, rather than in kind, with regard to their psychometric properties and nature of task. (T/F) Why? _____

_____

9. For all practical purposes it can be assumed that projective tests are immune to faking. (T/F) Why? _____

_____

10. The final interpretation of projective test responses may reveal more about the examiner than it does about the examinee's personality dynamics. (T/F) Why? _____

_____

11. Projective devices frequently require special statistical procedures for ascertaining such psychometric characteristics as reliability. (T/F) Why? _____

_____

12. In the context of projective testing, fantasy productions with high aggressive content are consistently associated with high aggression in overt behavior. (T/F) Why? _____

_____

13. The relation between ambiguity of stimuli and projective productivity appears to be linear, in that the less structured the stimuli, the more likely they are to elicit projection and tap deep layers of personality. (T/F) Why? _____

_____

14. When experienced clinicians are allowed to interpret projective protocols in their own way, their evaluations of the respondents' personalities usually match independent case history data significantly better than chance. (T/F) Why? _____

_____

15. There is ample evidence that responses to unstructured test stimuli can be best explained by the projective hypothesis. (T/F) Why? _____

_____

ANSWERS TO TRUE/FALSE:

1. False	5. False	9. False	13. False
2. False	6. True	10. True	14. True
3. True	7. True	11. True	15. False
4. True	8. True	12. False	

MULTIPLE CHOICE: TEST YOURSELF

1. Compared to the more objective measures of personality, projective techniques are _____

_____.

   a. less structured
   b. more difficult to evaluate
   c. less reliable
   d. all of the above

2. The original scoring procedures for the Rorschach can best be described as _____

_____.

   a. based primarily on the intuition of Rorschach
   b. refined through statistical manipulation
   c. based on an informal and subjective application of criterion keying
   d. relatively simple, straightforward, and easy to master

3. Research has shown that the scoring of the Rorschach _____

_____.

   a. is not influenced by the verbal aptitude of the respondent
   b. is influenced by factors quite extraneous to personality
   c. underemphasizes the use of color
   d. none of the above

4. The major emphasis in well-developed quantitative systems for scoring the Rorschach has

   been on _____

   _____.

   a. identification of cerebral dysfunction
   b. detection of test taker attempts to fake responses
   c. assessment of cognitive style and perceptual organization
   d. inclusion of biographical data in the scoring indexes

5. Recent efforts to improve the Rorschach as a psychometric instrument have centered on

   _____.

   a. more standardized procedures for administration and scoring
   b. additional emphasis on structural variables
   c. more data-based interpretations
   d. all of the above

6. When compared to the Rorschach, the Holtzman Inkblot Technique (HIT) _____

   _____.

   a. allows for greater response productivity
   b. is more standardized
   c. uses fewer stimulus cards
   d. all of the above

7. The Thematic Apperception Test (TAT) involves _____

   _____.

   a. presenting the respondent with a series of incomplete statements
   b. creating stories after exposure to vague pictures
   c. responding to a set of multicolored inkblots
   d. a set of 250 forced-choice-type questions

8. Compared with the Rorschach, the TAT is _____

   _____.

   a. more structured
   b. less structured
   c. less influenced by examiner variables
   d. unaffected by the respondent's motivation

9. "My mother...," "What worries me...," and "I am..." are all examples of items that might

   appear on _____.

   a. the TAT
   b. a word association test
   c. a sentence completion test
   d. the Kent-Rosanoff Free Association Test

10. Word association tests have been scored on the basis of _____
_____ .

    a. popularity of responses
    b. reaction time
    c. detection of impairment of thought processes
    d. all of the above

11. Playing with toys while being observed, drawing pictures of people, and drawing familiar

things can be classified as _____ .

    a. expressive techniques
    b. pictorial techniques
    c. psychometric instruments
    d. all of the above

12. The major weakness of such traditional projective techniques as the D-A-P is _____
_____ .

    a. undetected faked responses
    b. inadequate validation data
    c. dearth of clinical experience with these tests
    d. excessive time required to administer them

13. The reliability of most projective techniques is _____
_____ .

    a. lower than desirable
    b. difficult to assess
    c. heavily dependent on the training of the clinician who administers and scores the
       procedure
    d. all of the above

14. The "projective hypothesis" _____
_____ .

    a. assumes that the individual's responses reflect significant and lasting personality
       attributes
    b. has been supported surprisingly well by empirical findings
    c. has become less and less favored by clinicians
    d. all of the above

15. Projective techniques are best used for _____
_____ .

    a. detecting deep-seated emotional disorders
    b. accurate assessment of global personality characteristics
    c. developing leads for further exploration
    d. evaluating verbally gifted individuals

MINIPROJECTS/SUGGESTED OUTREACH ACTIVITIES:

1. The topic of projective techniques is a vast and intriguing one and there are hundreds of
books and articles that you could read to become more familiar with it, should you wish to

do so. The suggested readings that follow were chosen, out of the many possible ones, because of their relative recency, thoroughness, and conciseness, within their respective formats:

   A. The review article entitled "Projective Tests," by W.G. Klopfer and E.S. Taulbee (*Annual Review of Psychology,* 1976, *27,* 543-568), would provide an excellent quick survey of the field.

   B. The book entitled *Assessment with Projective Techniques: A Concise Introduction,* edited by A.I. Rabin (New York: Springer, 1981), presents more detailed coverage of all the major projective techniques by experts in each method. It also contains a very good chapter by Walter Klopfer on "Integration of Projective Techniques in the Clinical Case Study."

2. A sizable portion of what has been written and said about projective techniques has been written and said about the Rorschach. Exner's three-volume work, entitled *The Rorschach: A Comprehensive System* (New York: Wiley, 1978, 1982, 1986), is undoubtedly the most thorough and scholarly of the current sources on the subject. However, that work is well beyond the scope of a "miniproject" and would, in fact, only be appropriate for those who want to become serious "Rorschachers." If you want a brief, yet excellent, introduction to the technique, Aronow and Reznikoff's 1983 book, *A Rorschach Introduction* (published by Grune and Stratton but now available only through The Psychological Corporation), would suit that purpose quite well. Another good source of current information about the Rorschach, and other projective techniques and personality tests, is the *Journal of Personality Assessment.* The evolution of this quarterly publication of the Society for Personality Assessment, which started out as a mimeographed newsletter published by Bruno Klopfer called *The Rorschach Research Exchange* and later became the *Journal of Projective Techniques,* is in itself a reflection of the development of the field of personality assessment.

3. If you would like a more direct acquaintance with projective instruments, and if you can obtain a set of TAT cards and a manual, select about 10 of the pictures and write stories based on them, according to the directions in the manual. After you have finished writing the stories, set them aside for a couple of days and then reread them and analyze them as objectively as you can, using the manual and any other TAT references you can locate (see the textbook and/or Rabin's book, cited in Miniproject # 1 B for this chapter). Note particularly whether the "needs" and "presses" expressed in your stories bear any relationship to your mental and/or physical state at the time you wrote them or whether they reflect "themes" that concern you on an ongoing basis.

4. Another activity you might wish to undertake to deepen your understanding of the material in Chapter 19 is a replication of Chapman and Chapman's demonstration of the phenomenon of "illusory validation" (*Journal of Abnormal Psychology,* 1967, *72,* 193-204). After you have read the article describing the experiments, you could either try to duplicate the materials they used or fashion your own, along similar lines, and present them to a small sample of college students, preferably in majors other than psychology.

5. The continued popularity of projective techniques, even in light of the unabated criticisms they have received for their psychometric weaknesses, is evident in a number of surveys of psychodiagnostic test usage (see, for example, the Piotrowski *et al.* survey in the *Journal of Personality Assessment,* 1985, *49,* 115-119). In order to ascertain this phenomenon directly, you could survey clinicians in your area, with a questionnaire, asking them to report on the frequency of their use of the major techniques cited in Chapter 19.

ANSWERS TO MULTIPLE CHOICE/TEST YOURSELF ITEMS:

1. d	4. c	7. b	10. d	13. d
2. c	5. d	8. a	11. a	14. a
3. b	6. b	9. c	12. b	15. c

Chapter 20
OTHER ASSESSMENT TECHNIQUES

CHAPTER OUTLINE

CHAPTER SUMMARY

Chapter 20 considers a diverse array of personality assessment tools that differ from the self-report inventories and projective techniques described earlier in the text. These instruments, which include "objective" performance tests, situational tests, and techniques for the assessment of self-concepts and personal constructs, are used mainly in research, although some can also serve as clinical aids. In addition, the present chapter describes nontest techniques used in personality appraisal, including naturalistic observation, interviewing, ratings, and the analysis of life-history data, and previews some specialized measurement devices from the emerging fields of environmental and health psychology.

"Objective" performance tests, sometimes described as "indirect" tests, are task-oriented techniques that require perceptual, cognitive, or evaluative responses. These tests are similar to projective techniques in that their purpose is disguised, but differ from the latter in that the tasks they present are structured and, at least from the test taker's viewpoint, appear to require a "correct" solution. A large number of "objective" performance tests, e.g., the Gottschaldt Figures and the Embedded Figures Test, deal with perceptual functions that have proved fruitful in personality research, such as flexibility of closure and field dependence. The second major category of objective performance tests is comprised of techniques, such as the Humor Test of Personality and the Barron-Welsh Art Scale, that call for evaluative judgments by the respondent as a means of assessing personality characteristics.

Situational tests are techniques that place the test taker in a circumstance that simulates "real life." The most notable forerunners of such tests were the situations that Hartshorne and May devised in the course of the Character Education Inquiry (CEI) investigations they led in the late 1920s. The CEI tests were designed to measure behavior characteristics such as honesty and self-control in children; they produced results that underscored the situational specificity of those traits. The quintessential examples of situational tests are the techniques devised as part of the assessment-center program introduced by the U.S. Office of Strategic Services (OSS) during World War II. These techniques, which include situational stress tests and leaderless group discussions among others, were later adapted for other uses, such as the selection of high level executives in industry; they have proved to be quite effective when they approximate worksamples of the criterion behavior they are designed to predict. One ubiquitous type of situational test, which is enjoying heightened popularity in the selection and training of people whose jobs require interpersonal skills, is the roleplaying or improvisation technique wherein the individual is instructed to play a part either overtly or by reporting what he or she would do or say in a given situation.

Several current approaches to personality assessment concentrate on the way people view themselves and others. The Washington University Sentence Completion Test, for example, measures the trait of self-conceptualization, designated as ego development or I-level, that is so prominent in Loevinger's theoretical approach to personality development. The Coopersmith Self-Esteem Inventories are an example of a published instrument for the measurement of evaluative self-concept, a construct that is thought to influence the development of many affective as well as cognitive traits. Other broadly oriented techniques especially developed for assessing self-concepts include the Adjective Check List (ACL) and the Q sort procedure originated by Stephenson. Two representative examples of techniques used for investigating how individuals perceive others are the Semantic Differential, developed by Osgood for his research on the psychology of meaning, and the Role Construct Repertory Test (Rep Test) developed by G.A. Kelly and intimately related to his personal construct theory.

Direct observations of behavior are an essential supplement to standardized tests in the assessment of personality. Naturalistic observations, interviewing, ratings, nominating techniques, checklists, and Q sorts are some of the most prominent approaches that have been devised or adapted for gathering and reporting observational data in personality appraisal. Although much can be done to improve the accuracy and communicability of these procedures, their input is extremely valuable because they allow for more extensive and flexible sampling of behavioral data than do standardized tests.

Life-history data are a critical component of the information base that must be gathered by clinicians and others who are involved in the assessment of individuals. Although interviewing can and does supply much of these data, the biographical inventory can be an important alternative or additional source of information on the individual's life history. Biographical inventories bring the advantages of uniformity and economy to the gathering of background data. In addition, when their items are selected and weighted by criterion keying, and then cross-validated, such inventories have proven to be good predictors of performance for the specific purposes or contexts for which they were designed. A particularly effective adaptation of the biographical inventory technique is the behavioral consistency method developed by the U.S. Office of Personnel Management for the evaluation of job applicants. This procedure, which allows applicants to cite any job-relevant achievements, whether or not they occurred in occupational settings, is especially appropriate for assessing the qualifications of women and minority groups.

A variety of assessment techniques, ranging from self-report inventories to adjective checklists, are being explored in order to evaluate people's attitudes toward features of both natural and built environments. Only a few of these techniques, which are part of the burgeoning and multifaceted field of environmental psychology, are published instruments. Two of these, described in the text, are the Environmental Response Inventory (ERI) and the Leisure Activities Blank (LAB) developed by McKechnie. Other applications of testing related to the environment include measures of performance deterioration under unusual and stressful conditions, such as the Automated Portable Test System (ATPS), instruments to assess environmental status, such as the Home Observation for Measurement of the Environment (HOME), and measures of social climate as perceived by persons in a certain milieu, such as the College Characteristics Index (CCI).

Another rapidly growing field, which bridges the gap between psychology and medicine, is that of health psychology. Within that field, a number of new behavioral measurement instruments are in various stages of development. These instruments are aimed at providing systematic and standardized information about individuals for use in medical practice and in public health programs. The Jenkins Activity Survey (JAS), for example, was developed to assess Type-A behavior, which has been linked to coronary heart disease. The Millon Behavioral Health Inventory (MBHI) is a more broadly based instrument that attempts to assess coping styles, attitudes toward illness and treatment, and other personality tendencies of patients that may be relevant to decision-making in general medical settings. Another application of psychometric techniques to medical problems is represented by health status measures, such as the Sickness Impact Profile (SIP), the Index of Well-Being, and the Well-Life Expectancy index.

COMPREHENSIVE REVIEW

STUDY QUESTIONS:

1. List and describe the characteristics of "objective" performance tests of personality.

2. Discuss the notion of field dependence and describe some of the research findings related to that construct.

3. Cite two examples of tests that call for evaluative judgments by the respondent and discuss how they can be applied to personality assessment.

4. Describe the methodology and major findings of Hartshorne and May's Character Education Inquiry (CEI).

5. Describe two examples of situational tests that were developed through the assessment-center program of the Office of Strategic Services (OSS) and discuss their value in personality assessment.

6. Discuss the various current uses for roleplaying or improvisation techniques in individual assessment.

7. Discuss the background and purpose of the Washington University Sentence Completion Test.

8. Describe how the Adjective Check List (ACL), the Q sort, and the Semantic Differential technique can be used in the assessment of self-concepts.

9. Discuss the theoretical basis and procedures of the Role Construct Repertory Test (Rep Test).

10. Discuss the functions of naturalistic observations and interviews in personality assessment.

11. Compare and contrast ratings and the nominating technique as they are used in the evaluation of individuals.

12. Discuss how biographical inventories can be used in the evaluation of job applicants.

13. Describe two types of assessment techniques that are used in studying the relationship between individuals and their environments.

14. Discuss the construct of Type-A behavior and describe the Jenkins Activity Survey (JAS) as an example of an instrument designed to assess it.

15. Describe the Millon Behavioral Health Inventory (MBHI) and one example of a measure of health status and discuss the functions each of those instruments can serve.

FILL IN THE BLANKS: Key Terms, Concepts, and Names

1. "_ _ _ _ _ _ _ _ _ _" _ _ _ _ _ _ _ _ _ _ _ _ _ tests of personality, sometimes described as "indirect" tests, are relatively simple, structured tasks, typically of a perceptual or evaluative nature, whose purpose is disguised from test takers.

2. *Cognitive styles* refer to people's preferred and typical modes of perceiving, remembering, thinking, and problem solving; regarded as broad stylistic behavioral characteristics, they cut across abilities and personality and are manifested in many activities.

3. Instruments such as the Gottschaldt Figures and the _ _ _ _ _ _ _ _ _ Figures Test have been used to assess personality characteristics through an analysis of _ _ _ _ _ _ _ _ _ _ _ functions.

4. Witkin and his associates identified a relatively stable and consistent cognitive trait designated as __ __ __ __ __   __ __ __ __ __ __ __ __ __ __, which refers to the extent to which individuals' perceptions are influenced or disrupted by conflicting contextual cues and is apparently related to a number of personality variables.

5. The __ __ __ __ __ Test of Personality and the __ __ __ __ __ __–__ __ __ __ __ Art Scale are two of the measures that have used __ __ __ __ __ __ __ __ __ __ judgments by the respondent as a means of assessing personality characteristics.

6. *Situational* tests of personality place the test taker in a circumstance that simulates "real life" in order to sample complex criterion behavior of an emotional, interpersonal, or attitudinal nature.

7. Some of the earliest situational tests were those constructed by Hartshorne, May and their associates in the course of the __ __ __ __ __ __ __ __   __ __ __ __ __ __ __ __ __ __ __ __ __ __ (CEI), which was an extensive project that investigated such traits as honesty and self-control in children.

8. The __ __ __ __ __ __ __ __ __ __ __–__ __ __ __ __ program introduced by the U.S. Office of Strategic Services during World War II resulted in the development of a number of techniques later adapted for other settings. One of those techniques, designed to sample behavior under frustrating or emotionally disrupting conditions, was the __ __ __ __ __ __ __ __ __ __ __   __ __ __ __ __ __ __ test; another was the use of a __ __ __ __ __ __ __ __ __ __   __ __ __ __ __ to carry out assigned tasks, such as transporting men and materials across a brook, without designating the specific responsibilities of group members.

9. In the *Roleplaying* technique, which is used most extensively and systematically in clinical psychology, the individual is explicitly instructed to play a part either overtly or by reporting what she or he would do or say in a given situation.

10. In the Washington University Sentence Completion Test, __ __ __ __ __ __ __ __ __ and her associates undertook to measure the trait of __ __ __ __–__ __ __ __ __ __ __ __ __ __ __ __ __ __ __ __ __, designated as ego development or I-level, which is defined as the capacity to "assume distance" from oneself and one's impulses.

11. The __ __ __ __ __ __ __ __ __ __ Self-Esteem Inventories are one of the best known and most widely used measures of evaluative self-concept.

12. In the investigation of self-concepts, two of the most widely used techniques are the
_ _ _ _ _ _ _ _ _ _ _ _ _ _ _ _ _ _ _ (ACL), which consists of items
ranging from "absentminded" to "zany," and the _ _ _ _ _, wherein the respondent
classifies a set of cards, with statements or trait names on them, into piles ranging from
most to least characteristic of himself or herself.

13. The *Semantic Differentiation*, first developed by
Osgood for research on the psychology of meaning, provides a standardized and quantified
procedure for assessing the connotations that any given concept has for the individual
through ratings of each concept along a series of bipolar adjectival scales.

14. The _ _ _ _ _ _ _ _ _ _ _ _ _ _ _ _ _ _ _ _ _ _ Test (Rep Test)
was developed by Kelly to help the clinician identify some of the client's important
constructs about people, but has been modified and used extensively in personality
research. One of the important indices that can be derived from the Rep Test is designated
as _ _ _ _ _ _ _ _ _ _ _ _ _ _ _ _ _ _ _, which is based on the number
of constructs used by an individual and is regarded as a measure of cognitive style.

15. Personality assessment cannot rely entirely on standardized tests and must be
supplemented by direct *observation* of behavior and by life-history data
usually gathered through *interviewing*.

16. In the assessment of individuals, evaluations from observers can be reported through simple
_ _ _ _ _ _ _ _, which are often used to obtain criterion information, or through a
variation known as the _ _ _ _ _ _ _ _ _ _ _ technique, which is especially useful in
gathering peer assessments, as well as from _ _ _ _ _ _ _ _ _ _ _, such as the ACL,
and decks of _ – _ _ _ _ items.

17. Ratings are subject to a number of constant errors, such as the _ _ _ _ effect, or
tendency of raters to be influenced by a single favorable or unfavorable trait, the error of
_ _ _ _ _ _ _ _ _ _ _ _ _ _ _ _ _, which results in a bunching of ratings in the
middle of the scale, and the _ _ _ _ _ _ _ _ _ error, which refers to the reluctance of
raters to assign unfavorable ratings. One way to correct the latter two types of errors is to
use rankings or other _ _ _ _ _ _–_ _–_ _ _ _ _ procedures.

18. _____ inventories represent an attempt to obtain life-history data under uniform conditions and when interviews are not feasible. A special application of this technique, originally developed by the U.S. Office of Personnel Management, is the _____ _____ method used to differentiate applicants in terms of qualifications that are critical for a job.

19. Two important applications of measurement techniques to environmental psychology are in the assessment of environmental _____, used to gauge the effects of different environments on individual characteristics, and measures of _____ environment and _____ _____, such as the College Characteristics Index (CCI).

20. _____ _____ is concerned with the measurement of performance deterioration under unusual and stressful conditions, such as oxygen deficit and weightlessness. One battery designed to assess various performance functions under such conditions, in a wide range of field settings, is the _____ _____ Test System (APTS).

21. The _____ _____ Survey (JAS) is a self-report inventory developed to assess _____-_ behavior, which is characterized by traits such as extreme competitiveness, striving for achievement, aggressiveness, and impatience.

22. The _____ _____ _____ Inventory (MBHI) was designed to evaluate personality tendencies that may substantially affect a person's reaction to treatment and the course of an illness.

23. The _____ _____ _____ (SIP) and the Index of Well-Being are examples of measures of _____ _____ and can be used in individual assessment as well as in research on medical problems.

ANSWERS TO FILL-IN-THE-BLANKS: (Key Terms, Concepts, and Names)

1. "objective" performance (tests of personality)
2. cognitive styles
3. Embedded (Figures Test)/perceptual (functions)
4. field dependence
5. Humor (Test of Personality)/Barron-Welsh (Art Scale)/ evaluative (judgments)
6. situational (tests)
7. Character Education Inquiry (CEI)
8. assessment-center (program)/situational stress (test)/ leaderless group

9. roleplaying (technique)

10. Loevinger/self-conceptualization

11. Coopersmith (Self-Esteem Inventories)

12. Adjective Check List (ACL)/Q sort

13. Semantic Differential

14. Role Construct Repertory (Test) (Rep Test)/cognitive complexity

15. (direct) observation (of behavior)/interviewing

16. ratings/nominating (technique)/checklists/Q-sort (items)

17. halo (effect)/(error of) central tendency/leniency (error)/ order-of-merit (procedures)

18. biographical (inventories)/behavioral consistency (method)

19. (environmental) status/(measures of) perceived (environment and) social climate

20. behavioral toxicology/Automated Portable (Test System) (ATPS)

21. Jenkins Activity (Survey) (JAS)/Type-A (behavior)

22. Millon Behavioral Health (Inventory) (MBHI)

23. Sickness Impact Profile (SIP)/(measures of) health status

TRUE/FALSE and WHY?

1. A number of projective techniques, most notably the Rorschach, are essentially tests of perceptual functions. (T/F) Why? _T_____

_____

2. Surveys of studies of the field-dependent-independent continuum suggest that field independent persons are generally more effective and well adapted than those who are field dependent. (T/F) Why? _____

_____

3. There is a considerable accumulation of data that suggests that scores on the Barron-Welsh Art Scale are consistently related to certain personality variables. (T/F) Why? _____

_____

4. The responses of children who were studied in the CEI tended to vary not only across situations and contexts, but also within the school setting, from one teacher's classroom to another. (T/F) Why? _____

_____

5. The Leaderless Group Discussion (LGD) and some of the more elaborate situational tests have proven to be valid devices for assessing broad personality traits. (T/F) Why? _____

_____

6. Although roleplaying has come to be used prominently in behavior modification programs, it is clear that participants tend to remain calm and detached even in anger-arousing situations. (T/F) Why? _____

_____

7. According to the theory formulated by Loevinger, it would be accurate to say that self-report inventories, such as the MMPI, are actually measures of self-concept. (T/F) Why? _____

_____

8. Many investigators have found that the relationship between self-concept and behavior can be demonstrated most clearly if the self-concept is assessed with a single, global measure. (T/F) Why? __F_____

_____

9. Naturalistic observations differ from situational tests in that the former do not involve control of the stimulus situation and usually provide a more extensive behavior sample than the latter. (T/F) Why? __T_____

_____

10. Adept interviewers concern themselves only with what has happened to the individual in the past and what is presently happening to him or her. (T/F) Why? _____

_____

11. The accuracy and validity of ratings can be vastly improved through the use of numbers or general descriptive adjectives and also by ascertaining that the rater has known the person to be rated for a long time. (T/F) Why? _____

_____

12. Peer assessments have generally proven to be one of the most dependable rating techniques. (T/F) Why? __T_____

_____

13. A limitation of many biographical inventories developed for specific jobs by empirical methods is their narrow applicability. (T/F) Why? _____

_____

14. Research on Type-A behavior suggests that the construct is multidimensional and that its components do not correlate highly with each other. (T/F) Why? _____

_____

ANSWERS TO TRUE/FALSE:

1. True	5. False	9. True	13. True
2. False	6. False	10. False	14. True
3. True	7. True	11. False	
4. True	8. False	12. True	

MULTIPLE CHOICE: TEST YOURSELF

1. "Objective" performance tests can usually be distinguished by their _____ .

   a. emphasis on task orientation
   b. use of structured tasks
   c. use of tasks with apparently "correct" solutions
   d. all of the above

2. The Gottschaldt Figures and the Embedded Figures tests are basically tests of _____ .

   a. perceptual functions
   b. aesthetic preferences
   c. motivational traits
   d. none of the above

3. The Embedded Figures Test _____

   a. is difficult to administer
   b. is a purely visual, paper-and-pencil measure of field dependence
   c. is a personality measure useful in clinical assessment
   d. lacks a form suitable for use with adults

4. Low scores on aesthetic preference tests, such as the Barron-Welsh Art Scale, may indicate

   a. a tendency to yield to social pressure
   b. independence of judgment
   c. adventurousness
   d. both b and c

5. The instruments that Hartshorne, May, and their associates constructed for the CEI can be

   described as an early form of _____ .

   a. aesthetic evaluation tests
   b. improvisation techniques
   c. situational tests
   d. self-concept tests

6. The majority of CEI tests were concerned with _____.

     a. self-concept
     b. rigidity
     c. altruism
     d. honesty

7. The OSS devised a number of "lifelike" tests to assess special military personnel during World War II. These tests included _____

_____.

     a. situational stress tests
     b. roleplaying techniques
     c. leaderless groups
     d. all of the above

8. The major reason why situational tests are not used more often is that _____

_____.

     a. they are illegal
     b. their individual range of applicability is rather limited
     c. they are not nearly as accurate as formal objective tests
     d. none of the above

9. The use of situations that demand improvisation as an aspect of the overall evaluation of a client or job applicant _____

_____.

     a. is becoming more popular
     b. has been found to be basically unreliable and invalid
     c. is illegal
     d. is ineffective

10. According to Loevinger, the various response sets that are evident in self-report personality inventories are manifestations of one's _____.

     a. self-conceptualization
     b. impulsiveness
     c. self-esteem
     d. behavioral repertory

11. The Semantic Differential is basically a technique for the measurement of _____

_____.

     a. honesty
     b. verbal fluency
     c. evaluative connotations
     d. perseverance

12. Naturalistic observations have been used most often by _____
    _____.

    a. clinicians in psychiatric hospitals
    b. child psychologists
    c. OSS personnel
    d. counselors

13. The main function of the interview is to _____
    _____.

    a. provide an opportunity for observation
    b. elicit life-history data
    c. rate the interviewee
    d. detect roleplaying or faking

14. A constant error which reduces the effective width of rating scales is _____
    _____.

    a. the halo effect
    b. the error of central tendency
    c. the leniency error
    d. both b and c

15. Which of the following is an instrument designed to assess a health-related construct? ____
    _____.

    a. Environmental Response Inventory (ERI)
    b. Leisure Activities Blank (LAB)
    c. Jenkins Activity Survey (JAS)
    d. Q sort

MINIPROJECTS/SUGGESTED OUTREACH ACTIVITIES:

If you have done even a relatively small portion of the miniprojects and outreach activities suggested in this guide, in addition to studying the entire textbook, you could probably use a prolonged rest at this point. Should you choose to rest, you can start now and read no further than the end of this paragraph. The last suggestion for those who opt for a vacation, yet plan to stay in the field of psychology, is to retain your copy of the textbook for your basic professional library, as it is likely to come in handy time and again in the future.

For those who are dedicated to the pursuit of knowledge about psychological testing and assessment to a point above and beyond the call of duty, the following suggestions are meant to be enjoyable as well as informative:

1. Survey Chapter 20 one more time and make up your own miniproject. The scope of the chapter encompasses a number of fascinating topics, such as the psychology of self-concepts, improvisation techniques, and Kelly's personal construct theory, among others. The chapter also covers two emerging fields, i.e., environmental and health psychology, which for reasons that are obvious are certain to grow in importance through the coming decades and are well worth studying. If you choose to make up your own miniproject, you will find a good supply of references with which to start your pursuit of the topic that interests you right in the textbook.

2. Imagine that you are in charge of the selection of applicants for a prestigious medical school. You have decided to do away with traditional testing, in favor of situational tests. Applicants are being invited in groups of 10 to come to the campus for a two-day period of evaluation. Devise a series of situational tests that might be tried in order to select the top 20 percent of the applicants who would have the greatest chance of succeeding in the program and becoming "good" doctors. How would you evaluate the validity of your tests?

3. Select an appropriate time and place to conduct a naturalistic observation of one person. You might use a coffee shop, a library, or a public park, for example. Devote all of your attention to the person you have chosen to observe for about half an hour and note all of his or her activities, while remaining inconspicuous. Write a detailed word-picture of what you have observed and review its contents to see what evaluative hypotheses, if any, you could gather from your observation.

4. One of the most enjoyable texts that you are likely to encounter in the field of psychology is the book written by Webb *et al.* on *Nonreactive Measures in the Social Sciences* (2nd ed., Boston: Houghton Mifflin, 1981). This book presents a number of ingenious applications of naturalistic observation that can be used to conduct social psychological research in an unobtrusive fashion. The book is not only well written but, for those fond of the genre, it is as much fun to read as a detective novel.

5. Although most people are not concerned with reliability, validity, or any other psychometric considerations, human beings do spend a good deal of time evaluating each other in countless ways. As a final exercise, outline the assessment techniques you knowingly, and not so knowingly, use in your everyday life. Choose a particular aspect of your life, such as your method for assessing a potential marriage partner, boss, or friend, and then evaluate your method.

ANSWERS TO MULTIPLE CHOICE/TEST YOURSELF ITEMS:

1. d	4. a	7. d	10. a	13. b
2. a	5. c	8. b	11. c	14. d
3. b	6. d	9. a	12. b	15. c

Appendix

TABLE OF AREAS UNDER THE NORMAL CURVE

HOW TO USE THE TABLE OF AREAS UNDER THE NORMAL CURVE

Table Headings

In the first column of the Table $z = \frac{x}{\sigma}$, where x is the distance between any point on the baseline and zero, or the mean, and σ (sigma) is the standard deviation of the normal distribution. The first column lists values of z from 0.00 to 3.70. Column A lists the area of the curve that is encompassed *between* the mean (0) and any z values. Since the normal curve is symmetrical, when z is at the mean (0.00), half of the curve (.5000) is above z and half is below z. If the curve is cut at any point other than the mean, the area in the larger portion is given in Column B and the area in the smaller portion is given in Column C.

Explanation of the Table

Part One - Diagrams: In Diagram I (Figure 9), we look up a z value of +1.25 and find the area between that z and the mean to be .3944 (Column A). Because the normal curve is symmetrical, any given z distance subtends the same area above the mean or below the mean. Therefore, in Diagram II, a z value of −1.25 again gives us an area of .3944 between z and the mean. To find the proportion of the area in Diagram I that falls *above* a z of +1.25, we subtract .3944 from .5000, and obtain .1056. To find the proportion of the area falling *below* +1.25, we add .3944 to .5000, obtaining .8944. These values are shown in Diagram III. Diagram IV shows the results with a z of −1.25. In this case, the larger portion falls *above* z but is also found by adding the value in Column A to .5000 (.3944 + .5000 = .8944) and the smaller portion falls *below* z and is found by subtracting .3944 from .5000. Columns B and C of the Table have carried out those computations for us. You can verify your results by finding the entries in Columns B and C for the z value of 1.25. You can also, as an exercise, look up the areas under the curve that are shown in Figures 4-3 and 4-6 of the textbook (pp. 77 and 90, respectively) for z values of ±1.00, ±2.00, and ±3.00 in order to make sure that you have learned how to use the Table.

Part Two - Levels of Significance: Up to this point we have dealt with the normal curve merely as a model of a theoretical distribution that can be used to find the position of one measurement from a population or a sample whose distribution approximates the shape of our model. When the normal curve is applied to hypothesis testing, we use it to ascertain the probability that the critical value (z) we have obtained could have resulted by chance. Since z values simply give the proportion in one end of the curve, when we test a hypothesis that permits variation in either direction, we have to *double* the proportion that falls beyond the z value to find the probability level associated with the critical value obtained. (See, for example, Exercise # 8 in Chapter 5 of this *Guide*, where the value in Column C of the Table, which is the probability (p) for a z of 2.20, is 0.0139. Because score differences could occur in either direction, p has been doubled to obtain the answer to that problem.) This situation is described as a "two-tailed test," and it is the most common way in which the significance of findings is tested. In contrast, if we had a specific unidirectional hypothesis, as we might in conducting an experiment where we have reason to expect results to fall in a given direction, we would be doing a "one-tailed test." In such cases, if the findings were in the direction that was specified, the p for the critical values obtained would not be doubled.

For further information about the normal curve and its use in hypothesis testing, see pp. 114-115 and 133-134 of the textbook. You may also want to refer to a good basic statistics textbook, such as the sixth edition of Guilford and Fruchter's *Fundamental Statistics in Psychology and Education* (New York: McGraw-Hill, 1978).

Figure 9 – Diagrams of Areas Under the Normal Curve

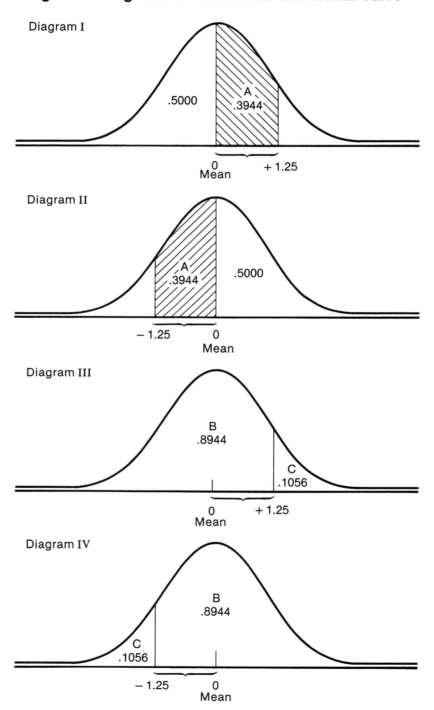

Table of Areas Under the Normal Curve

(1)	(2)	(3)	(4)
	A	B	C
$z = \frac{x}{\sigma}$	Area from Mean to $\frac{x}{\sigma}$	Area in Larger Portion	Area in Smaller Portion
0.00	.0000	.5000	.5000
0.01	.0040	.5040	.4960
0.02	.0080	.5080	.4920
0.03	.0120	.5120	.4880
0.04	.0160	.5160	.4840
0.05	.0199	.5199	.4801
0.06	.0239	.5239	.4761
0.07	.0279	.5279	.4721
0.08	.0319	.5319	.4681
0.09	.0359	.5359	.4641
0.10	.0398	.5398	.4602
0.11	.0438	.5438	.4562
0.12	.0478	.5478	.4522
0.13	.0517	.5517	.4483
0.14	.0557	.5557	.4443
0.15	.0596	.5596	.4404
0.16	.0636	.5636	.4364
0.17	.0675	.5675	.4325
0.18	.0714	.5714	.4286
0.19	.0753	.5753	.4247
0.20	.0793	.5793	.4207
0.21	.0832	.5832	.4168
0.22	.0871	.5871	.4129
0.23	.0910	.5910	.4090
0.24	.0948	.5948	.4052
0.25	.0987	.5987	.4013
0.26	.1026	.6026	.3974
0.27	.1064	.6064	.3936
0.28	.1103	.6103	.3897
0.29	.1141	.6141	.3859
0.30	.1179	.6179	.3821
0.31	.1217	.6217	.3783
0.32	.1255	.6255	.3745
0.33	.1293	.6293	.3707
0.34	.1331	.6331	.3669

Table of Areas Under the Normal Curve

(1)	(2)	(3)	(4)
	A	B	C
$z = \frac{x}{\sigma}$	Area from Mean to $\frac{x}{\sigma}$	Area in Larger Portion	Area in Smaller Portion
0.35	.1368	.6368	.3632
0.36	.1406	.6406	.3594
0.37	.1443	.6443	.3557
0.38	.1480	.6480	.3520
0.39	.1517	.6517	.3483
0.40	.1554	.6554	.3446
0.41	.1591	.6591	.3409
0.42	.1628	.6628	.3372
0.43	.1664	.6664	.3336
0.44	.1700	.6700	.3300
0.45	.1736	.6736	.3264
0.46	.1772	.6772	.3228
0.47	.1808	.6808	.3192
0.48	.1844	.6844	.3156
0.49	.1879	.6879	.3121
0.50	.1915	.6915	.3085
0.51	.1950	.6950	.3050
0.52	.1985	.6985	.3015
0.53	.2019	.7019	.2981
0.54	.2054	.7054	.2946
0.55	.2088	.7088	.2912
0.56	.2123	.7123	.2877
0.57	.2157	.7157	.2843
0.58	.2190	.7190	.2810
0.59	.2224	.7224	.2776
0.60	.2257	.7257	.2743
0.61	.2291	.7291	.2709
0.62	.2324	.7324	.2676
0.63	.2357	.7357	.2643
0.64	.2389	.7389	.2611
0.65	.2422	.7422	.2578
0.66	.2454	.7454	.2546
0.67	.2486	.7486	.2514
0.68	.2517	.7517	.2483
0.69	.2549	.7549	.2451

Table of Areas Under the Normal Curve

(1)	(2)	(3)	(4)
	A	B	C
$z = \frac{x}{\sigma}$	Area from Mean to $\frac{x}{\sigma}$	Area in Larger Portion	Area in Smaller Portion
0.70	.2580	.7580	.2420
0.71	.2611	.7611	.2389
0.72	.2642	.7642	.2358
0.73	.2673	.7673	.2327
0.74	.2704	.7704	.2296
0.75	.2734	.7734	.2266
0.76	.2764	.7764	.2236
0.77	.2794	.7794	.2206
0.78	.2823	.7823	.2177
0.79	.2852	.7852	.2148
0.80	.2881	.7881	.2119
0.81	.2910	.7910	.2090
0.82	.2939	.7939	.2061
0.83	.2967	.7967	.2033
0.84	.2995	.7995	.2005
0.85	.3023	.8023	.1977
0.86	.3051	.8051	.1949
0.87	.3078	.8078	.1922
0.88	.3106	.8106	.1894
0.89	.3133	.8133	.1867
0.90	.3159	.8159	.1841
0.91	.3186	.8186	.1814
0.92	.3212	.8212	.1788
0.93	.3238	.8238	.1762
0.94	.3264	.8264	.1736
0.95	.3289	.8289	.1711
0.96	.3315	.8315	.1685
0.97	.3340	.8340	.1660
0.98	.3365	.8365	.1635
0.99	.3389	.8389	.1611
1.00	.3413	.8413	.1587
1.01	.3438	.8438	.1562
1.02	.3461	.8461	.1539
1.03	.3485	.8485	.1515
1.04	.3508	.8508	.1492

Table of Areas Under the Normal Curve

(1)	(2)	(3)	(4)
	A	**B**	**C**
$z = \frac{x}{\sigma}$	**Area from Mean to $\frac{x}{\sigma}$**	**Area in Larger Portion**	**Area in Smaller Portion**
1.05	.3531	.8531	.1469
1.06	.3554	.8554	.1446
1.07	.3577	.8577	.1423
1.08	.3599	.8599	.1401
1.09	.3621	.8621	.1379
1.10	.3643	.8643	.1357
1.11	.3665	.8665	.1335
1.12	.3686	.8686	.1314
1.13	.3708	.8708	.1292
1.14	.3729	.8729	.1271
1.15	.3749	.8749	.1251
1.16	.3770	.8770	.1230
1.17	.3790	.8790	.1210
1.18	.3810	.8810	.1190
1.19	.3830	.8830	.1170
1.20	.3849	.8849	.1151
1.21	.3869	.8869	.1131
1.22	.3888	.8888	.1112
1.23	.3907	.8907	.1093
1.24	.3925	.8925	.1075
1.25	.3944	.8944	.1056
1.26	.3962	.8962	.1038
1.27	.3980	.8980	.1020
1.28	.3997	.8997	.1003
1.29	.4015	.9015	.0985
1.30	.4032	.9032	.0968
1.31	.4049	.9049	.0951
1.32	.4066	.9066	.0934
1.33	.4082	.9082	.0918
1.34	.4099	.9099	.0901
1.35	.4115	.9115	.0885
1.36	.4131	.9131	.0869
1.37	.4147	.9147	.0853
1.38	.4162	.9162	.0838
1.39	.4177	.9177	.0823

Table of Areas Under the Normal Curve

(1)	(2)	(3)	(4)
	A	B	C
$z = \frac{x}{\sigma}$	Area from Mean to $\frac{x}{\sigma}$	Area in Larger Portion	Area in Smaller Portion
1.40	.4192	.9192	.0808
1.41	.4207	.9207	.0793
1.42	.4222	.9222	.0778
1.43	.4236	.9236	.0764
1.44	.4251	.9251	.0749
1.45	.4265	.9265	.0735
1.46	.4279	.9279	.0721
1.47	.4292	.9292	.0708
1.48	.4306	.9306	.0694
1.49	.4319	.9319	.0681
1.50	.4332	.9332	.0668
1.51	.4345	.9345	.0655
1.52	.4357	.9357	.0643
1.53	.4370	.9370	.0630
1.54	.4382	.9382	.0618
1.55	.4394	.9394	.0606
1.56	.4406	.9406	.0594
1.57	.4418	.9418	.0582
1.58	.4429	.9429	.0571
1.59	.4441	.9441	.0559
1.60	.4452	.9452	.0548
1.61	.4463	.9463	.0537
1.62	.4474	.9474	.0526
1.63	.4484	.9484	.0516
1.64	.4495	.9495	.0505
1.65	.4505	.9505	.0495
1.66	.4515	.9515	.0485
1.67	.4525	.9525	.0475
1.68	.4535	.9535	.0465
1.69	.4545	.9545	.0455
1.70	.4554	.9554	.0446
1.71	.4564	.9564	.0436
1.72	.4573	.9573	.0427
1.73	.4582	.9582	.0418
1.74	.4591	.9591	.0409

Table of Areas Under the Normal Curve

(1)	(2)	(3)	(4)
	A	**B**	**C**
$z = \frac{x}{\sigma}$	**Area from Mean to $\frac{x}{\sigma}$**	**Area in Larger Portion**	**Area in Smaller Portion**
1.75	.4599	.9599	.0401
1.76	.4608	.9608	.0392
1.77	.4616	.9616	.0384
1.78	.4625	.9625	.0375
1.79	.4633	.9633	.0367
1.80	.4641	.9641	.0359
1.81	.4649	.9649	.0351
1.82	.4656	.9656	.0344
1.83	.4664	.9664	.0336
1.84	.4671	.9671	.0329
1.85	.4678	.9678	.0322
1.86	.4686	.9686	.0314
1.87	.4693	.9693	.0307
1.88	.4699	.9699	.0301
1.89	.4706	.9706	.0294
1.90	.4713	.9713	.0287
1.91	.4719	.9719	.0281
1.92	.4726	.9726	.0274
1.93	.4732	.9732	.0268
1.94	.4738	.9738	.0262
1.95	.4744	.9744	.0256
1.96	.4750	.9750	.0250
1.97	.4756	.9756	.0244
1.98	.4761	.9761	.0239
1.99	.4767	.9767	.0233
2.00	.4772	.9772	.0228
2.01	.4778	.9778	.0222
2.02	.4783	.9783	.0217
2.03	.4788	.9788	.0212
2.04	.4793	.9793	.0207
2.05	.4798	.9798	.0202
2.06	.4803	.9803	.0197
2.07	.4808	.9808	.0192
2.08	.4812	.9812	.0188
2.09	.4817	.9817	.0183

Table of Areas Under the Normal Curve

(1)	(2)	(3)	(4)
	A	B	C
$z = \frac{x}{\sigma}$	Area from Mean to $\frac{x}{\sigma}$	Area in Larger Portion	Area in Smaller Portion
2.10	.4821	.9821	.0179
2.11	.4826	.9826	.0174
2.12	.4830	.9830	.0170
2.13	.4834	.9834	.0166
2.14	.4838	.9838	.0162
2.15	.4842	.9842	.0158
2.16	.4846	.9846	.0154
2.17	.4850	.9850	.0150
2.18	.4854	.9854	.0146
2.19	.4857	.9857	.0143
2.20	.4861	.9861	.0139
2.21	.4864	.9864	.0136
2.22	.4868	.9868	.0132
2.23	.4871	.9871	.0129
2.24	.4875	.9875	.0125
2.25	.4878	.9878	.0122
2.26	.4881	.9881	.0119
2.27	.4884	.9884	.0116
2.28	.4887	.9887	.0113
2.29	.4890	.9890	.0110
2.30	.4893	.9893	.0107
2.31	.4896	.9896	.0104
2.32	.4898	.9898	.0102
2.33	.4901	.9901	.0099
2.34	.4904	.9904	.0096
2.35	.4906	.9906	.0094
2.36	.4909	.9909	.0091
2.37	.4911	.9911	.0089
2.38	.4913	.9913	.0087
2.39	.4916	.9916	.0084
2.40	.4918	.9918	.0082
2.41	.4920	.9920	.0080
2.42	.4922	.9922	.0078
2.43	.4925	.9925	.0075
2.44	.4927	.9927	.0073

Table of Areas Under the Normal Curve

(1)	(2)	(3)	(4)
	A	B	C
$z = \frac{x}{\sigma}$	Area from Mean to $\frac{x}{\sigma}$	Area in Larger Portion	Area in Smaller Portion
2.45	.4929	.9929	.0071
2.46	.4931	.9931	.0069
2.47	.4932	.9932	.0068
2.48	.4934	.9934	.0066
2.49	.4936	.9936	.0064
2.50	.4938	.9938	.0062
2.51	.4940	.9940	.0060
2.52	.4941	.9941	.0059
2.53	.4943	.9943	.0057
2.54	.4945	.9945	.0055
2.55	.4946	.9946	.0054
2.56	.4948	.9948	.0052
2.57	.4949	.9949	.0051
2.58	.4951	.9951	.0049
2.59	.4952	.9952	.0048
2.60	.4953	.9953	.0047
2.61	.4955	.9955	.0045
2.62	.4956	.9956	.0044
2.63	.4957	.9957	.0043
2.64	.4959	.9959	.0041
2.65	.4960	.9960	.0040
2.66	.4961	.9961	.0039
2.67	.4962	.9962	.0038
2.68	.4963	.9963	.0037
2.69	.4964	.9964	.0036
2.70	.4965	.9965	.0035
2.71	.4966	.9966	.0034
2.72	.4967	.9967	.0033
2.73	.4968	.9968	.0032
2.74	.4969	.9969	.0031
2.75	.4970	.9970	.0030
2.76	.4971	.9971	.0029
2.77	.4972	.9972	.0028
2.78	.4973	.9973	.0027
2.79	.4974	.9974	.0026

Table of Areas Under the Normal Curve

(1)	(2)	(3)	(4)
	A	B	C
$z = \frac{x}{\sigma}$	Area from Mean to $\frac{x}{\sigma}$	Area in Larger Portion	Area in Smaller Portion
2.80	.4974	.9974	.0026
2.81	.4975	.9975	.0025
2.82	.4976	.9976	.0024
2.83	.4977	.9977	.0023
2.84	.4977	.9977	.0023
2.85	.4978	.9978	.0022
2.86	.4979	.9979	.0021
2.87	.4979	.9979	.0021
2.88	.4980	.9980	.0020
2.89	.4981	.9981	.0019
2.90	.4981	.9981	.0019
2.91	.4982	.9982	.0018
2.92	.4982	.9982	.0018
2.93	.4983	.9983	.0017
2.94	.4984	.9984	.0016
2.95	.4984	.9984	.0016
2.96	.4985	.9985	.0015
2.97	.4985	.9985	.0015
2.98	.4986	.9986	.0014
2.99	.4986	.9986	.0014
3.00	.4987	.9987	.0013
3.01	.4987	.9987	.0013
3.02	.4987	.9987	.0013
3.03	.4988	.9988	.0012
3.04	.4988	.9988	.0012
3.05	.4989	.9989	.0011
3.06	.4989	.9989	.0011
3.07	.4989	.9989	.0011
3.08	.4990	.9990	.0010
3.09	.4990	.9990	.0010
3.10	.4990	.9990	.0010
3.11	.4991	.9991	.0009
3.12	.4991	.9991	.0009
3.13	.4991	.9991	.0009
3.14	.4992	.9992	.0008

Table of Areas Under the Normal Curve

(1)	(2)	(3)	(4)
	A	B	C
$z = \frac{x}{\sigma}$	Area from Mean to $\frac{x}{\sigma}$	Area in Larger Portion	Area in Smaller Portion
3.15	.4992	.9992	.0008
3.16	.4992	.9992	.0008
3.17	.4992	.9992	.0008
3.18	.4993	.9993	.0007
3.19	.4993	.9993	.0007
3.20	.4993	.9993	.0007
3.21	.4993	.9993	.0007
3.22	.4994	.9994	.0006
3.23	.4994	.9994	.0006
3.24	.4994	.9994	.0006
3.30	.4995	.9995	.0005
3.40	.4997	.9997	.0003
3.50	.4998	.9998	.0002
3.60	.4998	.9998	.0002
3.70	.4999	.9999	.0001

Source: *Statistical Methods for the Behavioral Sciences,* copyright 1946 and renewed 1973 by A. L. Edwards. Reproduced by permission of Holt, Rinehart & Winston, Inc.